# Towards Methodologically Inclusive Research Syntheses

Primary research in education and social sciences is marked by a diversity of methods and perspectives. How can we accommodate and reflect such diversity at the level of synthesizing research? What are the critical methodological decisions in the process of a research synthesis, and how do these decisions open up certain possibilities, while closing down others?

This book draws upon methodologically diverse literature on research synthesis methods and primary research methods to develop a framework for synthesizing research. It presents a Methodologically Inclusive Research Synthesis framework to facilitate critical and informed decision-making among the producers and users of research synthesis.

Three guiding principles for a quality research synthesis are proposed: informed subjectivity and reflexivity, purposefully informed selective inclusivity, and audience-appropriate transparency. The book then provides a thorough discussion of how these principles might be enacted in the following six phases:

- identifying an appropriate epistemological orientation
- identifying an appropriate purpose
- searching for relevant literature
- evaluating, interpreting and distilling evidence from selected studies
- constructing connected understandings
- communicating with an audience.

A wide range of techniques and perspectives from postpositivist, interpretive, participatory, critical and postmodern traditions are considered in the book, and new areas of debate are opened by exploring numerous aspects of research syntheses from a methodologically inclusive perspective. The book will be valuable reading for researchers and postgraduates in education and social sciences.

**Harsh Suri** is a lecturer in Higher Education at the University of Melbourne, Australia.

Routledge Research in Education

*For a complete list of titles in the series, please visit www.routledge.com*

SAAP

WITHDRAWN

# Towards Methodologically Inclusive Research Syntheses

Expanding possibilities

Harsh Suri

Routledge
Taylor & Francis Group

LONDON AND NEW YORK

First published 2014
by Routledge
2 Park Square, Milton Park, Abingdon, Oxon OX14 4RN

Simultaneously published in the USA and Canada
by Routledge
711 Third Avenue, New York, NY 10017

*Routledge is an imprint of the Taylor & Francis Group,
an informa business*

*British Library Cataloguing in Publication Data*
A catalogue record for this book is available from the British Library

*Library of Congress Cataloging in Publication Data*
A catalog record for this book has been requested

ISBN: 978-0-415-82869-7 (hbk)
ISBN: 978-0-203-38319-3 (ebk)

Typeset in Galliard
by Saxon Graphics Ltd, Derby

Printed and bound in Great Britain by
TJ International Ltd, Padstow, Cornwall

To my family for their encouragement, love and support in bringing this book to fruition.

# Contents

# List of figures

# List of tables

# Foreword

I have developed reasonably good skills in searching literature and one of the enjoyments is reading articles not necessarily related to the particular search, but that just look interesting. This leads to a large number of readings over a career and some have changed the way I look at the world. One of these was an article by Donald Fiske and Louis Fogg, published in 1990.

They evaluated 402 reviews of 153 papers submitted to 12 editors from seven journals of the American Psychological Association journals. A major question posed by Fiske and Fogg was which part of an article was most likely to lead to rejection or acceptance – the title, affiliation of the authors, the abstract, introduction, literature review, methods, results, or conclusions. It turned out that the quality of the conclusion was among the most if not *the* most critical discriminating part of a manuscript. Specifically whether the interpretations of conclusions are warranted or not by the data, whether the story in the discussion is acceptable and convincing, and whether the findings were interpreted or left dangling. The message is – it's the story, it's the story.

I have since used this article repeatedly with students who are beginning their theses by asking them at most of their supervision meetings 'so what's the story today?'. I also use this article as an 'editor' and a 'reviewer' of academic journals to help discriminate among the publishable and the not publishable, and I use it to implore readers of this book to constantly recall that it's about the convincability of the story.

Of course, the convincability is a major function of the quality of the question, review, design and interpretation. One of my worries, however, is that we see these latter as critical in their own right and forget that they are means to an end. The quality of a study relates to the convincability of the story – and there are many texts that elaborate the preconditions such as reliability, replicability, generalizability, and so on. Similarly, one of the most critical aspects of credibility is how the story builds on the corpus and stories of those who have come before.

Too often literature reviews are tacked on to provide a justification usually formed around the idea 'that was them, now here is me'. Some journals have debated omitting the literature review (to save space, which implies it is seen as just a space filler). This book highlights an integrated approach to considering the discipline of reviewing, and thus to maximize the credibility of the story that is to be defended. The major contribution is that Harsh Suri does this for the many diverse forms of studies found across our disciplines. The claims are not peculiar to a particular method.

In many ways, literature reviewing is akin to testing a model or theory where the articles are the raw 'data'. A major problem that is then confronted is 'which' data? Particularly since the technology boom of the Internet the access to journals and the accountability pressures of 'Publish or Perish' (it should have been 'Publish or Paris') the number of papers has exploded and it is hard to keep up with the publications in our field. The claims about how to best 'synthesize' the riches in the literature have thence become a discipline itself.

An important milestone in synthesizing literature came in the mid 1970s. In 1976 Gene Glass described three levels of data analysis: primary analysis, which is the original analysis of data; secondary analysis, which is the re-analysis of these data (e.g. for answering new questions with old data), and meta-analysis which, refers to a synthesis of primary studies for the purpose of integrating the findings. At that time Glass noted the rapidly expanding discussions of research studies, and the growth of research publications at an astounding rate. This rate continues and could easily overwhelm the policy maker, the researcher, and the student of most research topics. As interestingly, the publication of meta-analyses over the 38 years has been very consistent (about 25 per year) – and this is only in education related to achievement outcomes – the growth has been greater in medicine and psychology. In a recent search on the Internet (January, 2013), there were 263,000 references to an article with 'meta-analysis' in the title.

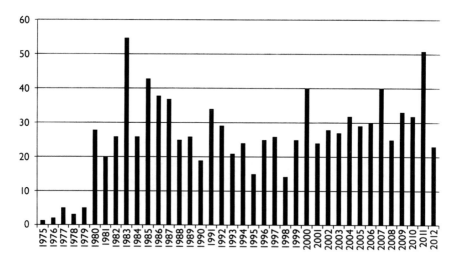

*Figure 0.1* Meta-analyses published in education related to achievement outcomes

My own venture started with a colleague. In 1977, in the first year of my first 'real' job, Brian Hansford asked me to explain what meta-analysis was. I clearly failed, as he said, why don't we do one to really see what is it like? We decided on about five topics that had sufficient literature that interested us. For no other good reason we decided on the relationship between self-concept and achievement. One hundred and twenty-three articles later we wrote our meta-analysis. Like many meta-analyses of that time, it was more about the data than about defending a story. The topic, however, sufficiently intrigued me that I later wrote a book on the topic (Hattie, 1992), in some degree to redeem my theory-free attempts at meta-analysis.

Even today, meta-analyses are published as if the data are the story, although the majority have moved passed this criticism. Now meta-analyses have been used to test various models, to develop models, and to develop and defend fascinating stories. For example, Kluger and de Nisi (1996) used 607 effect-sizes from 131 studies to show that feedback had a marked effect on performance. Their more critical contribution was their feedback intervention theory based around task learning, task motivation, and meta-tasks (e.g. self-regulations processes) and they showed how feedback decreased as attention moved up this hierarchy closer to the self and away from the task. I have used this model as an anchor in my own work to understand the variability of feedback effects in the classroom (Hattie and Timperley, 2007).

One of the limitations, however, of meta-analysis is that it only synthesizes a certain form of article – the article must have means and standard deviations dependent on administering some form of measure to people either over time or over groups (e.g. intervention and control groups). There have been modifications (e.g. there is a healthy synthesis of single subject studies and the use of odds-ratios) and a powerful statistical underpinning (Hedges and Olkin, 1985). But there is a major lack – the method does not synthesize qualitative studies. This book shows how the principles of synthesis, many derived from meta-analyses can be applied to synthesis of qualitative studies.

Consider, as one example, the story relating to the impact of teachers' subject matter knowledge. There have been two meta-analyses on this topic although there is a plethora of studies making claims about the criticalness of teachers knowing their subject, and knowing the pedagogical subject matter. Most authors write about the topic in terms of – it is obvious that teachers' subject matter knowledge matters; it is almost a badge of acceptance in the community to make this claim. The typical claim is that it is obvious that teachers who know their subject matter are more effective than those who do not (such as math teachers teaching history, those with PhDs in the content domain outperforming Diploma studies who may have taken a couple of content courses).

The two meta-analyses (one in science and one in math) show very low effects (d=.09). The problem is that there is little hint about why this effect is so low; there are no nuances, no leads, and the wrong conclusion is that subject matter knowledge does not matter. The message, instead, is that so far it may not matter but surely the aim then is to understand the conditions when it does matter – as that is the condition we want to create, esteem, and study. Mary Kennedy (2008) noted that the past literature was uneven, captured only narrow slices of literature, and too often eliminated qualitative studies. (Suri notes that this desire to synthesize qualitative studies can be traced back to the 1988 study by Noblit and Hare.)

Kennedy argues that synthesizing qualitative studies is not merely useful for learning about social meanings but also for making claims about causal influences – especially via revealing the mechanisms and process of influence. She completed a well-specified search process and located 23 qualitative studies that met her criteria. She seeks alternative explanations, sets out clear guidelines for interpreting findings, and identifies four major outcomes – the influence of stipulated content knowledge (e.g. content courses), studies of assessed content knowledge, influence of specific teacher education courses, and influence of whole teacher education programs.

Kennedy concludes that the findings from the qualitative studies agree with the quantitative studies in overall impact of teachers' subject matter knowledge (it is very low), but points to possible explanations. For example, she notes the tremendous power of classroom and school contexts over practice, too often teacher education courses provide only general ideas 'without the kind of detailed guidance teachers need to translate these concepts into specific strategies', teachers may 'know it' but seem to not know how to turn this into specifics about lessons, work, or assessments, and the relation is not always in one direction – knowledge does not stay fixed in teachers' minds after they leave college but continues to evolve as it interacts with both beliefs and the teaching experience itself. Kennedy is critical of the lack of detail about sampling rationale, the lack of awareness about controlling for confounding variables, documenting contexts and mitigating circumstances, and invites authors to take a more sceptical stance toward their own interpretations and evidence. The development of synthesis processes and exemplars of qualitative studies must be among the most exciting developments of the last decade.

The message so far is simple. Research synthesis is primarily about telling a story that has high convincing power. Such power is based on defensible sampling of studies, reliability of coding, replicability, and the appropriateness of generalization. The developments of synthesis, especially meta-analysis, has been meteoric, and the new move to develop similar systematic methodologies to synthesize qualitative studies is exciting.

Harsh Suri makes a major contribution to the field of literature reviews by bringing together these many topics in a rigorous manner. She notes the lack of links across the various forms of synthesis, and shows how her work builds on other attempts to also make these links – such as the EPPI centre, the What Works Clearing House, the Best Evidence Synthesis, and others. She develops the framework of Methodologically Inclusive Research Synthesis (MIRS) to guide the reader through the major claims about conceptualizing research synthesis, and then through each phase of the synthesis process – and does this with attention to the various methods that are available in our literature. She pulls ideas from many different perspectives while acknowledging the processes and politics of research synthesis (e.g. the three links cited above are all government sponsored).

She notes how evidence is one of the more contested terms, and questions the current claim that randomized control studies 'are the gold standard'. She quotes Thomas's (2004) observations that there is little empirical evidence from RCTs to support the hypothesis that the progress in medicine is caused by RCTs, and that most important discoveries are accompanied by a mix of inspirational thinking and serendipitous events. As Scriven (2005) does, I too place convincability as a higher aim ('beyond reasonable doubt') and RCTs can help make a claim convincible but they may not be enough, and other methods can lead to convincability. For example, a poorly designed RCT (e.g. based on five studies) is hardly convincing when the corpus of studies in the field is more like many thousands. There are too many RCT studies (and syntheses of RCTs) based on tiny samples. Instead of method as gold standard, Suri plays much attention to 'quality', such as informed subjectivity and reflexivity, and not losing the diversity that can be found in many studies.

There is a seeming paradox throughout the book in that the earliest attempts at synthesis involved 'mixed methods' – traditional reviews involved interpretations of qualitative and quantitative research, but maybe with the advent of meta-analysis the separation became larger (than it needs to be).

Similarly there is a seeming paradox in the controls for bias. In many senses a reader of a literature review wants to know the bias of the reviewer in the sense of hearing their story, their interpretation – as literature reviews need to be more than compendiums of articles. Suri cites the maxim that the person who does not have some vested interest in a subject is one who knows nothing about it. But as Campbell and Stanley (1966) have promoted, the point of research design is to control for those sources of bias that can provide plausible rival hypothesis for the conclusions of the author. Too many novices interpret this to mean that there is a cookbook of biases that one must control for, whereas it is primarily those that provide alternatives that must be controlled. One of my observations from reading close to 1000 meta-analyses is the poverty of arguments for the importance of the moderators or biases that are 'controlled'. Indeed moderators are noted more by their absence in many meta-analyses other than those that are easy to measure (age, quality, ethnicity, gender).

Across all the issues raised in this book, the emphasis continually is on quality of interpretation. Suri argues for quality relating to the search, the purpose, the interpretation, the methods, and her major contribution is the nature of coherence and logic of argument across these many claims. Her Epilogue epitomizes her approach – she aims to open discussions, to suggest new ways of thinking about literature reviewing, and to be ready for even more exciting approaches. This book does not provide an encompassing model, a set of definitive declarations, but in the true spirit of moving the field forward it brings coherence to the questions that are now open to us.

John Hattie
Director, Melbourne Education Research Institute
University of Melbourne

## References

Campbell, D. T. and Stanley, J. C. 1966. *Experimental and quasi-experimental designs for research*. Chicago, Illinois: Rand McNally.

Fiske, D. W. and Fogg, L. 1990. 'But the reviewers are making different criticisms of my paper! Diversity and uniqueness in reviewer comments'. *American Psychologist*, 45(5), 591–598.

Hansford, B. C. and Hattie, J. A. 1982. 'The relationship between self and achievement/performance measures'. *Review of Educational Research*, 52(1), 123–142.

Hattie, J. 1992. *Self-concept*. Hillsdale, NJ: Lawrence Erlbaum Associates.

Hattie, J. and Timperley, H. 2007. 'The power of feedback'. *Review of Educational Research*, 77(1), 81–113.

Hedges, L. V. and Olkin, I. 1985. *Statistical methods for meta-analysis*. Orlando: Academic Press.

Kennedy, M. M. 2008. 'Contributions of qualitative research to research on teacher qualifications'. *Educational Evaluation and Policy Analysis*, 30, 344–367.

Kluger, A. N. and DeNisi, A. 1996. 'The effects of feedback interventions on performance: A historical review, a meta-analysis, and a preliminary feedback intervention theory'. *Psychological Bulletin*, 119(2), 254–284.

Scriven, M. 2005. 'Can we infer causation from cross-sectional data?', invited speaker, School Level Data Symposium, National Research Council, Washington DC, December.

# Preface

When I started reading about research synthesis methods in the late 1990s, there was a rich body of literature on quantitative methods for synthesizing research. The literature on synthesizing qualitative research was relatively sparse and often not discussed within the dominant literature on statistical methods for synthesizing research. In the last two decades, there has been an exponential growth in the publications, especially from health care and public policy, on methods for synthesizing, qualitative and mixed-methods research. This book describes a methodologically inclusive research synthesis framework (MIRS) that has been developed by adapting and synthesizing ideas and techniques from the extensive and diverse literature on research synthesis methods and primary research methods. The MIRS framework is intended as a coherent conceptualization of research synthesis methods, expressed through the identification of critical decisions and thorough discussion of varied options associated with individual decisions in the process of a rigorous research synthesis.

Through the MIRS framework I have constructed a connected understanding, expressed as a set of diverse theoretical and practical considerations, to inform the theory and practice of research synthesis methods. In developing this framework I have been methodologically inclusive at several levels by:

- addressing issues arising from synthesizing methodologically diverse primary research;
- drawing on ideas and strategies from a variety of research synthesis methods and exemplary research syntheses;
- adapting ideas and techniques from a range of primary research methods, especially qualitative research methods, to the process of a research synthesis;
- taking into account how processes and politics of research synthesis may intersect with the interests of different stakeholders.

This book has hugely benefitted from the constructive feedback provided by anonymous reviewers and audience of manuscripts submitted to scholarly journals and conference presentations. Earlier drafts of several sections of this book have been presented and published in different outlets which include the following:

In press – with John Hattie. 'Meta-analysis and research synthesis in education'. *Oxford Bibliographies Online.*

First published online 2012. 'Epistemological pluralism in qualitative research synthesis'. *International Journal of Qualitative Studies in Education.*

2011. 'Purposeful sampling in qualitative research synthesis'. *Qualitative Research Journal*, 11(2), 63-75.

2010. 'Methodologically inclusive research synthesis'. *AERA Annual Conference*, Denver.

2009 – with David Clarke. 'Advancements in research synthesis methods: From a methodologically inclusive perspective'. *Review of Educational Research*, 79(1), 395-430.

2008. 'Ethical Considerations in Synthesising Research: Whose Representations?' *Qualitative Research Journal*, 8(1), 62-73.

2007. 'Evidence-based education: From an epistemologically inclusive perspective. Enhancing Higher Education, Theory and Scholarship'. *HERDSA Annual Conference*, Adelaide, Australia.

2004. 'Synthesising research for diverse purposes: Moving beyond "What Works?"'. *AARE Annual Conference*, Melbourne, Australia.

2003. 'Celebrating diversity and inclusivity in research synthesis'. *Advances in Qualitative Methods Conference*. Banff, Canada.

2003. 'Paradigmatic positioning of research syntheses'. *Biennial AQR Conference*. Sydney, Australia.

2002. 'Essential features of methodologically inclusive research syntheses'. *AERA Annual Conference*. New Orleans.

2001. 'Synthesis of literature on research synthesis methods'. *Biennial AQR Conference*. Melbourne, Australia.

2001 – with David Clarke. 'Understanding mathematics classrooms through the synthesis of multiple analyses of a common data set'. *MERGA Annual Conference*. Sydney, Australia.

2000. 'A critique of contemporary methods of research synthesis'. *Post-Script*, 1(1), 49-55.

1999 – with David Clarke. 'Revisiting methods of literature synthesis'. *AERA Annual Conference*. Montreal, Canada.

1999. 'A methodologically inclusive model for research synthesis'. *AARE-NZARE joint Annual Conference*. Melbourne, Australia.

1999. 'The process of synthesising qualitative research: A case-study'. *AQR Biennial Conference*, Melbourne, Australia.

1998. 'A critique of contemporary methods of research synthesis'. *AARE Annual Conference*, Adelaide, Australia.

Throughout this book, in preference to providing prescriptive answers or conclusions, I have attempted to open spaces, raise questions, explore possibilities and contest taken-for-granted practices. Rather than prescribing how a research synthesis ought to be conducted or evaluated, my goal is to support critical reflection among producers and users of research syntheses. I have attempted to do this by raising questions to structure and inform critical decision-making throughout a synthesis process. I hope this book will stimulate debate and discussion about numerous aspects of research syntheses from a methodologically inclusive perspective.

# Acknowledgements

My deepest appreciation goes to my PhD supervisors, Professor David Clarke and Dr Gaell Hildebrand, for their guidance, support and generous sharing of ideas. I thank my PhD examiners, anonymous reviewers of my earlier papers on research synthesis methods and colleagues at various conferences and seminars for their constructive critique and feedback. My special thanks go to Dr Darrel Caulley, Professor John Hattie, Dr Tony Jones, Dr Warren Sellers and Mr Jose Salazar for their insightful feedback on earlier drafts of this book.

# Chapter 1

# Contextualizing this book

How is the term research synthesis used in this book? What is the purpose of this book? Who is the intended audience for this book?

Analysis and synthesis of evidence in three modes can contribute to knowledge construction in research. These three modes are primary analysis, secondary analysis and research synthesis. *Primary research* involves going into an experimental situation, the field, archives or cyberspace to collect raw evidence or data to pursue one's own research questions. The analysis and interpretation of this raw data is referred to as primary analysis and the individuals conducting such research are called primary researchers. *Secondary research* involves re-analysing and re-interpreting raw evidence or data collected by other primary researchers for their own primary research. This re-analysis or re-interpretation could be pursued to address the same, or different, questions using different analytic tools or interpretive positions. In this book the term 'primary research' is frequently used as an umbrella term for primary research and secondary research. *Research synthesists* are different from primary researchers and secondary researchers in the sense that they analyse or interpret primary research reports rather than collecting, analysing or interpreting any raw data or evidence. The evidence, methodological perspectives and techniques employed in each of the three modes of knowledge construction can be qualitative, quantitative or a combination of both (Suri 2011).

Typically, literature reviews form a part of every research report. Researchers conduct literature reviews to contextualize the rationale, theoretical framework, methods and findings of their own studies. Research synthesis is a special type of research review that is not only descriptive, informative and evaluative, but also *connective* (Mays et al. 2005). 'Synthesis refers to making a whole into something more than the parts alone imply' (Noblit and Hare 1988, p. 28). The purpose of a research synthesis is to produce *new* knowledge by making explicit connections and relations between individual studies that were not visible before. It involves purposeful selection, review, analysis and synthesis of primary research on a similar topic. Many research syntheses also include evidence from the relevant secondary research and research reviews in the field. In a rigorous synthesis, readers are provided sufficient information about the synthesis process so that they can make informed decisions about the extent to which the synthesis findings may be adapted to their own contexts. This type of information about the process is frequently missing in typical literature reviews and some other forms of research reviews (Suri 2012).

## Published literature on research synthesis methods

There has been a rapid growth in the number and variety of reports in educational research. Each topic tends to be examined by different researchers in diverse contexts, employing a wide range of methods, resulting in disparate findings on the same topic. Making useable sense of such complex bodies of research can be an overwhelming experience for most stakeholders with an interest in educational research. These stakeholders include policy-makers, administrators, teachers, funding agencies, researchers, students, parents and the wider community.

Research syntheses play an important role in disseminating research knowledge and in shaping further research, policy, practice and public perception. They are frequently cited in scholarly journals (Cooper and Hedges 2009). Issues of methodological rigour in research syntheses are as crucial as they are in primary research (Slavin 2008). During the last four decades, there has been a growing body of literature on research synthesis methods marked by several commendable methodological advances (Sandelowski et al. 2012).

Among early efforts of enhancing rigour in synthesizing research in education, the most well-known improvement has been the formal proposition of 'meta-analysis' as a statistical method for integrating quantitative summaries from individual primary research reports (Glass 1976, p. 3). As several meta-analysts have critically examined and refined various aspects of meta-analytic syntheses in the last four decades, these procedures have become more sophisticated and sensitive. The vast literature on meta-analytic methods has contributed substantially in systematizing and refining the entire process of research synthesis. Meta-analyses and meta-analyzable studies have a particular appeal among politicians because of their ability to provide quantitative generalizations. With the current thrust for Evidence-Based Education (EBE), randomized controlled trials (RCTs) and meta-analyses are being particularly favoured by several politicians, senior administrators and funding agencies (Wiseman 2010). However, meta-analyses can synthesize only a limited portion of contemporary research in most areas of education. Meta-analytic procedures can integrate only those findings that can be reduced to a common index, often an effect size, of a conceptually similar outcome measure. A political push for meta-analyses and meta-analyzable studies has evoked strong responses from several educational researchers who challenge the narrow conception of educational research and EBE that excludes valuable evidence from various qualitative research traditions (Luke et al. 2010).

In the last two decades, many researchers from education and health care have been adapting ideas and techniques from interpretive and critical traditions to inform research synthesis processes. Useful guidelines have been published for synthesizing qualitative research in education and social sciences from a critical interpretive perspective (e.g. Major and Savin-Baden 2010). A large number of publications, from health care and public policy researchers, have focused on synthesizing qualitative research or methodologically diverse research (Hannes and Macaitis 2012). Useful methodological lessons can be learnt from a number of published narrative syntheses of quantitative and qualitative research in top-tier journals like the *Review of Educational Research* (*RER*). Insightful commentaries have also been published by critical scholars, especially from education, on the politics, process, use and abuse of research reviews. Several synthesists are calling for increased involvement of consumers of research in formulating and refining questions and protocols for syntheses (e.g. Rees and Oliver 2012).

Each of these individual bodies of literature makes a worthy contribution by providing guidelines to synthesize particular types of primary research reports with certain types of synthesis purposes in mind (Kastner et al. 2012). However, there is a paucity of literature that establishes links and examines complementarities and incompatibilities between different existing research synthesis methods. Also, there is a relative dearth of literature that explores adaptation of a variety of qualitative research perspectives and techniques to the process of a research synthesis.

In recent years, there has been increased activity and interest in this space. As a reviewer of this book noted, there is a degree of similarity between this book and publications from the Evidence for Policy and Practice Information (EPPI) centre. This is not surprising as colleagues from the EPPI Centre and I have been grappling with the same issue of how to conduct more rigorous research syntheses that are inclusive of qualitative research since the late 1990s. This is evident from our various conference presentations and publications on this issue. However, even though we have engaged with the same broad question, we have approached it from different perspectives. The focus of EPPI centre's work has been on systematization of review methods as suggested by the title of their recent book, *An introduction to systematic reviews* (Gough et al. 2012). However, *methodological inclusivity* has been the focus of my work since 1998. Their book describes the current state of systematic reviews. This book takes the discussion further by contesting the prevalent discourse to engage researchers in pushing the boundaries of the prevalent conceptions of a research synthesis. It is this *provocative* engagement with the published literature on research synthesis methods and primary research methods that is a distinguishing feature of this book.

As suggested by the subtitle of this book, the goal here is to *expand possibilities within research synthesis methods*. It is the in-depth engagement, informed by critical sensibilities, with issues less represented in the published literature on research synthesis methods that sets this book apart from other texts on this topic. While the preliminary discussions of many issues in this book have been published before, this book takes these discussions further by raising new questions, contesting taken-for-granted practices and exploring possibilities many of which have not been discussed in previously published books on research synthesis methods. The extent to which the book engages with a variety of techniques and perspectives associated with a wider spectrum of qualitative research traditions makes it distinct. This is important as educational research is marked by a diversity of epistemological perspectives, methods and techniques. The sheer variety of lenses employed to expand possibilities in research synthesis methods, with an openness that invites further critiques and modifications, makes this book unique.

## Methodologically Inclusive Research Synthesis (MIRS) framework

As the rhetoric of Evidence Based Education (EBE) is becoming popular, it becomes crucial to explore multiple ways of 'justifying evidence-based claims'. This book is one such exploration.

---

### Overarching question pursued in this book

Contemporary educational research is marked by diversity, complexity and richness of purposes, methods and perspectives. How can we accommodate and reflect such variety and complexity at the level of synthesizing educational research?

---

To address this question, we need an approach to research synthesis that is sufficiently inclusive and sensitive to accommodate and reflect the methodological and epistemological diversity in contemporary educational research. The Methodologically Inclusive Research Synthesis (MIRS) framework, presented in this book, is an attempt to respond to this need.

---

The **Methodologically Inclusive Research Synthesis (MIRS)** framework is intended to be a coherent conceptualization of research synthesis methods expressed through the identification of critical decisions and thorough discussion of varied options associated with each decision in the process of a rigorous research synthesis.

---

The MIRS framework is a synthesis of diverse theoretical and practical considerations to inform the theory and practice of research synthesis methods. It is not an alternative method for research synthesis. Rather, it is a framework developed to support critical reflection among producers and users of research syntheses. In developing this framework, methodological inclusivity has been considered from multiple angles:

- by addressing issues arising from synthesizing methodologically diverse primary research;
- by drawing on ideas and strategies from a variety of research synthesis methods and exemplary research syntheses;
- by adapting ideas and techniques from a wide range of primary research methods, especially qualitative research methods, to the process of a research synthesis;
- by taking into account how processes and politics of research synthesis may intersect with the interests of different stakeholders.

This book does not claim a comprehensive coverage of the possibilities within research syntheses for several reasons. First, contemporary educational research methods and perspectives are changing at such a rapid rate that any claim of comprehensiveness will be outdated by the time the work is published. Second, no single individual can rightfully claim expertise in all forms of research synthesis. Third, I humbly accept my limited experience and knowledge in various primary research methods and research synthesis methods. This book exemplifies a 'non-mastery approach...that can tolerate its own failure of knowledge and the detour of not understanding'. This book thus represents my 'situated, partial, and perspectival knowing that, while not knowing everything, does know something' (Lather 1999, p. 4). Nonetheless, this book makes a worthy contribution to the continuing development of the field of research synthesis by constructing a *new connected understanding*.

## Writing conventions used in this book

### Organization of different topics

The mutually informing relationship of individual chapters of this book is mapped in Figure 1.1. The 11 chapters of this book are broadly clustered into four parts. The first part is this introductory chapter.

   In the second part of this book, i.e. Chapter 2 and Chapter 3, the literature on contemporary methods of research synthesis and primary research in education is reviewed to establish a need for a methodologically inclusive research synthesis (MIRS) framework. Primary research methods and research synthesis methods should be, and to some extent are, mutually informing. Hence, any story about the developments in research synthesis methods is best told within the background context of developments in primary research methods and vice-versa. Chapter 2 highlights the growing complexity and diversity in contemporary educational principles, practices and primary research methods. This chapter concludes by asserting that compatibility between methods of primary research and research

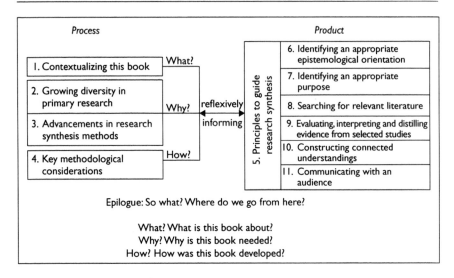

*Figure 1.1* Relationship between individual chapters of this book

synthesis necessitates that such richness and diversity of methods is also celebrated at the level of research synthesis. Chapter 3 describes key developments in research synthesis methods from a methodologically inclusive perspective that draws from diverse literature on research synthesis methods. This chapter establishes the need for a framework that purposefully weaves threads from diverse literature on research synthesis methods and primary research methods to expand possibilities within research syntheses.

In the third part of this book, Chapter 4, critical decisions involved in developing the MIRS framework are described. This chapter demonstrates how the same considerations were enacted in developing the MIRS framework, for purposefully synthesizing the literature on research synthesis methods and primary research methods, which are advocated through the MIRS framework itself.

In the fourth part of this book, Chapter 5 to Chapter 11, different aspects of the MIRS framework are described. Chapter 5 describes guiding principles for a research synthesis. Key considerations and critical decisions within each of the six phases of a research synthesis process are presented in Chapter 6 to Chapter 11 which address the following broad questions:

- *Identifying an appropriate epistemological orientation.* What possibilities open up (and close down) for syntheses that are positioned along distinct epistemologies?
- *Identifying an appropriate purpose.* What are some critical considerations in identifying an appropriate purpose for a research synthesis?
- *Searching for relevant literature.* What issues should be considered when identifying suitable approaches and techniques to search and retrieve relevant studies from the literature?

- *Evaluating, interpreting and distilling evidence from selected studies.* What issues should be considered when evaluating the retrieved primary research reports for inclusion into a research synthesis? What issues should be considered when interpreting and distilling relevant and trustworthy information from the selected primary research reports?
- *Constructing connected understandings.* What issues should be considered when constructing understandings by connecting the information distilled from individual research reports?
- *Communicating with an audience.* How can research synthesists effectively communicate the process and product of their synthesis to diverse audiences?

The book concludes with an epilogue in which the research community is urged to think beyond our current comfort zones about the implications of methodologically inclusive research syntheses for educational research, policy and practice.

### Strategic questions

The purpose of this book is to sensitize producers and users of research syntheses to a wide range of methodological choices that can impact upon the synthesis findings. Such sensitization is intended to facilitate informed production and utilization of research syntheses. Throughout this book, questioning is used as a deliberate and appropriate tactic to highlight the many implicit and explicit critical choices in a synthesis process. Each chapter begins with an overarching question to orient the reader in anticipation of the broad issues addressed in the chapter. This question is addressed from different perspectives throughout the chapter. Many sections include a series of questions to stimulate purposeful reflection focused on key issues pertinent to that aspect of a synthesis process.

### Meanings associated with key terms

Several key terms used in this book have been associated with diverse connotations, varied levels of specificity and fuzzy boundaries in the literature on research methods. Such fluidity allows concepts and ideas to grow in several dimensions with increasing complexity (Bernstein 1986). Nonetheless, a lack of consensus on the definitions of terms often leads to a greater need for defining terms to facilitate meaningful communication. Throughout this book, key terms have been defined to communicate the meanings and scope associated with them within the context of this book rather than according them universal meanings.

### Paraphrasing and direct quotes

While recognizing that 'borrowing words from others is always problematic; that meanings are never static and words are always in motion' (Segall 2001, p. 585), direct quotes have been extensively used from the published representations of researchers with allegiance to a wide range of methodologies in three different ways:

- to succinctly represent their views without losing their subtle nuances;
- to deliberately interrogate the narrow contexts in which they have been used, in order to support a methodologically inclusive perspective towards research synthesis;
- to purposefully adapt these quotes, beyond their intended domains of application, through my subjective interpretations in order to construct new ways of thinking about methodologically inclusive research syntheses.

## Summary

Research syntheses play an important role in disseminating research knowledge and in shaping further research, policy, practice and public perception. Commendable efforts have been made to enhance rigour in research syntheses. However, the literature on research synthesis methods from interpretive, participatory and critical perspectives is relatively sparse and often not discussed within the dominant literature on meta-analysis. Further, there is a paucity of literature that builds connections between these different parts of the literature on research synthesis methods. This book presents the MIRS framework that has been conceptualized by adapting and synthesizing ideas and techniques from the extensive and diverse literature on research synthesis methods and primary research methods.

# Chapter 2

# Growing diversity in primary research

What is the nature of contemporary principles, practices and primary research methods in education? What is the case for a methodologically inclusive discussion about the advancements in research synthesis methods? What is the rationale for a methodologically inclusive research synthesis framework?

This chapter illuminates the current multi-dimensional pluralism of principles, practices and primary research methods in education. By highlighting this diversity and complexity, it is argued that a methodologically inclusive discussion of research synthesis methods is essential to maintain their compatibility with the current principles, practices and research in education.

## Variety of epistemological viewpoints

Many researchers distinguish between the qualitative and quantitative paradigms or approaches to research (e.g. Wiseman 2010). Many other researchers contest the adequacy of these terms in representing different approaches to research because the terms quantitative and qualitative are considered to be more suited for describing differences at the level of data or method (e.g. Cassell 2010). Nonetheless, the terms quantitative and qualitative have come into common usage to distinguish between two major approaches to research. Quantitative studies tend to examine measurable causal-effects or correlations to uncover why or what with minimal bias by controlling for extraneous variables. Qualitative research describes, interprets, verifies, evaluates, deconstructs or changes processes, systems, policies, practices, theories or prevalent understandings. Qualitative researchers typically employ an emergent design to understand how a phenomenon is experienced by participants in its natural setting to build a complex and holistic account while reflexively tapping into their own subjectivity (Creswell 2013). Mixed-methods research often utilizes strategic combinations of quantitative and qualitative methods and draws on pragmatism or a quantitative or qualitative worldview depending on which form of data plays a dominant role in the analysis (Teddlie and Tashakkori 2003). In this book, the terms quantitative and qualitative have been broadly used to highlight this distinction without explicitly mentioning mixed-methods in many places where it was not seen to offer a sufficiently distinct worldview.

Within the umbrella of qualitative research, there is a growing diversity of philosophical frameworks and approaches (Lincoln et al. 2011). Many researchers are drawing from critical, postmodernist and poststructuralist viewpoints that are marked by 'skepticism about the rules of consensus' (Marshall and Peters 1999, p. 244). Since the 1990s, there has been a rapid growth in the discussions surrounding narrative inquiry, standpoint theories, politics associated with research and diverse forms of representing research. A growing diversification of qualitative research is blurring the boundaries between research and non-research (Denzin and Lincoln 2011).

Often researchers draw on the concept of a paradigm to position themselves epistemologically. The term 'paradigm' is frequently related back to Kuhn who used it to refer to a web of beliefs or theory within which a scientific discourse occurs (Kuhn 1962). Many contemporary researchers note that multiple paradigms co-exist and are drawn upon by different researchers in different research studies. As illustrated in Table 2.1, there are a number of paradigmatic classifications proposed by different methodologists. All of the terms used in this table have been copied verbatim from the relevant references. Each of these paradigms tends to be associated with its relevant set of criteria for trustworthiness.

In this book, like Cook and Campbell(1979), the term 'postpositivism' has been used to emphasize the probabilistic nature of all inquiry that is recognized within this approach. Postpositivists typically adopt an empirical and reductionist approach to statistically analyze relationships between measurable constructs in order to describe, explain or predict human or social behaviour. This was the dominant approach in education until the 1970s. I recognize that often the term positivist is used to describe this approach (e.g. Phillips et al. 2012). However, in this book I have refrained from using the term positivism as it is sometimes used with negative connotations.

Since mid-1980s, as evident from Table 2.1, educational research has been marked by a growing diversity of epistemological positions that have been structured differently by different methodologists. The same term, such as postpositivism, is used to refer to different epistemological positions by different methodologists. There are several more paradigmatic positions that are not listed in Table 2.1, such as pragmatism (Maxcy 2003), ecological paradigm and creative paradigm (Peile 1994).

The only common thread running through the various classifications illustrated in Table 2.1 is an emphasis on different conceptions of what is the nature of reality, what is worth knowing and what are legitimate ways of knowing. A lack of an absolute congruence across different rows illustrates how the paradigmatic differences can be understood and represented along several dimensions of variations. Each classification emphasizes key distinctions towards which the particular scholar in the relevant text wishes to sensitize us. Many methodologists

Table 2.1 Variety of paradigmatic classifications

| Classification (Methodologist) | Key dimensions along which the paradigms are distinguished |
| --- | --- |
| interpretivism versus positivism (Noblit and Hare 1988, p. 12) | Seek an explanation for social or cultural events based on perspectives and experiences of the people being studied versus seek cause-and-effect laws that are sufficiently generalizable to ensure that a knowledge of prior events enables a reasonable prediction of subsequent events |
| positivistic, interpretive or critical (Candy 1989, pp. 2-9) | Clusters of assumptions and broad orientations<br>Relative emphasis on reliability and validity |
| positivist, interpretive, critical, ecological or creative (Peile 1994, pp. 278-279) | Assumptions: cosmological, ontological, epistemological, ethical, spiritual and political |
| positivism/postpositivism, interpretive/constructivist, emancipatory (Mertens 1998, pp. 6-8)<br>Qualitative <----> quantitative (Wiersma 2000, p. 13) | Ontology (nature of reality)<br>Epistemology (nature of knowledge, relation between knower and would-be known)<br>Methodology (approach to systematic inquiry)<br>inductive inquiry <----> deductive inquiry<br>understanding social phenomena <----> relationships, effects, causes<br>atheoretical or grounded theory <----> theory-based<br>holistic inquiry <----> focused on individual variables<br>context-specific <----> context-free (generalizations)<br>observer-participant <----> detached role of researcher<br>narrative description <----> statistical analysis |
| positivism, postpositivism, critical theory et al., constructivism or participatory (Guba and Lincoln 2005, pp. 195-199) | Basic beliefs: ontology, epistemology, methodology<br>Selected issues: nature of knowledge, knowledge accumulation, goodness or quality criteria, values, ethics, inquirer posture, training<br>Critical issues of the time: axiology, accommodation and commensurability, action, control, relationship to foundations of truth and knowledge, extended considerations of validity, voice, reflexivity, postmodern textual representations |
| positivist, interpretivist, critical theory and pragmatic (Phillips et al. 2012, pp. 72-73) | Vary along the following characteristics: ontological, epistemological, axiological, methodological, validity and outcomes of inquiry |

Note: All the terms used in this table have been copied verbatim from the relevant references.

recognize the complexity and fuzzy nature of any paradigmatic classification (e.g. Lincoln et al. 2011).

Educational researchers also vary in their attitudes towards epistemological differences. Walker and Evers (1999) classify these different attitudes into three categories: 'oppositional diversity thesis' which regards different epistemologies as incommensurable, mutually incompatible and competing; 'complementarity diversity thesis' which regards different epistemologies as incommensurable and mutually incompatible but complementary; and 'unity thesis' or 'coherence epistemology', to which Walker and Evers themselves subscribe, which denies epistemological differences in favour of 'holistic scientific naturalism' with a 'unified account of validity and reliability' for all educational research (Walker and Evers 1999, pp. 41-54). Unity thesis recommends 'empirical adequacy', 'consistency', 'comprehensiveness', 'simplicity', 'learnability' and 'explanatory unity' as essentials for all educational research (Evers 1999, pp. 273-4).

Empiricists further vary in their attitudes towards epistemological debates in education. Some see them as 'metaphysical' and irrelevant to social sciences. Some use them for 'consciousness-raising' to contextualize the nature and caveats of their own research and do not mind these debates as long as their empiricist notions of rigour are not challenged. Yet others see them as 'an intellectual disruption-or eruption-of substantial proportions and, analogous to a volcano, wreaking havoc on the academic and political terrain of educational research' (Paul and Marfo 2001, p. 526).

In responding to epistemological differences, educational researchers can be 'fragmenting' by communicating only with those with a similar epistemological stance; 'polemical' by working to advance one's own stance with little intention of learning from others; 'defensive' by remaining firmly rooted in one's own epistemology and wishing others would follow their own epistemology; or they can engage in 'fallibilist pluralism' which involves looking inwards towards our own fallibility while respectfully engaging with other viewpoints without trivializing the differences (Schwandt 2005, p. 290). In this book, I have subscribed to a complementarity diversity thesis while engaging with fallibilist pluralism.

## Multi-dimensional variations in primary research methods

Contemporary primary research methods in education are marked by multi-dimensional variations (Luke et al. 2010). The landscape of educational research methods is partitioned differently depending on the key distinctions that an individual methodologist wishes to emphasize. With any effort of structuring the diversity in educational research, we find a diversity in structures. My portrayal of the diversity and complexity in contemporary educational research, as presented in this chapter, is one of the many ways in which this landscape can be portrayed.

Educational research studies examine a wide range of formal and informal teaching and learning situations. Informal learning could take place at home, libraries, museums or within wider communities through various experiences or mass media such as radio, TV or the Internet (Leander et al. 2010). Some researchers classify primary research according to the research site: a real or virtual classroom, school, community centre or laboratory. Even within classroom-based studies, research may be partitioned according to the following questions:

- Whose agency was foregrounded?
- What was the subject or content matter being dealt with?
- What was the demographic constitution of the class?
- What were physical characteristics of the classroom?

In a research report, often the representational structuring of any classroom or the reported context of an educational phenomenon is guided by the purpose of the study. Decisions about which aspects of the structure are important and worth mentioning and which aspects are not so important are influenced by the purpose of the study. Different target audience for educational research include policy-makers, general public, teachers, curriculum developers, educational administrators, politicians, researchers and parents. Some researchers assert that the purpose of educational research should not be limited to mere delivery of information. They argue that educational research should not only recommend change, but also be the catalyst for change and teacher empowerment by directly engaging teachers as co-researchers or by honing in teachers' skills in noticing to enrich their own practices (e.g. Mason 2002). Educational researchers utilize diverse media and genres to communicate their findings. While many educational journals still prefer the scientific reporting format, many others are opening up to a variety of genres for reporting research. To engage wider community with their research, many researchers are also moving beyond academic journals to skilfully utilize a variety of media in order to reach a wider audience.

Commonly used tools or techniques for collecting evidence in educational research include tests, questionnaires, interviews, observations, documents, archived evidence and reflective journals. Each of these tools can further be classified into different types. Tests and questionnaires can be standardized, teacher-made or researcher-made with open-ended or multiple-choice items. Interviews can be formally planned with prior appointment or ad hoc, structured or unstructured, individual or group discussion, stimulated by different types of interviewer's questions, video recall, images or sounds. Interviews may also vary according to the duration, frequency and timing of the interview; relative positioning and relationship between the interviewer and interviewee; medium and immediacy of time, i.e., synchronous (e.g. face-to-face, telephonic or via videoconferencing) or asynchronous (e.g. via electronic discussion forums, individual emails or recorded after considerable time for contemplating on the researcher questions). Observations may be participant or non-participant, overt or covert, emic or etic, with different configurations of relative positioning and relationship between the observer and observed, formally planned with prior appointment or ad hoc, structured or unstructured, and vary in the duration, frequency and timing of the observation periods. Documents and archived evidence may be categorized according to their source and form of publication, accessibility and ownership. Reflective journals may be generated by research participants or by the researchers themselves.

Online methods of collecting data add another layer of complexity as the boundaries between public/private, overt/covert, individual/collective and virtual/real become more blurred and, at the same time, more critical (Suri and Patel 2012, Buchanan and Ess 2009). Evidence for research may be quantitative, qualitative or a combination of both with the number of participants or sample size being large or small. Large-N studies may be experimental, quasi-experimental or non-experimental with cross-sectional, longitudinal or retrospective data. In case studies, the case may be a nation, school, class, teacher, student, parent, administrator or community. Qualitative evidence may be recorded through researchers' field notes and still-images, video recorded or audio recorded.

Until this point in this chapter, the emphasis has been on variations across individual methods. However, these variations are seldom compartmentalized or distinct. This is an era of pluralism and eclecticism in methodological approaches employed by educational researchers. The relative importance attributed to individual dimensions of variations depends on the purpose of a study where some distinctions are likely to be important while some others may be trivial. Often there are several overlaps and no clear boundaries between individual methods. Many researchers draw on tools and techniques from different methodologies in the same piece of research rather than adhering to a single method in its pure form (Denzin and Lincoln 2011).

## A hard-line perspective of Evidence-Based Education

The growing popularity and diversity of qualitative research methods is not embraced by all researchers. Following the popularity of Evidence-Based Medicine (EBM), there has been a political pressure on educational researchers to promote Evidence-Based Education (EBE) in several countries, such as the UK, Canada, the USA and several European Nations (Phillips 2006). Many quantitative researchers see this as an unprecedented opportunity for moving educational research in the *right* direction. These quantitative researchers assert that the main reason why educational practice has not made progress, like medicine, is because it has failed to concentrate its 'resources and energies on a set of randomized experiments of impeccable quality' (Slavin 2002, p. 18). They urge educational researchers to follow the medical model and provide practitioners and policy-makers with a reliable and unbiased knowledge base (e.g. Slavin 2008).

However, there is little empirical evidence from Randomized Controlled Trials (RCTs) to support the hypothesis that the progress in medicine is caused by RCTs. Medicine has a strong factual evidence base and RCTs are popular in medicine. These two observations, on their own, cannot be assumed to have a causal relationship. Most important discoveries are accompanied by 'a mix of inspirational thinking and serendipitous events' with RCTs playing the mundane confirmatory role (Thomas 2004, p. 11). Even the confirmatory role of RCTs becomes problematic given that studies that report non-significant findings are less likely to be published. Feasibility and ethics of RCTs in many educational settings are questionable (Lather 2004). Implementing an educational intervention is often more complex than prescribing a drug (Ridgway et al. 2000). Many health-care researchers have also emphasized the need to include qualitative research in systematic reviews conducted to inform policy and practice (Pope et al. 2007).

Well-designed, rigorous, large-N, comparative studies can inform our understanding of educational interventions in useful ways. However, 'statistical tests of reliability and validity merely assess the psychometric properties of an examination'. They provide little information on whether the test examined all aspects of the desired outcomes. 'Tests that focus on only a subset of the desired range of performance can give misleading results' and it is possible that 'ostensible proficiency may well have been an artefact of the narrowness of the test' (Schoenfeld 2006, pp. 17-18). An exclusive technocratic and instrumental focus on measuring effectiveness of interventions against given outcomes overlooks the more important task of critically reflecting on the suitability and appropriateness of those given outcomes (Burbules and Warnick 2006).

An emphasis on internal validity of RCTs can sometimes seriously limit their external validity (Briggs 2008). RCTs report what worked in controlled trials rather than what works in natural settings (Ryan and Hood 2004). After removing extraneous variables, an intervention that is tested by an RCT often becomes very different from the intervention that is implemented in an actual classroom (Chatterji 2008). 'The effectiveness of any practical action usually depends not just on *what* is done but also on *how* it is done and *when*' (Hammersley 2004, p. 136, emphasis in original). It is also possible that a particular program is effective when implemented with the support of the designer of the program. However, when teachers are required to implement the same program without adequate support, it could hinder student performance. Many researchers are challenging the definitive nature of the knowledge-base that some hard-line quantitative researchers are claiming to produce.

Hard-line quantitative researchers feel that it is their responsibility to provide scientific evidence-base to the public (e.g. Herman et al. 2006). However, it is this very narrow definition of scientific evidence as used by these hard-liners that raises questions amongst the wider community about the scientific merit of any information that falls outside the realms of this narrow definition (Luke et al. 2010). While being supportive of quantitative research in general, many scholars contest an exclusive privileging of RCTs (eg. Green and Skukauskaite 2008).

Many eminent quantitative synthesists themselves do not subscribe to a hard-line perspective of EBE and believe that quantitative, qualitative and mixed-methods research, all play important and complementary roles (e.g. Cooper 2009). Yet, the hard-line quantitative perspective is becoming popular, especially in the USA, among several powerful stakeholders like government and funding agencies (Wiseman 2010). To contest this hegemony, this chapter has focused on representing the methodologically pluralist perspective of educational research.

## Strengthening the nexus between policy, practice and research

There are multiple perspectives on how to strengthen the nexus between research, practice and policy in education. Most scholars recognize that change must occur at multiple levels within the educational systems and different types of research are suited for narrowing the gap between research and practice at different levels (Luke et al. 2010). Many researchers advocate greater involvement of students, parents, teachers, local administrators, policy-makers and the wider community in setting up research agenda and in interpreting research findings (Yu 2011). Many methodologists emphasize the need to make all types of research more accessible with clear implications for teachers, policy-makers and all the agents for change whose practices are potentially influenced by the research (e.g. Kirk 1996). Researchers also stress the need to provide open access of educational research reports to practitioners, policy-makers and the wider community.

Some researchers regard policy changes as the major impetus for change. They have a top-down vision of change where they argue that policy-makers must facilitate global change by informing their decisions with research findings that are based on generalizable observations. Some qualitative researchers emphasize that educational policy and practice ought to be guided by research conducted within natural settings. Some argue that local decision-makers are often not interested in generalizations across a wide range of contexts many of which may be very different from their own contexts. Participatory and emancipatory researchers assert that teachers must be co-researchers in any research geared at informing their own practice. Emphasizing that change must occur as an inherent part of the research process, action researchers challenge the merit in constructing knowledge for its own sake and argue that knowledge must be constructed in the process of bringing about a reflective change (Heron and Reason 1997, Yu 2011).

Critical scholars assert that it is more important to inform policy-making by identifying 'what is not working and what should not be done' (Popkewitz 2004, p. 75). They emphasize that rather than providing conclusive answers, evidence-based practice can be more honestly and effectively implemented by working with practitioners and policy-makers to understand and use 'the fragmented, uncertain and contested nature of research knowledge' in education (Hodkinson and Smith 2004, p. 163). As the same body of evidence can be used to support several policies, they assert that ideology is as important as the methodological quality of research for informing policy (Phillips 2006). They call for recognizing not just the direct, but also indirect approaches to improving practice through research (Edwards 2000).

Emphasizing the highly complex nature of educational practice, many researchers recognize the need to draw on multiple theoretical frameworks and methodologies. To avoid polarization within the educational research community, we need more sites for genuine dialogues between different groups of researchers where each group can learn from the other (Moss 2005). This book is intended to stimulate such conversations about research synthesis methods.

## Summary

Contemporary research and practice in education is marked by growing diversity, complexity and eclecticism. Different methodological options can be matched to the research needs of different situations. There is a level at which it may be useful to note similarities between individual positions. At the same time there is also a level when it suits our purpose to distinguish between different positions. Given all this complexity and diversity in principles, practices and primary research methods within education, we have a case for a more inclusive discussion of advancements in research synthesis methods. This inclusive discussion is described in the next chapter. Recognizing this methodological diversity also builds a case for exploring a variety of methodologically inclusive possibilities in research synthesis methods. This book presents insights gained from one such exploration.

# Chapter 3

# Advancements in research synthesis methods

From a methodologically inclusive perspective, what are some key developments in the literature on research synthesis methods?

The vast, sometimes seemingly disparate, literature on research synthesis methods appears in several forms. From a methodological perspective, this substantial body of literature can be partitioned into the following six subsets with several overlaps:

1 *Statistical research syntheses.* Extensive literature on discussions and applications of statistical methods of comparing and integrating primary research reports, such as meta-analysis and best-evidence synthesis.

2 *Systematic reviews.* Literature on systematic reviews which emphasizes a priori protocols, comprehensive searches, transparency to reduce biases and involving stakeholders in the review process.

3 *Qualitative research syntheses.* Relatively sparse, but rapidly growing, literature on various methods for synthesizing qualitative research.

4 *Qualitative syntheses of qualitative and quantitative research.* Relatively sparse, but definitely growing, literature on various qualitative methods for synthesizing qualitative and quantitative research.

5 *Critical impetus in reviewing research.* Relatively sparse published discussions on a range of critical issues associated with the production and use of research syntheses, such as their forms and purposes, politics of representation, frequent sources of errors and biases, and suggestions for reducing some commonly found biases.

6 *Critiques, taxonomies and exemplars.* Critiques and taxonomies of published research syntheses and a variety of exemplary syntheses.

The first part of this chapter reviews each of these six subsets of literature from a methodologically inclusive perspective. Each section begins with a summary of how this subset of literature has advanced the methodology of research synthesis. This is followed by a critical commentary on its overall implications for research synthesis methods. The chapter concludes by identifying some transcendental trends in the literature on research synthesis methods.

## Statistical research syntheses

Glass coined the term 'meta-analysis' to refer to the process of statistical integration of primary research findings (1976, p. 3). While some meta-analysts reserve the term 'meta-analysis' to refer 'specifically to statistical analysis in research synthesis and not to the entire enterprise of research synthesis' (Cooper and Hedges 2009), this distinction is not recognized by all meta-analysts (e.g. Lipsey and Wilson 2001, Glass et al. 1981). In this book the term meta-analysis has been used broadly to refer to the entire process of a research synthesis employing statistical procedures. For example, the term meta-analysts is used to collectively refer to meta-analysts and best-evidence synthesists when referring to the perspective on which both the groups converge.

To reduce unstated subjectivity in a synthesis meta-analysts formulate clear hypotheses with operational and conceptual definitions of key constructs; state explicit criteria for the inclusion and exclusion of primary research; conduct explicit and comprehensive searches for relevant studies; follow explicit procedures for extracting relevant information from each study; convert summaries of individual studies to appropriate effect-sizes; attach appropriate weights to individual effect-sizes according to their sample sizes; statistically integrate these findings into a cumulative effect-size after adjusting for their variances; identify confidence intervals associated with the cumulative effect; and conduct outlier diagnosis and homogeneity analysis to identify potential moderators of the effect (Glass 2006, Suri and Hattie in press).

Meta-analytic literature contains sophisticated discussions of different types of effect-sizes suitable for different study designs; formulae that allow conversion between different effect-size indices; guidelines for estimating an effect-size when some information is not reported in the primary research report; appropriateness of various effect indices for analyzing different types of data (Borenstein 2009, Fleiss and Berlin 2009); strengths and weaknesses of various search strategies; different types of publication biases and search biases (Rothstein et al. 2004); strategies for identifying and taking into account potential publication biases (Sutton 2009); and several types of sensitivity analyses to examine the dependence of the synthesis findings on the assumptions made about the nature of the data (Greenhouse and Iyengar 2009).

Since the conception of meta-analysis, several meta-analysts in education have recommended that meta-analyses must be supplemented with rich narrative discussions of quantitative and qualitative information (Light and Pillemer 1984). Accordingly, different variations of meta-analysis have been proposed to include qualitative information, such as 'best-evidence synthesis' (Slavin 1986, p. 5) and Bayesian approaches (Louis and Zelterman 1994, Pope et al. 2007). Over the past three decades, numerous investigations have been conducted to examine the robustness of meta-analytic techniques and to explore strategies for refining these techniques by methodologists from diverse disciplinary backgrounds including statistics, psychology, education, health care, agriculture and physics. Meta-analyses are so widely prevalent in education, especially in the USA, that the method has been referred to as 'a minor academic industry, as well as a commercial endeavour' (Glass 2006, p. 436). Numerous meta-analyses have been published in the *Review of Educational Research* (RER). Reflecting this dominance of meta-analytic methods, in the American Educational Research Association's (AERA's) publication, *Handbook of complementary methods in education research* (Green et al. 2006), there are only two chapters devoted to research synthesis methods: 'Meta-analysis: The quantitative synthesis of research findings' (Glass 2006) and 'Research synthesis: Effect sizes' (Thompson 2006). Both of these chapters exclusively discuss meta-analytic methods with no recognition of any other form of research synthesis.

By systematization of the entire process of a research synthesis, meta-analysts make a worthy contribution in advancing the methodology of research synthesis. However, until recently, the meta-analytic literature gave little recognition to a variety of qualitative methods of primary research and research synthesis. The fundamental premise of a meta-analysis is that every primary research finding that is included in the meta-analysis should be converted into an effect-size. Meta-analyses are essentially 'backward looking' as studies with innovative designs or ideas are often excluded because they are difficult to compare with other studies (Kennedy 2007). Within the meta-analytic literature, even the discussions about including qualitative information tend to overlook the potential for qualitative research to inform synthesis findings more structurally; incommensurabilities between quantitative and qualitative research; and opportunities for conducting research syntheses oriented along different methodologies. It would be limiting to inform educational policies and practices exclusively by syntheses based on measurable concepts and statistical integration of verifiable relationships between two or more variables. In addition to meta-analyses, we need multiple forms of research synthesis that reflect the diversity and complexity in contemporary educational research. In recent years, several eminent meta-analysts have also acknowledged the need for rigorous qualitative research syntheses (e.g. Cooper 2009).

## Systematic reviews

Systematic reviews are frequently associated with the political movement of Evidence-Based Education (EBE) that is gaining momentum in several nations, such as the UK, USA, Canada and some members of the European Union. Systematic reviews are becoming common in disciplines such as health care, education, social sciences and public policy. Organizations, such as the Cochrane Collaboration (The Cochrane Collaboration 2011), the Campbell Collaboration (n.d.), EPPI-Centre (2009), Centre for Reviews and Dissemination (CRD 2011) and Best Evidence Encyclopedia (BEE 2011) have been set up to support production and dissemination of 'systematic reviews' of research. Some of these organizations are heavily funded and politically supported by government, corporate and philanthropic agencies. Particularly noteworthy are systematic reviewers' intentions to seek feedback from users of educational research when formulating synthesis questions; regularly update their reviews with the new relevant studies in the field; reduce duplication through explicit international collaborations; methodologically support groups interested in conducting systematic reviews; develop useful databases of intervention studies and systematic reviews to facilitate their dissemination and access; and utilize technology strategically to update and disseminate relevant information widely. Like meta-analysts, most systematic reviewers emphasize a priori synthesis protocols; explicit inclusion-exclusion criteria; explicit criteria for evaluating methodological quality of individual studies; comprehensive searches for all relevant studies; and objectivity and transparency throughout the synthesis process (Gough et al. 2012a).

There are two methodologically distinct perspectives prevalent among systematic reviewers. The first group is dominated by quantitative synthesists who recommend that ideally a systematic review must hold randomized controlled trials (RCTs) as the gold standard for individual studies (e.g. Campbell Collaboration n.d.). In 2010, the Society for Research Synthesis Methodology (SRSM n.d.) started publishing its journal *Research Synthesis Methods* (JRSM) to publish 'papers covering the development and dissemination of methods for designing, conducting, analyzing, interpreting, reporting, and applying systematic research synthesis' (Schmid and Lipsey 2011). It is interesting to note the dominance of quantitative procedures in the activities and publications of this society.

The second group of systematic reviewers have engaged with various issues associated with including qualitative research in systematic reviews; developing efficient search strategies, appraisal criteria and synthesis techniques for primary qualitative research; engaging various stakeholders in formulating and critiquing their reviews' questions, protocols and summary reports; and stressing that systematic reviews must be complemented with other forms of reviews to facilitate informed decision-making by different stakeholders. In the last decade, useful contributions have been made by this group (e.g. Pope et al. 2007, Petticrew and Roberts 2006, Gough et al. 2012b).

Critiquing from a methodologically inclusive perspective, many systematic reviewers exclude a large proportion of research on the grounds of poor methodological quality using an evaluation criteria that is biased against certain paradigmatic orientations. Such an unacknowledged bias raises serious questions about the validity and generalizability of review findings (Pawson 2006). Sometimes systematic reviewers discuss qualitative research as a broad category and do not adequately distinguish between different types of qualitative research (Dixon-Woods et al. 2005). Even in their inclusion of qualitative research, systematic reviewers often include only interpretive qualitative research and seek ideologically neutral evidence. The rhetorical effect of terms like 'evidence-based practice', 'systematic reviews', 'clarity', 'comprehensive', 'reliable', 'objectivity', 'replicable' not only discredits any opposition, but also has the political impact of favouring postpositivism. Ironically, these key terms that are the trademark of systematic reviews are operationalized differently by different groups of systematic reviewers. The problem here is not the subjectivity associated with these terms, but the systematic reviewers' denial of subjectivity itself (Hammersley 2004). The problem lies in openly discrediting ideological research with an implicit political agenda (Gallagher 2004).

Many systematic reviewers unproblematically value objectivity and transparency of process, a priori protocols and exhaustive searches. Accordingly, advantages of emergent synthesis designs and purposeful sampling are less discussed in this body of literature. In reality, transparency itself is always subjective, partial and purposefully informed where each way of showing is mirrored by a way of concealing, which may or may not be deliberate. Prescribing a priori rules to enhance objectivity, transparency and clarity could worsen the quality of reviews by discouraging reflection on important process decisions (MacLure 2005, Kennedy 2007). 'Instead of the systematic/unsystematic distinction what is required is a non-evaluative typology dealing with different kinds of focus that reviews can have' (Hammersley 2003, p. 5). The MIRS framework is an attempt to offer one such typology.

## Qualitative research syntheses

In this section, the term qualitative research synthesis is used to refer to efforts of synthesizing qualitative research. Asserting that the efforts involved in a rigorous research synthesis are comparable with those required in a rigorous primary research study, qualitative research synthesists distinguish systematic efforts of synthesizing qualitative research from the intuitive reviews of literature that meta-analysts refer to as traditional discursive reviews. Among the early methods for synthesizing qualitative research, Noblit and Hare's (1988) 'meta-ethnography' is the most cited method. Distinguishing features of their approach include an emphasis on being 'interpretive rather than aggregative'; 'constructing interpretations, not analyses' (p. 11); being inductive rather than using a prior conceptual framework; employing purposeful sampling rather than exhaustive sampling for selecting primary research studies; being consciously aware of one's own subjectivity; and paying attention to the target audience's discourse (Noblit and Hare 1988).

Noblit and Hare (1988) used the term 'metaphor' to refer to 'themes, perspectives, organizers, and/or concepts revealed by qualitative studies'. They recommended 'metaphoric reductions' to 'achieve both abstraction and complexity, and create translations that preserve the relations between concepts' (p. 14). These metaphoric reductions are then translated into one another and expressed as analogies through 'idiomatic translations' of salient categories of meaning. A meta-ethnography takes different forms depending on how individual accounts are related to each other: 'as a reciprocal translation (essentially similar and subject to direct translation), as a refutation (involving translation of refutations as well as accounts), or in a line of argument (an analogy about a set of parts to some whole)' (pp. 81-82). Based on this initial assumption about the relationship between individual accounts, a meta-ethnographer makes appropriate translations, checks this initial assumption, and constructs a text that presents the synthesis process and product in a suitable form for the target audience (Noblit and Hare 1988).

Since the mid 1990s, there has been a growing interest in synthesizing qualitative studies especially in the areas of health care and public policy. A variety of methods have been proposed for synthesizing qualitative research from interpretive and critical-realist perspectives which vary along several dimensions (Barnett-Page and Thomas 2009). Some methods have been developed to facilitate a fuller understanding of a phenomenon (Jensen and Allen 1996) but others are aimed at generating mid-range theory (Zimmer 2006, Eastabrooks et al. 1994) or 'lines-of-action' (Hannes and Lockwood 2011a) to inform practical decision-making. While some synthesists recommend purposeful sampling for selecting studies, others recommend comprehensive searches and inclusion criteria. Some recommend including epistemologically similar qualitative studies in a synthesis, others recommend including studies from diverse epistemologies. And while many qualitative research synthesists recommend a grounded-theory like approach of axial coding for identifying themes emerging across studies, others note that a grounded-theory like approach to synthesizing research can sometimes become very resource-intensive and may not be viable. To improve efficiency in a research synthesis, some synthesists recommend starting with an a priori conceptual framework and modifying it as new themes emerge from the data (Carroll et al. 2011, Dixon-woods 2011).

In recent years, several monographs have exclusively focused on issues associated with synthesizing qualitative research. While most of these monographs have been authored by synthesists from health care and public policy areas (e.g. Sandelowski and Barroso 2007, Paterson et al. 2001, Hannes and Lockwood 2011b), Major and Savin-Baden (2010) provide useful guidelines for synthesizing qualitative research in education and social sciences from a critical interpretive perspective.

Critiquing from a methodologically inclusive perspective, this group has made an important contribution towards improving the status and quality of qualitative research syntheses by addressing important questions such as the following: What are suitable purposes for conducting syntheses of qualitative research? What are suitable criteria for evaluating qualitative research in an interpretive synthesis? What strategies can be adopted for enhancing trustworthiness of a qualitative research synthesis? What are some caveats of a qualitative synthesis? However, this subset of literature offers relatively sparse discussion of questions such as the following: How might different strategies for purposeful sampling be adopted to the context of a research synthesis? How can synthesists be inclusive of critical and participatory perspectives that are common in educational research? What are issues associated with including openly ideological research in a synthesis? How might synthesists draw on various arts-based, critical and post-modern sensibilities through every phase of a research synthesis?

## Synthesizing methodologically diverse research

Many research synthesists assert that important questions about educational, health and social phenomena must be informed by syntheses of qualitative, quantitative and mixed-methods studies. Some quantitative synthesists draw on qualitative evidence to inform their quantitative synthesis or quantify the qualitative evidence for inclusion in quantitative synthesists. Many synthesists argue that qualitative approaches are more suitable for synthesizing methodologically diverse studies on a similar topic. A large proportion of rigorous reviews published in educational journals such as *RER* and *Review of Research in Education* (*RRE*) have been qualitative reviews of qualitative and quantitative research. Examples of publications about such methodologically inclusive qualitative syntheses include Zhao's classification of multi-paradigmatic 'meta-study' from sociology (Zhao 1991); Ogawa and Malen's 'exploratory case study approach' (1991b, p. 265), which draws on ideas from meta-analysis and the case survey method to synthesize research and non-research papers, along with its critiques published in the *RER* (Ogawa and Malen 1991a, Patton 1991, Yin 1991); Bair's 'integrative and expansionist' method of 'meta-synthesis', which she developed to synthesize research on attrition and persistence of doctoral students (Bair 1999); Pascarella and Terenzini's 'narrative explanatory synthesis' (2005) of a large number of methodologically diverse studies on how students are affected by college; and comparisons between various quantitative and qualitative approaches that have the potential to synthesize qualitative and quantitative evidence published by health-care researchers (Kastner et al. 2012). Some researchers argue that in preference to quantitative or qualitative research syntheses, often 'mixed methods research syntheses' are more suitable for providing 'more complete, concrete and nuanced answers' to complex synthesis questions (Heyvaert 2011).

Particularly noteworthy is Pawson's (2006) method of 'realist synthesis' to develop theory from successful as well as non-successful implementations of a program. Rather than making global generalizations, realist reviews seek to explain how different aspects of a program are likely to work in different circumstances. The synthesist begins by identifying the key theories underlying the specific phenomenon to formulate a more refined theory. Then the synthesist applies this theory successively to explain a number of successful and unsuccessful cases. With each application, the synthesist refines the theory. The salient features of Pawson's method include purposeful sampling; methodological inclusivity by including studies with diverse qualitative and qualitative designs; involvement of stakeholders in identifying the purpose; and tentative findings which inform decision-makers of the likely implications of different decisions made in different situations rather than what works (Pawson 2006).

Given the methodological diversity of educational research on most topics, qualitative synthesis of quantitative and qualitative research is an appealing concept. This subset of literature offers useful, practical suggestions on how to formulate a coherent understanding from the complex terrain of methodologically diverse studies on a topic. They offer promising directions for synthesists to pursue. Some questions that require further discussion include the following: How should a synthesist deal with the incommensurabilities or incompatibilities across diverse methods of primary research? How can synthesists choose a suitable set of criteria for evaluating the quality of methodologically diverse primary research reports? What are the issues associated with including reports that are openly ideological and/or use the arts-based methods that are gaining popularity within some circles in education.

## Critical impetus in reviewing research

Since the late 1990s, several articles published in reputable educational journals like *RER* and *British Educational Research Journal* (*BERJ*) have inspected, interrogated and expanded boundaries of the processes involved in the production and use of educational research reviews. Topics of such critical discussions include the complexities and tensions inherent in decisions that influence production and use of reviews, such as sponsorship, authorship, intended audience, structure, scope, selection criteria and nature of conclusions drawn (Foster and Hammersley 1998); reflexivity in reviews of reviews (Gillborn and Gipps 1998); reformulation of 'the categories of knowledge through the intersection of epistemology, culture, and politics in education' (Popkewitz 1999, p. 398); a genealogical examination of curriculum reviews published in the *RER* to reveal how the 'discursive practices embedded in the language in which our research reviews are framed creates the kind of thinking that constructs fields of inquiry in certain ways and not others' (Franklin 1999, pp. 358-359); an historical examination of the issues of 'voice, identity and representation', to question the unproblematic conception of voice as a 'liberatory or emancipatory strategy in re-viewing reviews' (Baker 1999, pp. 381); and an historical examination of the issues of *RER* published from 1931 (when it was know as *The Review)* to 1999 to identify the evolving trends in the various features of these reviews, such as the nature of included primary research in terms of the substantive content area, its scope and coverage, and methods employed, probable authors, intended audience, editorial presence, and forms of reviews (Grant and Graue 1999).

Reflecting critically on their editorial experiences, some past editors of *RER* and *RRE* have raised concerns over issues, such as the observation that there are factors besides quality of the manuscripts that sometimes influence the peer-review process of research reviews, e.g. 'uninformed reviews, ideological or political bias in the review process, ethical conflicts of interest, and the mistaken views of fairness held by the field' (Murray and Raths 1996, p. 418). They also observed that often little attention is paid to critiques of research reviews. The process and product of research reviews are inherently social and situated. Often, research reviews are not recognized as 'new' knowledge and are relatively *marginalized* in the 'institutionalized and increasingly marketized hierarchies of legitimate knowledge' (Apple 1999, pp. 344-5).

Recognizing the need to move beyond postpositivist reviews, there have been calls for reviews that highlight the cracks, tensions and fractures in our understanding about a phenomenon rather than building a comprehensive understanding of a field (Eisenhart 1998, p. 394); reviews, which reveal how 'we are all immersed within processes which are connected to and constitutive of the disparities and inequalities which characterize the educational landscape' (Meacham 1998, pp. 402-405); reviews, which are tools for 'recasting both the academic literature and the lived' and which could afford 'robust disorientation possible at the internal-external nexus of power' (1999, pp. 10-12); and poststructural reviews, which construct 'situated, partial, perspectival' understandings rather than constructing any totalizing grand meta-narratives (Lather 1999, p. 3).

In critiquing the hegemonic dominance of systematic reviews, critical scholars alert us to several contentious issues, such as: the problematics of formalization and systematization of research synthesis processes (e.g. MacLure 2005, Gallagher 2004); social and political 'dynamics of the ways in which evidence comes to be used' (Clegg 2005, p. 425); and 'diverse commentaries on audiences and readers, and on interconnections between research/researchers, policy/policy-makers, and practice/practitioners' (Hustler et al. 1998, p. 500). Many of these criticisms apply to most formal research synthesis methods and not just systematic reviews. It is crucial that all research synthesists and readers of syntheses engage with these critical conversations to enhance reflexivity in production and interpretation of research syntheses.

## Exemplary syntheses in education

Often, a clear distinction between knowledge from research, practice and policy is not feasible in education as all these domains of knowledge constitute, and are constituted by, each other (Ward 1983). Since the early 1980s, there have been several attempts to categorize different aspects of reviewing knowledge in education, such as: structure, types and synthesis of knowledge (Ward 1983); epistemological problems in knowledge synthesis (Strike and Posner 1983); categorizations of literature reviews (Cooper 1988, Boote and Beile 2005) and systematic reviews (Gough and Thomas 2012); and discussions of commonly-observed sources of errors and biases in research reviews in education (Dunkin 1996).

Every year, the *American Educational Research Association* (*AERA*) gives a Review of Research award in recognition of an outstanding review of research article appearing in *RRE* or *RER* (*AERA* 2012). A closer examination of these award-winning reviews reveals several common methodological features as listed in the boxed text. Most research synthesists would agree that these must be an integral part of every quality synthesis.

---

### Common methodological features of exemplary reviews

- conceptually substantiated and well-bound coverage of the substantive topic;
- rigorous critique of previous reviews;
- inductive approach to identifying common assumptions, theories, methods and findings emerging from extant research;
- critical analyses of extant research;
- coherent structuring of the report along meaningful themes;
- providing a unique conceptual framework or perspective to think about the topic, future research, practice and policy;
- providing clear implications for researchers, practitioners and policy-makers.

---

## Making some overarching trends explicit

Although a plethora of terms are being used with different connotations, all research synthesists uphold several assumptions. This section *explicitly* discusses some of these assumptions and illuminates some evolving trends in the literature of research synthesis methods under the following two subheadings:

- Complementary purposes of primary research and research syntheses
- Changing landscape of the literature on research synthesis methods

### Complementary purposes of primary research and research syntheses

A common belief underlying all research synthesis methods is that primary research and research syntheses have complementary purposes. While some questions are amenable to a research synthesis, others are more amenable to primary research methods. Primary research can capture greater detail of the context being studied. Often, a primary research study has the virtue of being close to its context and hence its findings are likely to be more transferable to similar contexts. It is naïve to assume that a research synthesis encompasses all aspects of its constituent studies. As a research synthesis draws on parts of primary research studies, it is inevitable to sacrifice some of the rich contextual information available in reports of primary research.

The 'value-addedness' of a research synthesis lies to a significant extent in its ability to bring to light new ways of looking at a set of primary research studies. The evidence of a research synthesis is more complex, refined and sophisticated. A research synthesis advances knowledge in a field by identifying some transcendental features and patterns across a number of studies. Transferability of an educational phenomenon can be enhanced by systematically examining a range of contexts in which it has been observed. Subtle nuances that form the essence of a phenomenon can become noticeable through systematic comparisons to make explicit similarities and variations between individual studies examining that phenomenon. Research syntheses play an important role in informing policy, practice, public perception and further research by making explicit connections between individual studies. Hence, issues of rigor are important in every research synthesis. Research synthesis is a methodology in its own right involving numerous tasks and critical decisions. Efforts and resources required in a rigorous research synthesis are comparable to those required in a rigorous primary research study. It is crucial that synthesists share, discuss, debate and critique different aspects of research synthesis processes to improve quality of research syntheses.

### Changing landscape of the literature on research synthesis methods

Advances in methods of primary research and research synthesis should, and to some extent do, mutually inform each other. A dialectic tension exists between the methods of primary research and research synthesis, where methodological developments in either mode influence methodological developments in the other mode. In Table 3.1, a summary of the nature of typical primary research in education is juxtaposed with the methods of research synthesis that became the norm a decade later. In the 1940s and 1950s, primary research on a given topic tended to consist of a relatively small number of primary research studies employing similar methods. These could be described aptly by ad hoc narrative reviews which were the norm in education until the 1960s. In the 1960s and 1970s, the tendency was for many individual topics within education to be examined by a large number of primary research studies that aimed to empirically investigate similar hypotheses with minimal biases. In the 1970s and 1980s, statistical methods of integrating findings across studies gained popularity. The aim of these methods was to objectively synthesize studies that addressed similar hypotheses. Since the 1980s, primary research in education has been marked by a diversity of purposes, perspectives and methods. With a growing acceptance of qualitative research methods, the elusive nature of objectivity is increasingly being recognized and questioned. A parallel drive for methodological inclusivity can also be observed in the evolution of methods of research synthesis since the late 1980s (Grant and Graue 1999). 'Clarity, explicitness, and openness' (Glass et al.

*Table 3.1* Evolving methods of primary research and research synthesis in education

| Primary Research | Research Syntheses |
|---|---|
| 1940s and 1950s: small number of studies employing similar methods | Until 1960s: ad hoc narrative reviews were the norm |
| 1960s and 1970s: large number of studies examining similar hypotheses | 1970s and 1980s: statistical methods of research integration gained popularity |
| From 1980s: growing eclecticism and diversity of purpose, methods and perspectives in primary research | From late 1980s: growing eclecticism and diversity of purpose, methods and perspectives in research syntheses |

1981, p. 20) are still valued. However, there is a growing recognition that these tenets may be pursued through a variety of quantitative, qualitative and mixed methods of sense-making. Thus, we notice a time lag of about a decade between primary research methods and their compatible research synthesis methods. Such a time lag is understandable as most syntheses are likely to include primary research conducted during the previous decade.

A decade ago, there was a relative paucity of published literature on the following issues: synthesis of qualitative research; qualitative synthesis of quantitative and qualitative research; involvement of key stakeholders, especially practitioners, in making critical choices throughout the synthesis process; and reflexivity in research syntheses. In recent years, the landscape of research synthesis methods has been changing rapidly to become more inclusive. The literature on synthesizing qualitative research is relatively young and can be improved by exploring adaptability of ideas, techniques and strategies from wider range of qualitative primary research methods to research synthesis processes.

Each method inherently involves judgement calls at various phases of a synthesis. Each of the methods described in the previous section has its individual strengths, weaknesses and domain of applicability. Each method makes useful contribution by providing guidelines for synthesizing a particular type of research reports and has its domain of applicability. Exploring adaptability of various methodological ideas, techniques and strategies from primary research methods to research synthesis processes can contribute, and often has contributed, towards improving the craft of research synthesis. This book presents a purposeful synthesis of diverse literature on methods of research synthesis and primary research to expand possibilities within research synthesis methods.

# Chapter 4

# Key methodological considerations

What were key methodological considerations in conceptualizing the MIRS framework?

This chapter describes critical choices made in the process of conceptualizing the MIRS framework. It represents my retrospective construction of the process expressed through the six phases of the MIRS framework. Many considerations and issues identified within the MIRS framework are applicable to any rigorous effort of knowledge synthesis.

## Identifying an appropriate purpose

### Overarching question underpinning the development of the MIRS framework

Contemporary educational research is marked by diversity, complexity and richness of purposes, methods and perspectives. How can we accommodate, reflect and celebrate such variety and complexity at the level of synthesizing educational research?

This is the essence of the quest underpinning development of the MIRS framework. At the early stages of this project, I wanted to propose *a single most comprehensive* and useful method for synthesizing several methodologically diverse primary research reports on a similar topic.

In developing this method, I intended to draw on the *best* aspects of *all* research synthesis methods and several primary research methods. To retain the strengths of a meta-analysis while overcoming some of its limitations, the structural framework of a meta-analysis was considered suitable for the new method. An exploratory emphasis was considered essential to remain open to various issues arising from engaging with diverse methods of research synthesis and primary research. An emerging design with evolving questions was necessary for enacting my ethical commitment to synthesize some less represented methodological perspectives within the dominant literature on research synthesis methods. Two forms of inquiry were pursued for this purpose. First, the transferability of perspectives and techniques across various methods of synthesizing research was explored. Second, the adaptability of ideas and techniques from diverse primary research methods to the process of a research synthesis was explored. Both of these inquiries revealed the paradoxical nature of my initial purpose.

### Literature on research synthesis methods

As I immersed myself deeper into the literature on research synthesis methods, I became conscious of several tensions within my initial purpose. First, I wanted to provide the most comprehensive set of guidelines that was firm but not rigid, useful but not restrictive, flexible but not vague. However, by claiming that it was possible to develop a single research synthesis method that would be most comprehensive and suitable for all synthesis purposes, I was myself being rigid and prescriptive. Second, I wanted to draw on the *best* aspects of *all* previously proposed research synthesis methods without undermining their individual worth. As I closely examined each method, I noticed not only similar and compatible features but also unique and incommensurable features across methods. I became more conscious of the prevailing complexities, variety of purposes, evidence types, and possible orientations of research syntheses. My initial purpose of developing a *single most comprehensive* method that could serve diverse purposes, encapsulate complexities prevalent in most areas of research, have sufficient scope, and be flexible enough to respond to the rapidly changing realms of educational practices and research methods, became self-defeating.

### Literature on primary research methods

I noticed that meta-analysts had thoroughly examined the adaptability of a range of ideas and statistical techniques to minimize bias in the process of a research synthesis. In comparison, the literature was relatively sparse on the adaptation of ideas and techniques from primary qualitative research methods to the process of a research synthesis. I turned my attention towards filling in this gap by exploring adaptability of ideas and techniques from a variety of primary qualitative research methods to the process of a research synthesis. This exploration revealed two conflicts within my initial purpose. First, a research synthesis method with the postpositivist structural framework of a meta-analysis could not encapsulate the interpretive epistemology endorsed by most qualitative researchers. Second, even though there were some similarities across individual primary qualitative research methods, there were also striking differences that were sometimes irreconcilable. With a growing awareness of the variations in perspectives and techniques under the broad umbrella of qualitative research, I recognized the problematics of compiling a common set of guidelines that were representative of all types of qualitative research. For instance, I realized that syntheses with interpretive, participatory and critical orientations would be different even if they were all generally positioned within qualitative research tradition.

Through both of these initial inquiries, I developed a better appreciation for the problematics inherent in proposing a single method of research synthesis to comprehensively and justifiably synthesize diverse types of evidence for different purposes. Also, I realized that a reductionist framework, structurally similar to that of a meta-analysis, is at odds with the interpretive spirit essential for synthesizing primary research in a field that is methodologically and substantively disparate.

At this stage of the project, the purpose was modified to develop a set of guidelines to facilitate informed decision-making by identifying various possibilities, and their respective consequences, throughout the synthesis process. These guidelines have been synthesized into a coherent framework that is referred to as the 'Methodologically Inclusive Research Synthesis' (MIRS) framework. In developing this framework, I have been methodologically inclusive by:

- addressing issues arising from synthesizing methodologically diverse primary research;
- drawing on ideas and strategies from a variety of research synthesis methods and exemplary research syntheses;
- adapting ideas and techniques from a range of primary research methods, especially qualitative research methods, to the process of a research synthesis;
- taking into account how processes and politics of research synthesis may intersect with the interests of different stakeholders.

---

**The specific questions addressed in this book**

- What are some critical considerations in the process of a research synthesis?
- What options open up, and close down, by making different methodological choices in a research synthesis?

---

## Identifying an appropriate epistemological orientation

I commenced this project with a postpositivist vision of a unified theory to reliably integrate empirical research conducted in a field. As I delved deeper into the literature on traditional qualitative primary research methods, I began to appreciate *multiple constructions of reality* as stressed in qualitative research literature. At the end of this project, I am more conscious of my ignorance and partiality of perspective with a greater recognition and celebration of my inconclusive transitional position in an ongoing journey. I find myself at a transitional stage with a sense of inclusivity that values purposeful, partial, multiple and transitional nature of any process of knowledge construction. As noted earlier in Chapter 2, different researchers vary in their attitudes towards epistemological differences. The very notion of methodological inclusivity is understood and enacted differently by different methodologists. In this book, I have enacted the principle of purposefully informed selective inclusivity in my efforts to draw from diverse philosophical, theoretical and methodological discussions. This position is markedly different from my initial postpositivist position of subscribing to a unity thesis. This book is positioned within an interpretive tradition informed by critical sensibilities.

## Searching for relevant literature

The exploratory nature of this project and the vast bodies of literature on research synthesis methods and primary research methods necessitated broad inclusion criteria from the outset. With a selective rather than a comprehensive goal, the focus of my coverage of the relevant literature was on drawing ideas from a wide spectrum of methodological perspectives. At the early stages of this project, extensive searches were conducted to cast a wide net and get a general feel for the literature on research synthesis methods. This was followed by purposeful sampling to identify recent texts from key players in the field and to explore those themes that were not covered well within the retrieved literature, but were seen as being important for enhancing inclusivity and rigour in research syntheses. Extensive searches were also conducted to identify the key themes and variations within the literature covered under the umbrella of qualitative research and mixed-methods research.

Multiple techniques were employed to first conduct extensive searches and then to focus these searches purposefully. Electronic searches were conducted on several databases (including ERIC, Web of Science, Australian Education Index, PsychInfo and Cinhal) and library catalogues of three Australian universities. Experts on individual methods of primary research were contacted to identify the key publications about their individual methods and to clarify my own understanding of different methods, especially different strands of qualitative research. Selected references from the bibliographies of retrieved publications were checked for further consideration. Also considered were recent publications citing selected publications, especially on qualitative research synthesis methods. Websites of major organizations supporting systematic reviews, such as the EPPI-centre, Campbell Collaboration and Cochrane Collaboration were also looked at regularly to keep up with the emerging developments.

Often references to the more recent issues of journals are not included in the electronic databases. To keep abreast with the latest discussions on methods of research synthesis and primary research, the Table of Contents of recent issues of several relevant journals were skimmed through. These journals include the *Review of Educational Research (RER)*, *Educational Researcher (ER)*, *Qualitative*

*Inquiry (QI), Qualitative Studies in Education (QSE), Qualitative Research (QR), Australian Educational Researcher (AER), British Educational Research Journal (BERJ), Evaluation and Research in Education, Oxford Review of Education, Harvard Educational Review (HER)* and *Educational Research Review (ERR).*

An exhaustive reading of all the literature published on methods of primary research and research synthesis was neither viable nor cost-effective. Every new piece of information influenced my conception of the MIRS framework to varying degrees. In this sense, the stage of data saturation or data redundancy was never reached. Rather, a sense of data sufficiency has been achieved from several angles. First, I realize that I have reasonably represented the adaptation of ideas and techniques from several distinct methodological orientations to the process of a research synthesis. Second, many fellow-researchers have expressed an interest in finding more information about the MIRS framework, which suggests that this book will be of interest to this group of audience. Third, informed by postmodern sensibilities, I have learnt to live in the uncomfortable space of sharing my partial understanding that is fluid and evolving. Rather than providing prescriptive methodological solutions, the goal of this book is to stimulate debate, discussion and critical consideration of a range of methodological issues associated with research synthesis methods.

For several reasons this project primarily draws on the literature published in the USA. During the early phases of this project, when extensive searches for literature on research synthesis methods were conducted, publications from the USA had dominated the literature on research synthesis methods. For instance, most books and articles formally proposing and critiquing research synthesis methods were published in the USA. Journals like the *RER*, which are exclusively devoted to research reviews, were not published in other countries like the UK (Foster and Hammersley 1998) or Australia. No award like the coveted *AERA's Review of the Year* was found in the UK or Australia.

I acknowledge that a high representation of publications from the USA has biased my coverage. This book would have taken a different shape if I had more access to methodological literature from different countries, especially in languages other than English. I have taken three steps to account for this bias. First, I have explicitly acknowledged it. Second, I have tried to be inclusive by skimming through the Table of Contents of key British and Australian journals and websites. Also, I have extensively covered recently published literature on systematic reviews from the UK and Europe. Third, I have drawn on critical sensibilities to interrogate the very text on which I have built my narrative.

## Evaluating, interpreting and distilling relevant information

Ideas from several vast bodies of literature have been synthesized in this book, not all of which have been equally represented. Also the nature and extent of information distilled from individual texts varies substantially. This section describes the key criteria and strategies that were employed in evaluating, interpreting and distilling relevant and trustworthy information from selected texts.

Trustworthiness of individual texts was appraised on the basis of how these texts, and their authors, were generally regarded by researchers espousing that particular methodology. Often, more attention was paid to texts that captured well the essence of a particular methodology. Nonetheless, sometimes I specifically attended to those texts which discussed issues that I believed were important but not typically discussed in the literature, such as texts stressing the need to complement discussions of statistical significance with practical significance. The underlying criterion that guided the extent to which I drew on a particular text was the extent to which that text helped me in expanding possibilities within research synthesis methods.

In the first draft of this book, I drew heavily from several books and articles exclusively devoted to meta-analytic methods to explore the adaptability of meta-analytic techniques and ideas for syntheses with diverse purposes. In particular I drew on the *Handbook of research synthesis and meta-analysis* (Cooper et al. 2009) and its previous edition. At the commencement of this project, the literature on interpretive, critical and participatory syntheses was relatively less represented in the mainstream literature on research synthesis methods. To fill in this gap, I read, interpreted and analyzed texts on qualitative research synthesis methods several times to explore how synthesists from various orientations can learn useful lessons from this sparse body of literature. Also, I drew heavily from key texts on qualitative research methods, such as the *Sage Handbook of qualitative research* (Denzin and Lincoln 2011) and its earlier editions.

Although I found the readings on mixed-methods insightful, I distinguished between the purposefully informed selective inclusivity on which this book is premised from the ecumenical approach frequently endorsed by proponents of mixed-methods (e.g. Tashakkori and Teddlie 2010). Research synthesists *can* usefully draw upon the rich literature on mixed-methods when synthesizing quantitative, qualitative and mixed-methods research reports especially by using a combination of quantitative and qualitative synthesis techniques. However, it is not essential in every rigorous synthesis to employ mixed-methods techniques or to include quantitative, qualitative and mixed-methods primary research. *A methodologically inclusive stance is adopted in this book by juxtaposing multiple ways of looking at research syntheses.* Unlike some supporters of mixed-methods, who advocate blending of qualitative and quantitative approaches in most studies, this book recommends purposefully informed selective inclusivity in research syntheses. Such purposeful adoption, and rejection, of a mixed-methods approach in research synthesis is increasingly being endorsed by several other methodologically inclusive research synthesists also (e.g. Pope et al. 2007).

When interpreting individual texts, I briefly summarized them and reflected on how that text had altered or reinforced my emerging conceptualization of the

MIRS framework. Each text I read guided my reading and interpretion of further texts. As my pre-understanding of the whole improved, my understanding of the particular also improved. Such a hermeneutic circle of understanding the part-and-whole facilitated reflexive interpretations of individual and collective texts.

I have interpreted and adapted ideas and techniques from the literature on a wide range of research synthesis methods and primary research methods. I acknowledge that many of my adaptations are from an outsider's perspective since I do not have the practical experience of employing these methods. These adaptations may have been different if I had actually used these methods in real contexts. My etic status allowed me to problematize some taken-for-granted concepts among the practitioners of that methodology. Nonetheless, I complemented my etic's perspective on different methods by regularly consulting with the practitioners of different methodologies. These consultations enhanced my emerging understandings by refining my processes of searching, selecting and making sense of the relevant literature.

After identifying key methodological ideas within each text, I explored ways in which these ideas could be adapted to different types of research syntheses. Each text was broadly coded according to its methodological focus. A new field was created for entering these codes within my Endnote referencing database. When necessary, I used multiple codes for individual texts. In the margins of each text, I wrote summary sentences of key points, brief comments to note my thinking at the time, finer codes capturing the essence of the particular section of that text, and/or issues and dilemmas relevant to the MIRS framework. For both levels of coding, I used an emergent coding scheme to identify typical and atypical methodological ideas and techniques. The following broad questions guided the process of distilling information from relevant texts:

### Texts on research synthesis methods

How can ideas and techniques presented here be adapted by synthesists with diverse methodological orientations?

### General research methods texts

What are some recent trends and changes in educational research? How can some primary research ideas and techniques be extrapolated to the process of a research synthesis? What criteria can be used to judge the quality for including/excluding primary reports? Of these, what criteria can be extrapolated to evaluate the quality of a research synthesis?

### Individual research methodology texts

What are some common purposes of research using this methodology? How can research reports using this methodology contribute to a synthesis on a particular topic? What type of questions can a research synthesis that is oriented along this methodology address? How can some ideas and techniques from this methodology be extrapolated usefully to the process of a research synthesis? What are some features of this methodology that cannot be adapted to the process of a research synthesis? What criteria can be used to judge the quality for including/excluding primary research reports from this methodology? Of these, what criteria can be extrapolated to evaluate the quality of a research synthesis?

These broad questions are in line with the exploratory and illustrative nature of this book with a clear focus on expanding possibilities within research synthesis methods.

## Constructing connected understandings

The following techniques were employed for constructing connected understandings across individual texts:

- preliminary content-analysis;
- interpretive and hermeneutic comparisons;
- writing as a method of inquiry;
- problematizing, interrogating, unpacking and adapting individual texts informed by critical sensibilities;
- seeking feedback on my emerging understandings from senior researchers and peers;
- maintaining postmodern doubt and tentativeness.

A preliminary thematic content-analysis was employed at the early stages: to partition the literature according to methodological foci of individual texts; to identify the relative prevalence and absence of literature on different research synthesis methods; and to note current trends in primary research methods. Attention was paid to the relative frequencies of various methodological ideas presented in the literature to build a broad picture. Then, the focus was shifted from 'how often' do individual methodological themes appear to the 'range' of methodological possibilities, i.e. 'what ideas' are present and absent in the contemporary literature.

I started by reading widely on contemporary issues, debates, techniques, theories and viewpoints in educational research to get a broad-picture, pre-understanding or a general feel for the area. As I delved deeper into the literature on disparate methods of research synthesis and primary research, I noticed some common threads running through different territories and I was excited about exploring potential transferability of features across boundaries. Also, I began to appreciate the subtle differences between different methods and nuances associated with the same terms when used in different contexts. Questioning the ostensible consensus or transparency of the terms and methods used, I became wary of making sweeping generalizations.

With every attempt to develop a methodologically inclusive framework, I felt I was going around in circles. After much reflection and discussion, I felt I was making the same mistake as many beginning researchers do with cross-case analyses. Miles and Huberman (1994) caution researchers against going to an abstract level before dealing with the specifics. In their exploratory multiple case-study approach, they recommend that first the evidence for each case must be collected, analyzed, interpreted and represented, while maintaining the integrity and entirety of the case, before moving on to the next stage of comparing across cases. One may conduct more than one case-study simultaneously or be interested in ultimately doing a cross-case analysis. Nonetheless, while studying an individual case, all efforts must be concentrated in understanding the uniqueness, typicality, and complexities associated with that case only (1994). Drawing an analogy between their case and my individual method of research synthesis or primary research, I decided to internalize concepts underlying individual methods before conceptualizing the MIRS framework. Then I developed the MIRS framework by synthesizing these individual summaries.

A researcher with limited resources can select an exemplary case and examine other cases for the extent to which they demonstrate or add to the description of the phenomenon in the exemplar case (Miles and Huberman 1994). Extrapolating this logic, for each method or topic, I identified a few exemplar references by snowball sampling and wrote the first draft of this book using information distilled from these references. This initial draft was modified and revised several times to enrich it with the information distilled from selected additional references on that topic. In particular, I looked for information that contradicted, augmented or reinforced my initial argument.

Baker (1999) urges synthesists to go beyond interpreting primary research reports to adapt, interrogate and distort what is given in order to create spaces for different perspectives. In this book I have used the meta-analytic literature as a departure point to create spaces for an inclusive perspective to research synthesis. I have adapted, interrogated and distorted the very text on which I built my main argument. Informed by critical sensibilities, I unpacked issues, techniques and themes distilled from the literature on individual methods to explore their potential adaptability to a methodologically inclusive framework.

I compared the information distilled from individual texts and my memos to identify similarities, dissimilarities, commensurabilities and incommensurabilities between different methods of research synthesis and primary research. In my interpretive efforts of finding a coherent synthetic structure for the MIRS framework, I was confronted by the enormous diversity across this pool of information. Through reflection and discussion, I recognized a tension between what I was doing and what I thought I must report. I wanted to share with the audience how the process of research synthesis looked to me when I saw it through different viewpoints. Although my thinking at the time was marked by postmodern doubt and tentativeness, I was still trying to write about the MIRS framework with a postpositivist confidence. Informed by poststructuralism, I recognized at that time that I did not know the shape that the final book would take. I drew on Richardson's notion of writing as 'a method of inquiry' (2000, p. 923) and used each relevant idea as a lens, as one way of looking at the process of research synthesis. Living with a postmodern doubt, I saw enormous opportunities of possibilities intertwined with this uncertainty.

Drawing on the notion of member-checking, feedback was sought from colleagues who had an expertise in different research methodologies to refine my emerging understandings about their particular methodology, which was particularly useful in:

- exposing me to details that are taken for granted within their methodology and are not explicitly mentioned in the literature;
- helping me to identify some gaps in my understanding of their methodology;
- identifying my misunderstandings and misrepresentations about their methodology as evident from my articulation of ideas and issues related to their methodology.

In addition to eliciting feedback from key stakeholders, the following strategies were employed for enhancing relevance, inclusivity and currency of this book:

- identifying disconfirming pieces of information;
- exploring rival connections;
- using multiple lenses and sensitivity analyses;
- maintaining a questioning gaze;
- reflexivity;
- updating with the recent literature.

To enhance the robustness of my connected understandings, I looked for information negating or contradicting prevalent thinking and my thinking at the time. Alternative positions have been presented when applicable. To facilitate complementarity of purposes within research syntheses, multiple lenses or frames of reference have been used to conceptualize the MIRS framework. Drawing from the notion of sensitivity analyses, I explored variations introduced by synthesizing information from different perspectives or worldviews.

Given the ideological and organic nature of this project, I did not strive for objectivity, strict adherence to a priori protocols or rigid consistency of method. Drawing from critical sensibilities, I questioned the very texts on which I was building my arguments. At times, in my early efforts of critiquing, extrapolating and adapting ideas from individual texts, my viewpoints became very biased. Feedback from critical friends helped me to sharpen and substantiate my own arguments. They also helped me to maintain a questioning gaze by encouraging me to doubt and interrogate my own emerging interpretations and connected understandings.

In a topical area of interest, synthesists can often find that other synthesists are also working on a similar topic. From a deficit model of advancing science where the only purpose of a scholarly piece of work is to fill in some 'gap', this might appear to diminish the value of the synthesis being undertaken because of potential replication. However, in practice, every synthesis makes a unique contribution to the discipline with its particular theoretical stance and coverage. From this viewpoint, multiple syntheses on the same topic are often complementary rather than repetitive. When I commenced this project, the literature on synthesis of qualitative research methods was sparse. During the course of this project, many eminent scholars have been working on various issues associated with synthesizing qualitative research. There are many overlaps between some of my conference papers presented during the course of this project and some of their recent publications. I see this as a form of member-checking where many of the issues I have raised are also being recognized by several members of the research community. However, unlike traditional member-checking, there has been a degree of reflexivity where the literature I was reading and the texts that I was presenting in the public domain were mutually informing, as is evident from the overlap between this book and the insights presented by Major and Savin-Baden (2010) in their monograph.

## Communicating with different audiences

Feedback from a number of research synthesists, primary researchers, policy-makers, teachers and lecturers was sought through serendipitous conversations and in discussions on numerous occasions where I presented my emerging understanding about research synthesis methods. These included various local, national and international forums, such as the annual or biennial conferences of the American Educational Research Association (AERA), Association for Qualitative Research (AQR), Higher Education Research and Development Society of Australasia (HERDSA), Australian Association for Research in Education (AARE), Advances in Qualitative Methods (AQM) and Mathematics Education Research Group of Australasia (MERGA). This book has also benefitted from the constructive feedback provided by a number of senior colleagues on earlier drafts of different sections of this book. This includes my PhD supervisors, research mentors, PhD examiners and anonymous reviewers of previously published journal articles and conference papers.

## Summary

During the course of this project, my specific questions, worldview, search strategies, criteria for interpreting and distilling information, nature of connected understandings and communication plan, all mutually informed and evolved simultaneously. I started from a postpositivist worldview and embraced interpretive, participatory and critical viewpoints as I went along. My conception of inclusivity evolved from 'a single most comprehensive method' to 'purposefully informed selective inclusivity'. A strategic combination of several sampling strategies and search channels was employed to retrieve the relevant literature. A range of ideas and techniques from interpretive and critical paradigms were drawn upon to interpret, distil, problematize, interrogate and adapt relevant information and to construct connected understandings. This conceptualization of the MIRS framework has been informed by critical feedback throughout this project from a number of users and producers of educational research.

# Chapter 5

# Principles to guide research synthesis

What are key principles for guiding a research synthesis?

The first three chapters of this book contextualized the need for developing a methodologically inclusive framework for research synthesis. The previous chapter elucidated key methodological decisions in conceptualizing the MIRS framework. This chapter discusses key principles underpinning this framework. The chapter begins with a discussion of three principles for guiding a research synthesis. This is followed by a discussion of the general nature of the six phases of considerations that have been identified to facilitate informed decision-making in a research synthesis. These phases are further elaborated in the rest of this book.

## Guiding principles for a quality research synthesis

I have identified three general guiding principles for a quality research synthesis:

1   informed subjectivity and reflexivity;
2   purposefully informed selective inclusivity;
3   audience-appropriate transparency.

Each guiding principle will be enacted differently depending on the overarching epistemological and teleological orientation of the synthesis. Further, each guiding principle will also be interpreted in terms of different actions within different phases of a synthesis.

### Informed subjectivity and reflexivity

Every research synthesis method, such as meta-analysis or meta-ethnography, has its domain of applicability. Drawing on the notion of informed subjectivity, synthesists must make methodological choices that are coherently aligned with their synthesis purpose. Throughout the synthesis process, the synthesist must evaluate various available options to make informed methodological choices that are most suited for the synthesis purpose. Rather than maintaining an objective distance from the synthesis process, synthesists ought to actively take into consideration the varied interests of different stakeholders in the field, including their own interests.

In practice, a dialectic and dialogic tension exists between the process and the product of a rigorous synthesis whereby both mutually inform and shape each other. Certain methodological decisions would provide particular insights into a phenomenon that may be different from those found through alternative methodological decisions. In a rigorous research synthesis, the synthesist ought to explicitly reflect on the interactive relationship and the dynamic interplay between the synthesis process and the synthesis product (Lather 1999). Being reflexive requires synthesists to become conscious of how the synthesis process is changing their own worldview and how their changing worldview is impacting upon the synthesis product. To make the synthesis report more compelling, synthesists ought to be explicit about where they are coming from and how their own positioning may have influenced the synthesis. The synthesist must substantiate why certain paths, in preference to other paths, were followed in a synthesis process (Zhao 1991).

Some might argue that informed subjectivity and reflexivity are at odds with the aspirations for disengaged objectivity espoused by some postpositivists. However, most educational researchers, regardless of their methodological orientation, advocate some level of reflexivity even if in the guise of different names. Even systematic reviewers with a postpositivist orientation recognize that 'it is impossible to abolish conflict of interest, since the only person who does not have some vested interest in a subject is somebody who knows nothing about it' (Campbell Collaboration 2001). All synthesists, including meta-analysts, recognize that a series of judgement calls are inevitable in every synthesis. Aspiring for objectivity to achieve certain neutral purposes is not essentially bad. However, a false impression of suggesting a degree of objectivity that is not feasible is objectionable. Even systematic reviewers using a priori protocols could be reflexive to some extent by reflecting upon how their a priori protocols are focusing their gaze, analysis or synthesis in certain directions while blinding them to other connections. Informed subjectivity and reflexivity are also included in the criteria for evaluating *RER* reviews. Authors of *RER* reviews are required to recognize their frame of reference and critically reflect on how it enabled, and disabled, them from addressing certain questions.

Postpositivist synthesists, like meta-analysts, go out of their way to avoid biases as any bias undermines their claims of objectivity and neutrality. As far as possible, all synthesists must take into account any biases introduced by their methodological and political choices. However, biases on their own, are not essentially bad or undesirable in all syntheses. Synthesists from interpretive, participatory and critical traditions can harness some of these biases to enhance depth, utility and impact of their syntheses. They can 'illuminate the nature of the bias and the social, cultural, and political forces that shaped it' (Moss 2005,

p. 280). Nonetheless, all synthesists must be wary of biases caused by unreflexive selectivity, that is, those biases that have not gone through the synthesist's reflexive scrutiny. These are different from the biases that have been reflexively considered by the synthesist.

One of the reviewers of my earlier papers posed the question, 'Could not two people reviewing exactly the same pool of research come up with quite different conclusions?' My response is, yes! Just as two primary researchers might conduct different studies of the same setting, two research synthesists might synthesize the same pool of research using different frameworks to come up with quite different conclusions. A good illustration of this point is Amundsen and Wilson's (2012) synthesis. A large proportion of studies included in their synthesis were also included in the previous reviews that examined effectiveness of educational development practices. Unlike the previous reviews, their review makes a distinct contribution by identifying the core practices and theoretical thinking underpinning educational development practices studied in those reports.

### *Purposefully informed selective inclusivity*

Inclusivity is an enabling constraint that requires us to recognize and honour differences. Inclusivity can be realized in numerous valid ways. Inclusion is always mirrored by exclusion. Thus, any form of inclusivity can be only partial inclusivity. The inclusivity recommended here is not an unrestrained and unthinking inclusivity. There is a clear distinction between purposefully informed critical subjectivity and a nihilistic 'anything goes' attitude. A commitment to methodological inclusivity heightens the need for critical, informed and purposeful selectivity.

It may sound paradoxical to advocate selectivity in a framework that is fundamentally concerned with inclusivity, but informed selectivity remains as important in the MIRS framework as it has always been in any rigorous research synthesis. Inclusivity and selectivity are not in simple opposition. Rather, there is an interesting dialectical tension between them. If we broaden the domain of what is brought together, then the process of excluding certain studies clearly becomes more complex. All decisions in a research synthesis must be guided by the principle of purposefully informed selective inclusivity.

Being inclusive of a range of qualitative research methods requires that we become sensitive to a variety of questions: Who is researching? Whose questions are being researched? What are the tools, techniques, and perspectives employed in research? What is the relationship between the researcher and the participants? All of these questions necessitate that we recognize overlaps and tensions between the varied interests of multiple stakeholders who are involved in educational research and practice.

Primary research and research synthesis can privilege academic knowledge over practitioners' experiences, tacit knowledge, and wisdom – all of which is a valuable source of knowledge and so must be considered when formulating policy and identifying principles of good practice. Any discussion of knowledge construction about educational practices is incomplete and oppressive if it undermines the rich experiential knowledge of different stakeholders, especially teachers and students, whose practices and experiences are the sites for educational research (Ryan & Hood, 2004; Schwandt, 2005). In addition to recognizing the complementary role of primary research and research syntheses, it is crucial to recognize how these domains of knowledge construction are complemented by the experiential knowledge of multiple stakeholders in educational practice, policy, and research. Research syntheses can strengthen the relationship among educational research, policy, and practice by engaging different stakeholders in reading and constructing succinct representations of primary and secondary research. In every research synthesis, we must pay careful attention to the varied interests of different stakeholders (Oliver et al. 2008).

### Audience-appropriate transparency

Research synthesists from diverse orientations emphasize the need to be explicit about critical decisions, and their justifications, in the process of a research synthesis. Depending on the ontological, epistemological and methodological underpinnings of a synthesis, the overarching principle of transparency may be justified with different motives. Transparency of process can provide readers 'opportunities for inspection, replication, verification, or refutation' (Ogawa and Malen 1991, p. 283). Often, guidelines for systematic reviews recommend transparency to enhance reliability by improving replicability (e.g. CRD 2011). Most systematic reviewers advocate transparency of process to enhance accountability, credibility and transferability of synthesis findings.

At the same time, contesting the innocence of 'making the invisible visible' and an implied discourse of distrust, Strathern (2000) urges us to attend to that which is concealed by visibility. Producers and users of research syntheses should be wary of the feasibility and desirability of absolute transparency in any research synthesis to the extent that it stifles creativity (MacLure 2005, Hannes and Lockwood 2011). Each telling is inevitably mirrored by not telling. The metaphor of transparency can wrongly imply that all one needs is a pair of eyes to see through the minds of the synthesists. Rather than adhering to some prescriptive notion of transparency, research synthesists must aim at an audience-appropriate transparency that is enacted purposefully. It requires the synthesist to make informed decisions about what aspects of the synthesis process must be explicitly stated to enhance the utility of the synthesis for the intended audience. Such an audience-appropriate transparency is often enacted in most rigorous reviews of research and not just systematic reviews (Sandelowski et al. 2012).

Audience-appropriate transparency and reflexivity in the process of a research synthesis allows readers to critically evaluate the similarities or dissimilarities of the synthesis context, and the synthesist's standpoint, with their own contexts and viewpoints. This can, in turn, facilitate informed transferability of the product.

The audience can adapt the synthesis product, in varying degrees, to their own contexts depending on the relative match with the synthesis context.

Transparency of process can be difficult when there are restrictions on the length of an article as is the case with most paper-based scholarly journals. Restricted by the length of the article, a synthesist faces the dilemma of what to share in order to optimally utilize the journal space in a way that is most suited for the intended audience of the journal. Many research synthesists overcome the constraints imposed by limited journal space by archiving details of the synthesis process on the internet and directing interested readers to the relevant website.

## Interactive phases of a research synthesis

Several judgment calls are an inherent part of every quality research synthesis. The product of a research synthesis is inevitably shaped by the decisions made throughout the synthesis process. In developing the MIRS framework, I have synthesized a variety of considerations that are applicable to research syntheses conducted for diverse purposes. These considerations are intended to assist research synthesists in reflecting on, explicitly delineating, and substantiating the critical choices they make in a research synthesis process. These considerations are also intended to assist readers of research syntheses in actively evaluating and adapting the information to their own contexts. These considerations are not absolute requirements for every quality research synthesis. If a synthesist chooses not to attend to a particular consideration, then it ought to be a deliberate, purposeful decision to do so, rather than a simple inadvertent omission.

Within specific domains of applicability, several methodologists have identified various tasks, decision-points, stages or phases in the process of a research synthesis or primary research study (e.g. Cooper 1982, Noblit and Hare 1988, Maxwell and Loomis 2003). After collating several such representations from diverse perspectives, I unpacked them to unravel the associated euphemisms and to problematize embedded metaphors and assumptions. These were then purposefully adapted and synthesized into the following six phases of considerations relevant to any quality research synthesis.

1    Identifying an appropriate epistemological orientation
2    Identifying an appropriate purpose
3    Searching for relevant literature
4    Evaluating, interpreting and distilling evidence from selected reports
5    Constructing connected understandings
6    Communicating with an audience

In the first phase, the synthesists identify a suitable overarching epistemological orientation for the synthesis while being reflexive about how their philosophical, theoretical and political orientations are intersecting with the synthesis process and product. In the second phase, the synthesists identify an appropriate purpose for the synthesis from a range of potentially useful purposes. In the third phase, the synthesists search for the relevant literature by identifying a suitable sampling logic and pursuing multiple channels for retrieving and selecting primary research reports to include in the synthesis. In the fourth phase, the synthesists interpret, evaluate and distil evidence from selected reports. In the fifth phase, the synthesists draw on these distilled interpretations to construct connected understandings across studies. In the sixth phase, the synthesists adopt suitable medium, genre and techniques to effectively communicate their synthetic understandings with multiple audiences. Considerations within each of these six phases are discussed in-depth in the next six chapters of this book.

To refer to each phase, I have deliberately used clauses beginning with action verbs in preference to nouns. This is to emphasize a dynamic approach to research synthesis that values the process as well as the product. The verbs associated with each phase (identifying; searching; evaluating, interpreting and distilling; constructing; and communicating) are presented in present continuous tense to stress the tentative and ongoing nature of each phase and to refrain from implying a sense of finality. Within each phase, I have refrained from a sense of objective distancing by emphasizing the role of the synthesist as a sensitive human instrument.

The term 'phases' has been used in lieu of stages to emphasize that these phases are not stages with discreet boundaries where each stage serially follows the previous stage. In practice, these phases are likely to overlap with tasks involved in more than one phase being carried out in tandem. Considerations within each phase may inform and refine the process of other phases. Various tasks within different phases may be sometimes carried out simultaneously. Such flexibility leaves scope for an inductive design rather than requiring that every synthesis has an a priori deductive design. Non-sequential and overlapping nature of different phases is emphasized in several formally proposed methods of research synthesis, especially those designed for synthesizing qualitative research (Pope et al. 2007).

The interactive nature of these six phases is diagrammatically illustrated in Figure 5.1. Double arrowed lines between consecutive phases have been used to stress that decisions within an individual phase are likely to inform, and be informed by, decisions within adjacent phases. In accordance with the principle of purposefully informed selective inclusivity, each phase is connected with a double arrowed line with the phase of identifying an appropriate purpose. This phase is positioned in the centre to emphasize that decisions about the purpose of a synthesis act as critical filters for decisions within different phases, and vice-versa.

The sequential nature of these phases is preferably conceptualized as an interactively iterative process where each phase tends to be revisited and refined several times. Decisions within each phase are best conceptualized as components of an interactive network, where each decision must be considered in the light of the others. The relative emphasis given to various decisions will be guided by the

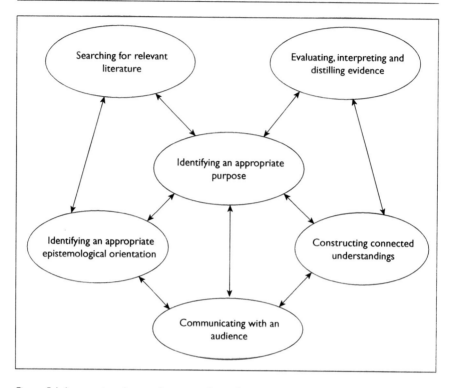

*Figure 5.1* Interactive phases of a research synthesis

particular context of the synthesis. Not all of the issues discussed within each phase will be equally relevant to all forms of synthesis. While some considerations are essential in every synthesis, the rest will apply only to some situations but not all.

## Summary

This chapter described the following three general guiding principles for a quality research synthesis: informed subjectivity and reflexivity; purposefully informed selective inclusivity; and audience-appropriate transparency. Practical implications of these principles have been presented as critical considerations clustered within six interactive phases of a research synthesis. Each of these phases is further elaborated in the rest of this book.

# Chapter 6

# Identifying an appropriate epistemological orientation

What possibilities open up (and close down) for syntheses that are positioned along distinct epistemologies?

Several primary research methodologists have argued that all researchers must examine and substantiate the appropriateness of the methodological, theoretical, political and moral assumptions they make in their studies. Researchers must also reflect on how these choices may have influenced their findings (Gaskell 1988, Kress 2011b). Sometimes researchers draw on the notion of a paradigm to situate their studies epistemologically and methodologically. Paradigms focus and facilitate understanding by providing a framework within which to work (Kuhn 1970). At the same time, paradigms also restrict our understanding to the parameters of the framework. Reaching a consensus on what is the most accurate paradigmatic classification is neither possible nor useful (Mertens 2005). Nonetheless, situating our research paradigmatically can help us to be more reflexive about how our study design interacts with our findings.

The diversity of epistemological orientations prevalent in contemporary primary research in education must also be practiced at the level of synthesizing research (Suri 2012). To emphasize the viability and desirability of a variety of epistemological orientations among research synthesis methods the phase *identifying an appropriate epistemological orientation for the synthesis* is explicitly discussed within the MIRS framework. Within this phase, the synthesist identifies an overarching epistemological orientation for the synthesis that is compatible with the intended purpose of the synthesis.

> **Key questions to consider**
>
> How would the overarching epistemological orientation of the synthesis influence my assumptions about:
>
> - the intended utility and purpose of the synthesis;
> - my relationship to the groups represented in primary research studies;
> - my relationship to the authors of the primary research studies;
> - suitable strategies for selecting and evaluating primary research studies;
> - appropriate techniques for interpreting and distilling information from selected primary research studies;
> - relevant strategies for constructing connected understandings and sharing them with the intended audience?

There is no best-fit orientation for all research syntheses. The overarching orientation of the synthesis ought to be guided by the anticipated utility of the synthesis, the nature of primary research in the field and the synthesist's methodological expertise. The synthesist must attempt to make explicit the reflexive relationship between the synthesis findings and the synthesist's own research disposition. This is not an easy task, as we often cannot see beyond our own frame of reference, and hence do not perceive our own standpoint. For example, a synthesist coming from a feminist philosophical stance may perceive gaps in studies differently from a synthesist who does not subscribe to a similar philosophy. While emphasizing the importance of 'making things visible', it is crucial to remember the problematics associated with this. 'Many things are obscure simply because the world is too much with us. Like the fish in water, the boy in love, or the sexist among like-minded friends, we lack the perspective to see things closest to us' (Dabbs 1982, p. 31).

This chapter illustrates through examples how synthesists might draw on published paradigmatic discussions to inform and situate their own syntheses. Many of the publications cited in this chapter relate to primary research methods. The arguments presented in these texts have been purposefully extrapolated and adapted to the process of a research synthesis in this chapter.

As illustrated in Figure 6.1, this chapter has seven main sections. The first section, which is in the centre of the figure, *recognizing diversity*, emphasizes the need to attend to the variety of epistemological orientations possible for a research synthesis and describes the broad framework used for structuring this chapter. The next four sections illustrate how research synthesists might draw from discussions about postpositivist, interpretive, participatory and critical traditions to inform their own syntheses. In comparison with postpositivist and interpretive syntheses, participatory and critical syntheses are less discussed in the published literature. Taking this into account, participatory and critical syntheses are

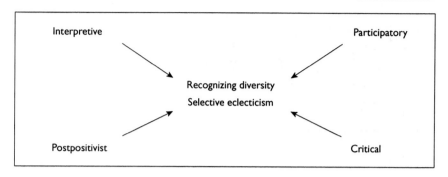

*Figure 6.1* Epistemological pluralism in research synthesis methods

discussed in greater detail in this chapter. This is followed by a discussion of the blurring genres and a selectively eclectic approach to drawing from paradigmatic discussions. In the centre of Figure 6.1, *selective eclecticism* and recognizing *diversity* are juxtaposed to highlight the dialectical tension between these two stances. In this figure, I have refrained from drawing boundaries between individual paradigmatic orientations to emphasize that there are overlaps and blurred boundaries between different paradigms. The final section draws on this discussion to illustrate how re/viewing research syntheses from distinct epistemological positions can open up useful possibilities.

## Recognizing diversity: An illustrative framework

In this chapter, there is no intention to prescribe the most appropriate paradigmatic classification of educational research syntheses. Rather, the intention here is to problematize the exclusive identification of research syntheses with any single paradigm. An illustrative framework of four epistemological orientations is used, in the next four sections, to demonstrate how syntheses with different paradigmatic orientations can serve varied, albeit equally useful, purposes. This framework is summarized in Table 6.1. This table is purposefully constructed to model how syntheses with distinct paradigmatic orientations may be situated with respect to each other. It is designed to highlight some essential differences that may characterize potentially useful developments in research synthesis methodology. In the most pragmatic sense, the table serves as a structuring and navigational device for my discussion of paradigmatic alternatives.

The first row in Table 6.1 illustrates distinct ontological positions for a synthesis. The second row illustrates different purposes that a synthesis can serve. The third row illustrates potential relationships that a synthesist can have with participants and authors of primary research. Evidence included in a research synthesis is interpreted and represented first by the participants of primary research, then by the authors of primary research and finally by the research

Table 6.1 Research syntheses with different paradigmatic orientations

| | Postpositivist syntheses | interpretive syntheses | participatory syntheses | critical syntheses |
|---|---|---|---|---|
| ontological position | objective factual world is out there | world is constructed through meanings that individuals and groups attribute to events | individuals and groups construct their own world views through participation | relativistic and transitional world views reflective of dominant power structures |
| amenable purposes | objectively explain, predict or describe in terms of probabilistic, generalizable laws, facts or relations between measurable constructs and variables | construct deeper and more comprehensive understanding about phenomena as experienced subjectively by different stakeholders | understand and/or improve ourselves and our local world experientially through critical engagement | problematize prevalent metanarratives to deconstruct and/or transform dominant discourses |
| informant-synthesist relationship | objective distancing of an unbiased expert | sensitive and reflective understanding with minimal power-imbalance | critical, selective and creative understanding, emphasizing realistic transferability to inform local practice | self-doubting and reflexive understandings of perspectives represented in, and missing from, primary research literature |
| common strategies | exhaustive sampling; a priori protocol and coding sheets; statistical variable-oriented analysis | purposive sampling; emergent design; holistic case-oriented analysis; summary-sheets, meta-matrices, reciprocal translations, etc. | purposive sampling; emergent design; eclectic data analysis; emphasis on practical and experiential knowledge | openly ideological, dialogic, dialectic selection and analysis of evidence, emphasis on historical and structural insights |
| quality criteria | validity and reliability | deep and authentic understanding | empower participants to improve locally | catalytic validity or crystallisation |
| suitable genres | scientific reporting format | comprehensive narrative with thick descriptions | interactive reporting | nuanced texts celebrating intertextuality |

synthesist. In this sense, both participants and authors of primary research serve as informants for a research synthesist. The fourth row of this table illustrates a range of strategies for searching and distilling relevant evidence and constructing connected understandings from the distilled evidence. The fifth row illustrates various quality criteria suitable for evaluating syntheses. The last row illustrates common genres that synthesists could employ to communicate with their audiences.

The four columns of Table 6.1 are elaborated further in the next four sections of this chapter. The next section describes key features of postpositivist syntheses that aim to synthesize research with minimal bias for providing generalizations across contexts. This is followed by a discussion of interpretivist syntheses which closely examine how individual accounts of a phenomenon relate to each other to facilitate an holistic understanding. Then experiential and transformative potential of syntheses with participatory orientation is discussed, followed by a discussion of how might research synthesists draw on the published literature within the critical traditions which includes postmodernism.

To illustrate how research syntheses with different paradigmatic orientations might differ, at times I have compared and contrasted alternative orientations. This might wrongly suggest that I am emphasizing compartmentalization of perspectives. I do not believe there are rigid boundaries between various orientations. However, to facilitate informed decisions regarding paradigmatic choices, it is crucial to understand the differences between various options. The explicit recognition of diversity directly addresses concerns regarding the possible unintended *rejection by omission* of positions less discussed in the published literature. Rigid adherence to any single perspective is neither prescribed nor recommended. Nonetheless, synthesists should be critically aware of the implications of the choices they make, where some of these choices are likely to involve drawing from more than one paradigm.

## Syntheses with postpositivist orientations

In this book, the term postpositivism is used as an umbrella term that is inclusive of positivist and postpositivist methods with randomized controlled trials or quasi-experimental designs. Postpositivists generally espouse a rationalist, empiricist, reductionist, realist position which seeks to explain, predict or describe the world in terms of generalizable laws, facts or probabilistic relations between behavioural constructs and contextual variables (Phillips et al. 2012). Quantitative systematic reviews, best-evidence syntheses and meta-analyses are examples of postpositivist syntheses. Such syntheses are frequently conducted: to estimate the overall effectiveness of an educational strategy; to estimate the prevalence of various measurable attitudes, preferences, perceptions, conceptions or misconceptions among certain populations; to estimate the degree of variation across studies examining a similar hypothesis; to identify conditions that maximize or minimize the probability of a particular finding; or to propose how these conditions may be related.

Often postpositivist synthesists seek to synthesize research objectively with minimal researcher bias: by designing a priori synthesis protocols to minimize biases introduced by the synthesist's subjective preferences; by defining conceptually and operationally all key constructs in behavioural terms at the outset; and by employing exhaustive sampling in order to be representative of the entire population of studies. Sometimes they blind primary research reports to reduce biases introduced in judging the quality of individual reports by preconceived notions about the source of the publication or the author of the individual primary research report. Also, they measure inter-rater reliability to judge the degree of objectivity and reliability associated with the key decisions in the synthesis process (Lipsey and Wilson 2001, Wilson 2009, Orwin and Vevea 2009).

Postpositivist synthesists commonly employ variable-oriented statistical analyses to reduce *Type II* error and to enhance objectivity in the process of analysis and synthesis; target global decision-makers and researchers as their audience; utilize scientific reporting format; and adapt Cook and Campbell's (1979) constructs of validity and reliability to address issues of rigour in research synthesis. Sophisticated discussions have been published about ways of reducing threats to internal validity, external validity, internal reliability and external reliability within postpositivist syntheses (e.g. Petticrew and Roberts 2006, Matt and Cook 2009). Advances in this field have also been supported by government funding to organizations which support the implementation and dissemination of quantitative systematic reviews (e.g. Campbell Collaboration n.d., The Cochrane Collaboration 2011, CRD 2011).

### Caveats of postpositivist syntheses

Most criticisms levelled against postpositivist primary research from exponents of alternative paradigms would also be applicable to postpositivist syntheses. For instance, a drive for universal laws generalizable to *all* settings can decontextualize findings to the extent that they may be no longer usefully applied to *any* setting. A reductionist, variable-oriented analysis often cannot capture the subtle nuances of the dynamic interaction between various contextual influences. Quantitative findings and scientific reporting formats can give a false sense of accuracy and objectivity that can be misleading. Postpositivist syntheses may contribute to the imbalance of power between various stakeholders by assuming a top-down approach to educational change (Clegg 2005, Wiseman 2010). In their defence, postpositivists note that many critics of postpositivism do not fully appreciate the contemporary postpositivist school of thought that is sensitive to the changing context of educational research. Many postpositivists hold that being a postpositivist does not essentially involve rejecting interpretivism or qualitative evidence.

Following are examples of some caveats specific to all syntheses, including postpositivist syntheses, which are recognized by exponents of postpositivism themselves. Synthesists tend to mix 'apples and oranges', i.e. they combine findings from samples that may not be comparable along several dimensions.

Synthesists have little control over a range of variables that might be related to the construct being measured. True experiments are impossible at the level of a synthesis and hence causal relationships cannot be inferred from a synthesis unless causal findings across a number of individual primary research studies are being generalized (Kennedy 2007).

## Syntheses with interpretive orientations

Even though the literature on interpretive syntheses was sporadic until two decades ago, a growing body of literature has been published since then. Interpretive syntheses have been discussed under various names, such as meta-ethnography (Noblit and Hare 1988), exploratory case-study oriented review of multivocal literatures (Ogawa and Malen 1991), cross-case analysis (Miles and Huberman 1994), aggregated analysis (Eastabrooks et al. 1994), meta-analysis of qualitative research (Jensen and Allen 1994), qualitative meta-synthesis (Zimmer 2006), interpretivist-oriented reviews (Eisenhart 1998), meta-synthesis (Bair 1999), meta-study (Paterson et al. 2001), thematic synthesis (Thomas and Harden 2008) and framework synthesis (Carroll et al. 2011).

Contesting an objective reality that is out there, interpretive synthesists hold that the world is socially constructed in terms of the meanings we attribute to events. Their goal is to improve 'communication and understanding across human groups' by interpreting the subjective experiences of different stakeholders (Eisenhart 1998, p. 393). Interpretive synthesists 'bring to light an underlying coherence of sense' (Taylor 1982, p. 153) by '(1) making the obvious obvious, (2) making the obvious dubious, and (3) making the hidden obvious' (Noblit and Hare 1988, p. 17). Typical questions addressed by an interpretive synthesist include the following: How do different stakeholders in different contexts experience a phenomenon? How do the contextual particularities interact with the perceptions of different groups and individuals? How do individual primary research reports on a topic reinforce, contradict or augment each other?

Recognizing the inevitable subjectivity in a synthesist's interpretive constructions of connections across individual reports, many interpretivists argue that every synthesis is an interpretive process even if the synthesist does not explicitly acknowledge it (Schwandt 1998). Interpretive synthesists begin by acknowledging the tacit knowledge, values and experiences they bring to the synthesis process. They recognize that each primary research report is the author's interpretation of the research participants' interpretation of the phenomenon being studied. By engaging in iterative negotiations between multiple meanings constructed at each layer of interpretation and representation, they try to reveal the multiple perspectives of different stakeholders with a sensitive understanding. They seek evidence that contests, reinforces or augments their emerging understanding of the phenomenon. With 'an attitude of openness, discovery and reflection', they construct 'multiple, coexisting, and even sometimes incongruous realities related to the phenomenon' (Paterson et al. 2001, pp. 7-10). To maintain the integrity of individual reports, some interpretive synthesists argue in favour of purposeful sampling and emergent designs. Interpretivists often utilize the genre of narrative descriptions to communicate with their audience.

### Caveats of interpretive syntheses

Most criticisms levelled against interpretive primary research from exponents of alternative paradigms would also apply to interpretive syntheses. Many postpositivists criticize the relativism embraced within interpretive, participatory and critical traditions, on the grounds that this relativism makes it difficult to arrive at unbiased, reliable, generalizable conclusions. Interpretive reports are often subjective descriptions of a phenomenon with deliberate attention to contextual particularities. These reports tend to be lengthy and may have less appeal to policy-makers and decision-making bodies who prefer succinct reports that provide concrete evidence to inform and support their decisions. Some participatory scholars argue that it is not enough merely to construct synthetic understandings *about* the groups represented in the primary research studies (as done in all non-participatory syntheses). Rather, synthesists ought to facilitate experiential learning by co-constructing synthetic understandings *with* the groups whose practices would be impacted upon by the synthesis. Some critical scholars denounce all non-critical syntheses for merely reifying the *false consciousness* of the groups portrayed in the primary research studies. Critical scholars urge synthesists to unpack these representations and understand the factors that enable these representations while disabling alternative representations.

Interpretive syntheses have also been criticized by a group of interpretive scholars who believe that any effort to synthesize research is at odds with the epistemological position of interpretivism. They argue that the goal of interpretivism is to understand the manifestation of a phenomenon in its natural setting. Interpretivists are well known for their holistic attention to interactions between various complementary and competing local influences. Interpretive researchers are continually responding sensitively to changing local contexts. This group of purist interpretive scholars asserts that all research syntheses attempt to identify plausible patterns of influences across a number of diverse settings. They argue that this goal is incommensurable with an interpretive epistemology. In response to this criticism, interpretive scholars who believe in the process of interpretive research synthesis argue that every study inherently involves synthesis at some level. For instance, most case studies involve abstraction of information across individual cases. In this sense, interpretive syntheses are no different from any other type of interpretive research (Jensen and Allen 1996).

Another layer of complexity associated with interpretive syntheses has been recognized by many interpretive synthesists themselves. This is the difficulty in identifying a standardized set of criteria for evaluating methodologically diverse interpretive primary research reports being considered for inclusion in a synthesis (Suri 2007, Wright and Coultas 2007, Cassell 2010). Again, this is analogous to the difficulty experienced by an interpretive researcher in deciding what relative priority or authority to accord to the multiple participant voices at the heart of a primary interpretive research study. As with a primary interpretive study, an interpretive synthesis must consider how its constituent research studies are situated within the broader context of educational research and in relation to the issue around which the various studies cohere. Rather than postpositivist criteria of homogeneity of variance or effect size, decisions of weight and representation in constructing the interpretive synthesis will be subject to criteria of coherence and faithfulness to the contingencies of the organizing question or issue.

## Syntheses with participatory orientations

Research synthesists can usefully draw from the participatory tradition to collaborate with various stakeholders in order to inform policy and practice that is pertinent to them. A participatory school of thought holds that individuals and communities construct, understand and change themselves and their local world experientially. 'To experience anything is to participate in it, and to participate is both to mold and to encounter; hence, experiential reality is always subjective-objective' (Heron and Reason 1997, p. 278). Within the participatory tradition, practitioners are encouraged to be analytical and critical about 'their own educational ideas and theories, their own work practices, and their own work settings' (Kemmis 1999, p. 151).

In the last decade, several systematic reviewers have embraced the idea of involving consumers of research reviews in appraising the protocols and reports of systematic reviews (EPPI-Centre 2009, The Cochrane Collaboration 2011). These efforts are commendable in that they involve potential users of a systematic review in identifying suitable topics and in reviewing the protocols and reports of the review. However, despite involving different stakeholders when formulating review questions, protocols and summaries, systematic reviews are sometimes criticized for disempowering practitioners and students by dichotomizing 'research and practice-based contexts with a simple one-way linear model of the relationship between the two' (Clegg 2005, p. 424). In recent years, at times, systematic reviewers have accorded a greater agency of control to stakeholders in making decisions about how the synthesis should proceed (Rees and Oliver 2012).

A truly participatory synthesis contests stereotypical hierarchies and encourages critical thinking through engaged participation of those whose practices and experiences are being researched. Those who are intended to experience a change are given a greater control over the synthesis and a greater agency to transform practices that directly impact upon them. A complementary collaboration model where the distinct skill sets and expertise of individual collaborators are valued is suitable for encouraging participation of different stakeholders in a research synthesis without burdening them with a heavier workload (Yu 2011, Ritchie and Rigano 2007). Rather than ironing out the differences, a participatory synthesis involves paying careful attention to learning opportunities that arise from the differences in language, perspectives and experiences of individual co-synthesists (Paugh and Robinson 2011). A participatory synthesis can become a site for teachers to 'problematize their educational practices by reflecting on their underlying meanings' using the relevant research domain as a mirror for 'developing "actionable knowledge" about their own classrooms' (Torrance 2004, p. 198). The academic co-synthesist can co-construct an understanding of the literature that is informed by the practitioners' perspective. Participatory synthesists could draw on the relevant literature to engage in all the components of 'reflective practice: knowing in action, reflection in action, and reflective conversation with the situation' (Schön 1992, p. 123).

Participatory synthesists would value practical experience, local knowledge and serendipitous leaps of intuitive understanding. The participants in participatory syntheses could be the authors of the primary research reports being synthesized; members of stakeholder groups who participated in those studies; or stakeholders wishing to critically engage with the literature to inform their own decisions. Academic synthesists could collaborate with these participants in order to co-synthesize the relevant body of research through a process of reciprocal learning and co-constructing connected understandings. A participatory synthesis of action research reports authored by teacher-researchers or reflexive practitioners, on how they effected changes within their contextual constraints, could provide useful information to policy-makers and other practitioners. Identifying patterns across these individual reports could provide useful input from this group of action researchers into theory-building.

The purpose of a participatory synthesis should be guided by the concerns, dilemmas and uncertainties that arise in the minds of the practitioners while reflecting on their own practices and beliefs. Preliminary findings of the synthesis product could be tested by the practitioners in their own work contexts which, in turn, could raise further questions. These emerging questions could guide the next stage of the synthesis process. Such a participatory synthesis process could dialectically improve the local practice and the prevalent academic discourse. A participatory synthesis could involve cycles of reflection: to formulate synthesis purpose; to conduct the research synthesis; to implement changes as suggested by the implications of the synthesis; to evaluate the implemented change and to compare these evaluations with the relevant research literature.

All those involved in a participatory synthesis should 'engage together in democratic dialogue' as co-synthesists and 'as cosubjects' (Heron and Reason 1997, p. 283). Using emergent, pragmatic and eclectic designs, participatory synthesists could employ purposeful sampling strategies for selecting studies which illuminate aspects of a phenomenon that are of immediate interest to the participant co-synthesists. They could use the delphi-technique for collecting, analyzing and building collective understandings of research to involve a homogeneous or heterogeneous group of participants with a common interest in a research topic. Participatory synthesists could construct critical, selective and creative understandings with realistic transferability to inform practice in local contexts of the participants. They could employ an interactive reporting format to encourage a participative audience. The synthesis could be evaluated in terms of the progress in thinking and transformation of the contexts of the individuals and the communities of those engaged in the synthesis process. For a practical example of some of these ideas, see Bassett and McGibbon who designed a 'critical, participatory and collaborative method' for scoping literature with individuals who had been actively 'drawing attention to barriers to health and well-being in rural, Aboriginal and African Canadian communities in Canada' (2012).

### Caveats of participatory syntheses

Most of the criticisms levelled against participatory primary research from exponents of alternative paradigms would also be applicable to a participatory synthesis. Critics of participatory research argue that by placing too much emphasis on experiential and local knowledge, participatory research and syntheses often fail to contribute to overall theory development and disciplinary knowledge (Nisbet 1999). Also, an examination of issues in which participants have a stake can often introduce unintentional biases and skewed results.

It is possible to provide examples of some caveats specific to all syntheses, including participatory syntheses, which might be raised from within the participatory tradition. 'In the participatory paradigm, practical knowing is an end in itself, and intellectual knowing is of instrumental value in supporting practical excellence' (Heron and Reason 1997, p. 287). Unlike their postpositivist counter-parts who seek generalizations, scholars with a participatory orientation value contextual and local solutions found through experiential learning. Purist participatory scholars could argue that solutions found by research participants through reflection on their own contextual practice might be more relevant and effective than solutions found by co-synthesizing research conducted by other researchers in different contexts.

## Syntheses with critical orientations

On the topic of syntheses with critical orientations, there is relatively little discussion in the published literature. Under the broad category of critical orientations, I have included Lather's (2006) deconstructivism. However, I acknowledge that there are two distinct teleological categories within this broad label: those who subscribe to emancipatory goals and those who subscribe to postmodern nihilism. I have endorsed Richardson's description of 'post-structuralism' as a 'particular kind of postmodern thought' (2001, p. 36).

Many contemporary critical theorists tend to draw on postmodern schools of thought which are characterized by an incredulity toward metanarratives and distrust of all 'stories which purport to justify certain practices or institutions by grounding them upon a set of transcendental, ahistorical, or universal principles' all and Peters 1999, p. 244). Postmodern scholarship is 'politically *ring*, methodologically *idiosyncratic*, and representationally *unbounded*' (Constas 1998, p. 40, emphasis in original). Accusing 'modern representation' of promoting 'deception, desecration, and domination', postmodernists hold a radically relativist and transitional worldview which is marked by contradictions and multiple realities where 'reality becomes a playful field of signs, signs of other signs and other signs of signs' (Gubrium and Holstein 1997, pp. 78-87). Many other critical theorists disagree with postmodern nihilism and are 'deeply concerned that critical and socially engaged research efforts are being undermined by [postmodern] autopoetic and self-referential academic activities in universities' (Greenwood and Levin 2000, p. 86).

Unlike Lather (1999) and Schwandt (1998), I have deliberately used 'research synthesis' as a blanket term, which includes critically oriented reviews, to reclaim its usage for an inclusive context rather than being limited to postpositivist contexts only. I have retained the term in order to 'both circulate and break with the signs that code it' (Lather 1993, p. 674) by rupturing the exclusive notion of research synthesis as an objective and reductionist aggregation of research findings.

Critical research synthesists hold that the prevalent conception of the world tends to be constructed through the dominant discourse and power structures that privilege those in power (Kress 2011a). They argue that research which is limited to representing perceptions of different stakeholders reifies 'false consciousness' (Lather 1986, p. 70) by ignoring the history of 'how values have developed over time and whose interests they serve, the effects of social and institutional contexts over time, and the impact of historical memory' (Eisenhart 2005, p. 260). Critical research synthesists would engage in promoting 'a "counterscience" of "indisciplined" policy analysis that troubles what we take for granted as the good in fostering understanding, reflection and action' (Lather 2004, p. 25).

Critical synthesists can highlight the inherently ideological nature of all research (Lather 1986); 'signify reformulated historical narratives, social meanings and problematics, interpellative obligations, analytics and assignments for educational inquiry' (Livingston 1999, p. 15); reveal 'the structures, powers, generative mechanisms and tendencies' within discussions of policy, practice and research in a field (Clegg 2005, p. 421); and disrupt conventional thinking to construct spaces for new ways of talking about policy, practice and research (Eisenhart 1998, Segall 2001, Kress 2011b). This involves re-examining to unsettle 'what we might take for granted as "already learned"' (Schwandt 1998, p. 410). A good example of a critical synthesis is Windschitl's theoretical analysis of research to illuminate the 'ambiguities, tensions and compromises' faced by teachers as they implement a constructivist pedagogy (Windschitl 2002, p. 131).

By paying attention to the presence and absence of various issues in the primary research reports, critical synthesists could raise 'important questions about how narratives get constructed, what they mean, how they regulate particular forms of moral and social experiences, and how they presuppose and embody particular epistemological and political views of the world' (Aronowitz and Giroux 1991, pp. 80-81). Framing their synthesis 'around notions of self-reflection, scepticism, refusal, imagination and learning', critical synthesists could resist current marketization of research by demonstrating a 'willingness publicly to raise embarrassing questions, to confront orthodoxy and dogma and to not be co-opted by governments or corporations' (Smyth and Hattam 2000, pp. 171-2). While being open to 'differences and the other', critical synthesists would not 'foreclose the possibility of solidarity' to 'allow many voices to speak, thus multiplying the possibilities for practice' (Sholle 1992, pp. 279-280). Postmodern synthesists would disrupt and problematize the metanarratives in a research domain in order to enhance multiple discourses that celebrate diversity and inclusivity by refusing 'over-simple answers to intractable questions' (Lather 1993, p. 674).

Examples of questions addressed by critical synthesists could include the following. What are the gaps in our understanding of a phenomenon? What methodologies or theoretical perspectives are likely and/or unlikely to be employed by primary researchers in the field? In the published literature, whose questions are prioritized? Whose questions have received little attention from primary researchers? How are the answers to such questions intertwined?

Critical synthesists would pay attention to not only what is said, but also what is not said while recognizing that the 'systems of inclusion/exclusion do not lie in direct parallel with vocal expression and silence, respectively' (Baker 1999, p.366); construct self-doubting and reflexive understandings of not only the perspectives represented in the primary research literature but also those missing from the published primary research; and highlight the gaps in the primary research domain with particular attention to how some groups have become invisible in the field with little representation. Critical synthesists could also collaborate with the groups who have been relatively silenced in the primary research in order to identify how the body of primary research has failed to adequately represent their interests (see e.g. Warschauer and Matuchniak 2010). Rather than deferring to the *authority of author*, postmodernist critical synthesists would recognize an author as someone who is in the process of making sense, a sense which is partial and temporal (Lather 1999, Richardson 2001).

Critical syntheses could employ critical theory, feminist theory, queer theory or other varied standpoint theories. They could employ a range of purposeful sampling strategies including sampling politically important cases to conduct syntheses that have high catalytic validity, i.e. that can act as catalysts for bringing about change. Openly ideological strategies for collecting and analyzing evidence with an emphasis on historical and structural insights would be suitable. Contesting the innocence of text and celebrating intertextuality, postmodernist synthesists would iteratively deconstruct the primary research texts to highlight the discontinuities and fractures in the prevalent research domain. Using emergent

s and 'writing as a method of inquiry', they would engage in representing
'e, nuanced, multiple texts which would create doubts about universal
generalizations and truth claims. Recognizing that there is no correct telling, they
would seek 'crystallization', rather than triangulation, by focusing on simultaneity
rather than linearity. Critical synthesists could use a range of representational
tools including 'creative analytic practices' and other emotive genres of writing to
promote action and change (Richardson 2000, pp. 923-934). Through an
'increasing proliferation of pastiche, irony and parody' (Aronowitz and Giroux
1991, p. 72), postmodernist critical synthesists could construct engaging and
multi-layered texts, performances and other forms of art to encapsulate diversity
and complexity. These synthesists could generate a text that 'turns back on itself,
putting the authority of its own affirmations in doubt, an undercutting that causes
a doubling of meanings that adds to a sense of multivalence and fluidities' (Lather
1996, p. 533).

### Caveats of critically oriented syntheses

Most criticisms levelled against critically oriented primary research from exponents
of alternative paradigms would also be applicable to critically oriented syntheses.
Realists and neo-realists criticize openly value-mediated, critical scholars for being
'too theory driven and biased' (Anderson 1989, p. 249), leaping 'into the abyss
of relativism' (Mayer 2000, p. 39), paralyzed by postmodernism (Hatch 2006),
lacking 'hard data' (Kelly and Lesh 2000, p. 44), and privileging 'speculation'
over 'knowledge' (Lakomski 1999, p. 182) as a result of which reputation of
educational research has been ruined within 'the scientific community' (Mayer
2001, p. 29). Critical scholars counter-argue that they do not privilege discourse
or text over observation. Rather, they focus on discourse as much as they focus
on observation (Denzin 2008). Rather than considering everything to be equal,
critical scholars emphasize that 'we do not have access to an extra-linguistic
reality' (Hodkinson and Smith 2004, p. 154).

It is possible to provide examples of some caveats of all syntheses, including
critically oriented syntheses, which might be raised from within the critical
tradition. For instance, any synthetic effort appears to be at odds with the radically
relativist postmodernist ontology. Some postmodernists counter-argue that
postmodernism 'does not – as some seem to think – automatically reject
conventional methods as false or archaic, it simply opens them to critique, as it
does the new methods of knowing, as well' (Richardson 2001, p. 35).

## Selective eclecticism

Thus far in this chapter, geographies of paradigmatic spaces have been organized
around mutually exclusive domains. However, the exclusive identification of a
particular research study with a unique paradigm can be constraining and
misleading as paradigms are often mutually informing (Lincoln et al. 2011). The

fragmentation of methodology into discrete labelled regions runs the risk of concealing the commonalities of the endeavour and the pervasiveness of particular issues and concerns.

Often, researchers display multiple overlaps in their practice of empirical research (Miles and Huberman 1994). Examples of such interbred paradigms in primary research include critical ethnography (Anderson 1989), critical realism (Clegg 2005), critical action research (Kemmis and McTaggart 2000), critical collaborative research (LeCompte 1995) and feminist empiricism (Haig 1999). In the context of primary research, many scholars recognize the merits of drawing from more than one paradigm. Such selective eclecticism can often enhance the depth, richness and utility of our research (Wickens 2010).

Multiple overlaps, blurred genres, hybrid approaches, crossing boundaries and interbreeding of paradigms are prevalent not only in primary research, but also in research synthesis. Research synthesists often draw on ideas from more than one paradigm to enhance utility of their syntheses. For instance, feminist scholars have sometimes utilized meta-analytic methods to highlight gender differences (e.g. Haig 1999). In the last three decades, many research synthesis methodologists have asserted that a synthesis that draws on both postpositivist and interpretive traditions is richer than a synthesis that is either postpositivist or interpretive (e.g. Light and Pillemer 1984). Systematic reviewers are increasingly trying to engage those who are intended to benefit from the synthesis in the synthesis process. Such an interbreeding of postpositivist or interpretive orientations with participatory orientations can enhance the impact of the synthesis product (Rees and Oliver 2012). Other examples that draw upon interpretive and critical orientations are Dixon-Woods et al.'s (2006) critical interpretive synthesis and Major and Savin-Baden's (2010) qualitative research synthesis.

Drawing from the tradition of mixed-methods, research synthesists can strategically draw on different combinations of quantitative and qualitative evidence forms and analysis techniques to serve different purposes (Heyvaert 2011). Like mixed-methods researchers, mixed-methods synthesists can dialectically examine tensions emerging from the juxtaposition of different paradigms; espouse a single paradigm such as pragmatism or transformative-emancipatory paradigm; or use different paradigms for different purposes (Tashakkori and Teddlie 2003). Syntheses oriented along pragmatism would focus on generating propositions of high practical utility. This is similar to the Joanna Briggs Institute's 'meta-aggregative approach to qualitative synthesis' where the goal is to propose clear 'lines of action' for practitioners or policy-makers to bring about the desired consequences (Hannes and Lockwood 2011, p. 1632).

Research synthesists are divided on the issues of commensurability between different epistemological and methodological positions (Heyvaert 2011). Selective eclecticism in a research synthesis requires sophisticated understanding of subtle nuances associated with each tradition (Hannes and Macaitis 2012). When drawing from more than one paradigm, a synthesist must critically reflect on the issues of commensurability and incommensurability within every phase of the synthesis. Depending on the purpose and the context of the synthesis, some differences will become important while some differences will become trivial. The mixing of paradigms in a synthesis ought to be guided by the purpose and the context of the synthesis. Selective eclecticism in research syntheses is particularly useful to encapsulate the diversity in contemporary educational research.

## Using this discussion as a departure point to expand possibilities

Epistemological considerations remain critical at every phase of a research synthesis. From the outset, it is crucial for the synthesists to be reflexive about the overarching epistemological orientation of the synthesis. This would influence, and be influenced by, formulation of the appropriate synthesis purpose. The overarching orientation would guide the sampling logic and the process of searching for relevant studies. The criteria for including some studies and excluding others would be guided by the synthesis purpose, as would the decisions related to how individual studies are represented in the synthesis product. Finally, the medium and the channels for sharing the synthesis findings with the intended audience would also vary depending on the overarching orientation of the synthesis.

Throughout the synthesis process, it is crucial that synthesists maintain a reflexive stance. While reflecting on how their epistemological positioning shapes what they see and what they don't see, it is also crucial that they reflect upon how their own epistemological position might be shifting in response to what they see. As an illustration, I now describe how my worldview changed as I tried to address the following broad question: Given that contemporary educational research is marked by diversity, complexity, and richness of purposes, methods and perspectives, how can such variety and complexity be accommodated and reflected at the level of synthesizing educational research?

Prior to commencing this project, I had conducted a meta-analysis that involved statistically integrating effect-sizes from individual studies and identifying variables that potentially moderated the effect-sizes. In my meta-analysis, I had excluded all qualitative research. I commenced this project with the purpose of finding the most comprehensive method of synthesizing research. Coming from a postpositivist paradigm, I had assumed that this method would be similar to Slavin's (1986) method of best-evidence synthesis where the qualitative research findings would supplement statistical integration of research.

As I became more conversant with the qualitative research traditions particularly from interpretive orientations, I realized that the richness of qualitative research could not be captured in a postpositivist synthesis with a common metric. At this stage, I tried to develop an interpretive method of synthesizing methodologically diverse research in a way that maintained the integrity of individual studies.

During my conversations with teachers and scholars from participatory and critically oriented traditions, I recognized that the academic focus of my pursuit unintentionally undermined practitioner knowledge. This made me question my own understanding: Whose questions are typically addressed by a research synthesis? What forms of knowledge are privileged in a research synthesis? What model of change underpins research synthesis methodology? Such questions helped me explore the notion of a research synthesis oriented along participatory traditions.

As I became more cognizant of the issues of incommensurability between different paradigmatic positions, I realized that no single method of synthesizing research could ever be comprehensive enough to synthesize research in ways that would be compatible with all epistemological positions. At this stage, I abandoned my pursuit for the most comprehensive method of synthesizing research. Instead, I set about developing a *framework* for synthesizing research to support critically informed decision-making among producers and users of research synthesis.

The example above describes how my epistemological position shifted in my pursuit for a methodologically inclusive approach for synthesizing research. When viewed from distinct epistemological positions, the same broad question had distinct interpretations. Each interpretation was valid from within that specific epistemological position even if incommensurable with the alternative interpretations. This chapter illustrates how syntheses oriented along diverse paradigms can serve distinct yet equally useful purposes. In practice, research synthesists would often be selectively eclectic and draw ideas from more than one paradigm to inform their own syntheses.

# Chapter 7

# Identifying an appropriate purpose

What are some critical considerations in identifying an appropriate purpose for a research synthesis?

This chapter discusses key considerations associated with the process of framing and refining the synthesis purpose. As illustrated in Figure 7.1, all these considerations are refracted through the epistemological positioning of the synthesis. In other words, the epistemological positioning of the synthesis influences:

- which potential stakes and collaborations are recognized;
- the perceived nature of the substantive area;
- the intended audience and utility;
- the pragmatic constraints identified;
- the ethical considerations taken into account.

The first five sections of this chapter discuss key considerations associated with these five factors listed above. The final section of this chapter discusses how all these considerations influence the synthesist's contextual positioning with respect to the synthesis and how they are inevitably considered within the environment of the synthesist's contextual positioning.

## Recognizing potential stakes and collaborations

Several groups can knowingly or unknowingly influence a research synthesis in certain directions. Likewise, the findings of a synthesis may intentionally or inadvertently affect or inform different groups (see Table 7.1). Reflecting upon the potential consequences of the synthesist's own contextual positioning, and those of potential collaborators and stakeholders, can improve the synthesist's sensitivity towards potential biases.

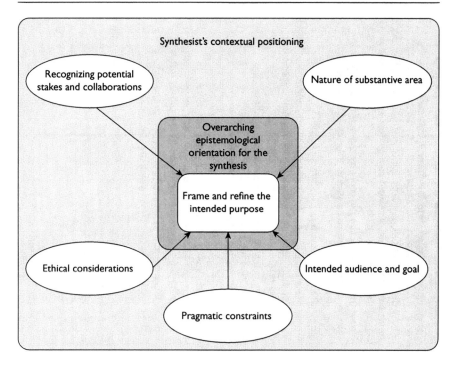

*Figure 7.1* Identifying an appropriate purpose

### *Potential stakeholders*

Reflecting on the potential for various influences on a synthesis could make synthesists aware of some obvious sources of biases. Recognizing the varied stake of different groups in a potential synthesis could sensitize the synthesist to anticipate diverse needs of different groups. The needs of individual groups may be overlapping, complementary and/or competing with those of others.

---

**Key questions to consider**

- Who are the various groups whose interests might be affected by a potential research synthesis?
- How might these groups influence the synthesis?
- What implications might the synthesis have on these groups?

---

Stakeholders in a synthesis are often anticipatory rather than retrospective. As illustrated in Table 7.1, several groups have a stake, at times overlapping stakes, in a research synthesis. Each row in the table lists a particular group and its

Table 7.1 Potential stakeholders in a research synthesis in education

| | Stakeholders | How could they shape/influence the synthesis? | The synthesis may affect them by influencing/informing: |
|---|---|---|---|
| A | students/learners | – whose learning experiences are being understood/discussed | – how their learning experiences are represented in the literature<br>– some of their decisions related to their learning experiences<br>– how they learn/are taught |
| B | parents/families of learners | – whose children's/family member's learning experiences are being understood /discussed | – how these experiences are represented in the literature<br>– some of their decisions related to their children's learning experiences<br>– how their family members learn/are taught |
| C | teachers/institutions (schools/universities) | – whose teaching experiences are being understood/discussed | – how these experiences are represented in the literature<br>– some of their decisions related to their teaching experiences<br>– how they teach |
| D | primary researchers in the substantive area | – whose research is being synthesized | – how their research is represented in the synthesis<br>– their direction for further research<br>– further funding for the domain of research |
| E | policy-makers | – whose policies may be evaluated | – further policies/global decisions |

*(Rows A–E, column 2, shared note):* They influence the synthesis inadvertently through their represent-ation in the data being synthesized, i.e. primary research reports.

| | Stakeholders | How could they shape/influence the synthesis? | The synthesis may affect them by influencing/informing: |
|---|---|---|---|
| F | wider community | – their perceptions influence what is considered important / desirable / right | – the broad thinking of citizenry and wider community<br>– the direction of further developments in education as often projects are directly/indirectly funded by tax-payers' money |
| G | commercial and political | – they may provide differential support to different types of syntheses to the extent of commissioning some | – political/commercial implications of interest to them<br>– their money/political power which may be put at risk |
| H | funding agencies | – they may fund particular types of research / research syntheses | – how primary research/innovations funded by them are perceived<br>– further directions for funding and practice |
| I | editorial boards and academic communities | – they collectively regulate the dissemination of primary research and research syntheses<br>– they regulate the status of varied forms of scholarship including research syntheses | – current and future academic conventions by providing methodological and substantive critique on the current status of research |
| J | professional synthesists | – they validate / legitimize methodology of research syntheses | – direction of further syntheses |

potentially reflexive relationship with a research synthesis. The last two columns in the table highlight the potential reflexivity of such relationships. Not only can these stakeholders be affected by the synthesis, but also they have the potential to influence the synthesis through their direct or indirect input at different stages.

The ordering of the rows in the table is not associated with any hierarchy. Members belonging to a particular group may also belong to other groups. Some individuals and groups may have multiple stakes or identities within the same synthesis. For example, policy-makers are often well positioned to commission research syntheses, thus taking on the role of a funding agency as well. Student bodies may also act as funding agencies by commissioning syntheses to look into issues that are particularly relevant to the welfare of student communities.

In Table 7.1, the first five rows (A-E) list groups who influence the synthesis indirectly through their representation in the relevant primary research reports that serve as the evidence for a research synthesis. The way a synthesis represents interests and issues of various groups could influence people's perceptions of these groups. A research synthesis can inform further practice, research and policy, which in turn, may influence teaching, learning, research or policy-making experiences of these groups (Popkewitz 1999).

The wider community (row F), through its collective and/or public voice, can sometimes indirectly influence the perceived importance of various educational issues. At the same time, a synthesis can influence thinking of the wider community. Often educational projects are funded directly or indirectly from public funds. A synthesis can inform the wider community about state-of-the-art of various domains of educational research.

While most of the groups in Table 7.1 are metaphorical stakeholders with their intellectual capital at stake, the commercial/political group (row G) is a literal stakeholder with their money and/or political power at stake. It is crucial that a synthesist is sensitive to various implications the synthesis may have for these literal stakeholders and the potential influence of these groups on the synthesis. Commercial stakeholders, like publishing companies, are likely to be interested in publishing and supporting syntheses that address relatively 'hot' or controversial topics. Many postpositivist synthesists aspire to provide unequivocal recommendations to decision-makers (e.g. Slavin 2002, CRD 2011). Criticizing this perspective, several critical scholars argue that researchers and synthesists must promote a culture of critical engagement with the research evidence, where the roles of ideology and politics are clearly recognized. From this perspective, synthesists must work with different stakeholders to find solutions while engaging with the uncertainties associated with the available research evidence (Schwandt 2005, Hodkinson and Smith 2004).

The groups represented in the last three rows (H-J) are funding agencies, editorial boards and academic communities, and professional synthesists. These groups often play a regulatory role by supporting syntheses and primary research of certain types more than others. A recent example is the level of funding being directed by the USA federal government to support systematic reviews, especially of randomized experimental and quasi-experimental studies. Synthesists can influence these groups by critiquing a range of methodological and substantive issues related to educational research and practice.

### Nature of potential collaborations

Drawing from the notion of participatory traditions, synthesists can explore the pros and cons of a wide range of collaborations between members of different groups whose interests may be associated with a potential synthesis. Such diverse collaborations can:

- encourage syntheses that address concerns of a wide range of stakeholders;
- facilitate syntheses informed by the perspectives of different groups;
- empower members of different groups by facilitating their participation in syntheses which may be of interest to them;
- enhance the impact of a synthesis by promoting participation of the agents of change who are crucial in implementing the recommendations made by the synthesis;
- contribute to wider dissemination of research syntheses;
- deepen academic synthesists' understandings of the collaborating stakeholders' concerns and understandings.

The nature of collaboration must be guided by the purpose of the synthesis. The collaborative team also has the potential to influence the purpose. For instance, a synthesist may collaborate with practitioners if the purpose of the synthesis is to inform practice. Such collaboration can direct the synthesis focus to questions that are of interest to practitioners. It can also serve as a form of member-checking in the interpretive process of the synthesis by providing a practitioner's perspective on, or validation of, the professional synthesist's interpretations. In another synthesis, a synthesist may collaborate with policy-makers to synthesize research for policy formulation. In yet another synthesis, a collaborative team of synthesists may consist of a professional synthesist, practitioner and a policy-maker to strengthen the links between policy, practice and research.

Different collaborators have the potential to enrich the synthesis by bringing in their own particular expertise. Each form of collaboration also introduces issues of power and varied interests that can add complexity to the synthesis process (Yu 2011). In a collaborative synthesis, synthesists must carefully negotiate issues arising from different perceptions of 'degree of jointness, definition of roles and responsibilities, flexibility of roles, similarity of standards and expectations, proximity of partners and depth of relationship' (Baldwin and Austin 1995, p. 60).

There are several complexities associated with the collaboration process between a team of research synthesists. Many of these issues find their parallels in primary research. However, the gravity of some of these issues is compounded by the novelty, fuzziness and long durations of time involved in the process of a research synthesis. In collaborative syntheses, synthesists should be able to 'provide evidence about the depth and quality of interaction among participants, including the process of meaning making' (Shulha and Wilson 2003, p. 656).

---

### Key questions to consider

- What are the pros and cons of the particular collaboration?
- What are each collaborator's respective interests and areas of expertise that are relevant to the particular synthesis?
- What are the potential overlaps, tensions or complementarities between the stakes of individual members of the collaborative team?
- Who will own the data? Who will publish? How will the issues of co-authorship or ownership of intellectual property be negotiated?
- How will potential mismatches between the agenda, purposes, interpretations, representations and/or interests of different collaborators be dealt with?

---

When seeking input from stakeholders, synthesists should, sensitively, be clear about the nature of input being sought and what can or cannot be negotiated; address power imbalances between different stakeholders; recognize heterogeneity within stakeholder groups; and ensure that less powerful groups do not feel further disempowered with the perception that their views are not being paid adequate attention (Petticrew and Roberts 2006, Rees and Oliver 2012).

## Nature of substantive area

In formulating an appropriate purpose, synthesists must pay attention to previous research reviews in the field, the current state of primary research in the field and the topicality of the field.

### Previous research reviews in the field

Often, research synthesists begin by reading previous research reviews in the field. Previous reviews, along with their bibliographic references, can provide useful information for developing a broad overview of primary research and research syntheses reported in the field. The following set of questions is useful in developing a preliminary understanding about purposes, orientations, coverage and impact of prior research and reviews in the field:

- What are key themes addressed by previous reviews? What aspects of the phenomenon are not clearly understood? Whose perspectives have been represented in previous reviews? Whose representations have been missing from the research literature?

- Who are the key stakeholders whose concerns have been the focus of previous reviews? Whose concerns have attracted little attention from primary researchers and research synthesists in the field? Who have been the intended audiences of the previous reviews?
- How have the previous research reviews influenced policy, practice, research and public perceptions in the relevant area?
- Why did the previous reviews have significant/little impact? What are some tentative or plausible reasons for this noticeable/little impact?

Informed by an understanding of the impact of previous syntheses in the broader context, the synthesist can speculate on how the proposed synthesis may be perceived by different stakeholders. The synthesist can refine the design of the proposed synthesis in a way that its likelihood of making the desired impact is enhanced. Recognizing the strengths and weaknesses of previous syntheses can help the synthesist to make informed decisions in the current synthesis.

---

### Key questions to contextualize the current synthesis

- How do the purpose and methods of the current synthesis differ from those of earlier reviews?
- How will this synthesis build on the connected understandings constructed in previous reviews?

---

A field may require a particular type of synthesis because other types of synthesis have already been conducted. At times one may need to build on or update prior syntheses conducted in the field (e.g. Hannes and Macaitis 2012). Purposeful synthesis of prior reviews can also be useful for 'very time- or resource-constrained situations' (Mays et al. 2005, p. 9) or in fields where a large number of reviews have been conducted. Interesting examples of such syntheses include Sipe and Curlette's statistical integration of 103 meta-analyses related to educational achievement (1997); Franklin's 'genealogical examination of the research reviews that appeared in the thirteen theme issues of the *RER* devoted to curriculum' (1999, p. 358); and Hattie's (2009) synthesis of over 800 meta-analyses of factors influencing achievement in school-aged kids which has been discussed by a large number of administrators, policy-makers, teachers and teacher educators in Australia and New Zealand.

### The current state of primary research in the field

Unlike primary researchers who generate their own data, research synthesists are confined to asking the questions that may be answered from the relevant primary research literature. In general, the overarching orientation of the synthesis should be compatible with the prevalent methodological orientations of the individual primary research studies. As an illustration, studies that are predominantly interpretive, lend themselves to an interpretive synthesis (Noblit and Hare 1988). However, such compatibility between the orientation of a research synthesis and dominant methodologies in primary research studies may not always be desirable if the purpose of the synthesis is to problematize the typical methods employed in the primary research studies. An excellent example of this approach is MacLure's methodological critique of 30 systematic reviews developed by the EPPI-centre in which she focuses on 'the silences in the discourse – at what systematic review leaves unspoken' (2005, p. 398).

Another aspect worth considering is the general relationship between individual primary research studies in the field. An aggregative synthesis may be applied to a relatively homogenous set of evidence. In a field where there is consensus on the desired outcome of schooling, a meta-analysis or an aggregative synthesis may be useful. However, a field with heterogeneous studies, which have employed diverse methodologies and examined different concepts, may be more amenable to an interpretive synthesis (Pope et al. 2007).

In an area that has been researched well, a confirmatory synthesis or a synthesis to systematically examine the commonalities and variations across individual primary research reports may be required. On the other hand, an exploratory synthesis may be useful to identify strands of research worth pursuing if the field has not been researched much. In a field where only a few methodologically sound primary research studies have been conducted, the synthesist might consider an in-depth synthesis of selected studies (Kennedy 2007).

---

### Aspects of the relevant primary research literature to consider:

- nature of predominant methodologies employed in the primary research studies;
- general relationship between individual studies;
- volume and scope of the relevant primary research.

---

### Topicality of the Field

Syntheses of hot topics, in which several stakeholders are interested, are likely to attract appropriate funding and have more impact (Elmore 1991). For instance, teachers across all year levels recognize the power of effective feedback and are interested in guidelines for providing it. Provision of effective feedback is often rated poorly in student feedback questionnaires administered in higher education institutions across many English-speaking nations. Given this widespread interest on this topic, it is not surprising that Hattie and Timperley's (2007) synthesis, which provides guidelines for providing effective feedback, is currently the most frequently read article of the *RER* and has already been cited in more than 1,100 articles according to Google Scholar. In addition to synthesizing research on a topical area, a rigorous synthesis can also contribute to enhancing the topicality of the relevant field by attracting a broad audience.

---

**Key questions to consider**

- How topical is the relevant substantive area of research?
- How can the synthesis contribute to enhancing the topicality of the field?
- How will the field benefit from a synthesis?

---

## Intended audience and goal

Research syntheses may be pursued for diverse intended audiences with varied goals in mind. Synthesists must foreground an intended audience and utility for the synthesis.

---

**Key questions to consider**

- Who is the intended audience for this synthesis?
- Whose questions will this synthesis address?
- Who is likely to benefit from this synthesis?
- What impact do I intend to make on this audience?
- What contribution do I hope to make?

---

### Target audience

It is better to synthesize research with the aim of answering the questions of a target audience rather than doing a synthesis and hoping to find an audience. Many research syntheses tend to inform a broad audience. Staying in touch with members of the intended audience can ensure that it is their questions that are being addressed by the synthesis (Patton 1991). Different stakeholders prefer different emphases in a research synthesis (Light and Pillemer 1984, Hannes and Lockwood 2011). Table 7.1 illuminates how a research synthesis may intentionally or unintentionally influence, and be influenced by, various groups with a potential stake in the synthesis. Table 7.2, illustrates how different groups are likely to be interested in syntheses that serve different purposes. The target audience of educational research syntheses could be broadly classified into four categories:

policy-makers; researchers focusing on the relevant area; practitioners; and those with peripheral interests in the topic.

Global decision-makers like policy-makers and administrators need generalizations which apply to diverse situations and students (Husen 1999). Useful synthesis questions to inform policy-making include the following: Whose interests have been overlooked by contemporary policy and research? Why have certain policies not had the intended impact? What configurations are most suited for the successful implementation of a program? (Hammersley 2000, Pawson 2006). What innovations have been effective or ineffective? What are the variables that potentially moderate the effectiveness of an innovation? What directions of research and practice should be supported further? What is the overall magnitude of a problem in terms of its prevalence and intensity? (Harlen and Crick 2004).

Academic researchers with a keen interest in the area tend to read syntheses to situate and inform their own research projects and are interested in syntheses that identify patterns of correspondence and disjunction in the findings, methods,

Table 7.2 Synthesis purposes illustrating interests of different stakeholders

| | Stakeholder (An example) | Illustrative Synthesis Purpose |
| --- | --- | --- |
| A | A council of postgraduate associations | Identify ways in which higher degree research students can be supported to bring down their attrition rates |
| B | Parent-teacher associations of a group of schools | Explore strategies that can make home environments more conducive for enriching children's learning experiences |
| C | An association of school administrators | Explore ways in which school administrators can respond to the needs of diverse students |
| D | Primary researchers interested in teacher education | What does research say about how people learn to teach? (Wideen et al. 1998) |
| E | Department of education | Review research on multiage classroom organization as an option for high-ability students (Lloyd 1999) |
| F | Groups interested in equity and access issues | Examine employment and postsecondary education outcomes for youth with disabilities leaving secondary schools (Phelps and Hanley Maxwell 1997). |
| G | Manufacturers of graphics calculators | Examine ways in which graphics calculators can enhance students' mathematical thinking |
| H | A funding agency like Spencer Foundation | How to enhance the methodological rigour of research being funded by an agency such as the Spencer Foundation? |
| I | Editorial boards of AERA sponsored journals | What is the methodological state-of-the-art of the research reports published in the AERA sponsored journals? |
| J | An inter-disciplinary consortium of meta-analysts | What are the common sources of errors or forms of incomplete information in quantitative research reports? |

contexts and theoretical orientations of primary research studies in the field; develop an holistic understanding of the field; identify gaps in the research domain; re-examine the literature with a fresh perspective; restructure the literature conceptually; and problematize the prevalent concepts and themes in the field (Hammersley 2003).

Practitioners, professional-developers and local decision-makers like to be provided with detailed information about viability and advantages of a program in contexts similar to their own (Hemsley-Brown and Sharp 2003). Examples of questions that are likely to interest them include the following: Is a particular educational strategy suitable for contexts similar to theirs? How can the strategy be adapted to their own contexts? How can its effectiveness be improved? Which groups of students benefit most from the strategy? How is the strategy perceived by different groups of students?

Practitioners like to know details of the scenarios in which an innovation is likely, or not likely, to work. Such vivid information can help practitioners in making informed decisions about the extent to which the findings of the relevant research are applicable to their own work contexts (Light and Pillemer 1984). Also such information can help professional developers to provide just-in-time support to practitioners. Synthesists with a potential for engaging practitioners in critical reflection through a set of key questions can be particularly useful. An excellent example of such a synthesis is Windschitl's 'theoretical analysis of constructivism in practice' to provide teachers with a framework in the form of 'critical questions that allow them to interrogate their own beliefs, question institutional routines, and understand more deeply the forces that influence classroom practice' about constructivism (2002, p. 131).

Members of the public are generally interested in syntheses that have implications for the wider society. Beginning graduate students, undergraduate students and those with peripheral interest in the field tend to be interested in getting an overall picture or essence of the field without getting into all the intricate details.

### Goal

The goal of a synthesis is frequently refracted through, though not limited by, its philosophical and theoretical orientation. Research syntheses may be pursued for various goals, such as to verify a hypothesis, generate a hypothesis, facilitate an holistic understanding, challenge prevalent generalizations or catalyze action. Goals may be broadly classified as integrative, interpretive, deconstructive, participatory and emancipatory.

A common goal for most research syntheses is some form of integration through generalization, conflict resolution or linguistic bridge building (Cooper 1988). Several formally proposed methods of research synthesis, such as meta-analysis and aggregative analysis (Eastabrooks et al. 1994), are geared towards identifying some transcendental themes that can be generalized across the contexts of several primary research studies. Research synthesists can enhance 'ecological transferability' across contexts, 'population transferability' across different individuals or groups, 'temporal transferability' across different time-periods and/or 'operational transferability' across different methods of data-collection and analysis (Teddlie and Tashakkori 2003, p. 38). Most research synthesists attempt some form of conflict resolution by exploring patterns of influence that may plausibly explain some variations in research outcomes of individual studies. Through linguistic bridge building, synthesists can construct connections between research reports that examine a similar phenomenon from different theoretical orientations; facilitate holistic understandings of various educational phenomena by drawing and weaving threads from a variety of disciplines; and support a wider dissemination of educational research across a range of disciplines.

Syntheses with interpretive goals can describe processes, relationships, situations, systems and people; develop new concepts; elaborate on existing concepts; provide insights; clarify and understand complexity; develop and verify assumptions and theories; evaluate policies, practices and innovations; describe how varied interests and experiences of different stakeholders interact; coherently organize typical and atypical experiences of a group to 'inspire empathy, interest, and understanding (rather than dislike, dismissal, or distrust)' (Eisenhart 1998, p. 395).

Syntheses with deconstructive goals can go beyond interpreting the narratives of primary research reports to interrogating 'how the narratives were made historically possible in the first place' (Popkewitz 1999, p. 397); create doubts about the prevalent metanarratives in the field in order to create more chaos and anarchy; shake our comfort zones of thinking about a phenomenon and force us to rethink a phenomenon in unfamiliar ways; 'provoke, challenge, and illuminate rather than confirm and settle' (Bullough and Pinnegar 2001, p. 20); portray diversity and conflict by focusing on 'contested, ambiguous, or inconsistent data' to uncover tensions and inconsistencies across studies (Eisenhart 2001, p. 23); and 'disrupt, rather than establish, definitions and boundaries ... [to] expand, rather than settle, the possibilities for human understanding and educational practice' (Eisenhart 1998, p. 397). Rather than resolving contradictions, smoothing over inconsistencies and achieving a sense of closure, deconstructive synthesists would ask 'what the text is *concealing* – what it had to suppress, or make a detour round, in order to achieve a sense of completeness' (Stronach and MacLure 1997, p. 53). Their task would be 'not to interpret but to consume – to revel in the plurality of uncertainties that claim no boundaries and seek no resolutions' (Aronowitz and Giroux 1991, p. 66).

Participatory synthesists can facilitate experiential learning by engaging in the synthesis process members of those groups whose practices are intended to be transformed through the synthesis. Such syntheses are also inherently emancipatory as they facilitate practitioners to have a voice in the construction of knowledge about their practice. Emancipatory synthesists would espouse the purpose of transforming the dominant discourse in order to emancipate or liberate the oppressed; have a sense of mission; and construct openly ideological, value-mediated, understandings to catalyze changes by re-examining how a domain of research literature has failed to adequately address concerns of a particular group of stakeholders (Mertens et al. 2010). Even a meta-analyst can serve an emancipatory purpose by harnessing the seductive power of big numbers to politicize an issue and highlight the concerns of a particular group (Haig 1999).

Syntheses of similar sets of studies with different goals can yield different insights. For instance, although many of the studies included in Amundsen and Wilson's (2012) conceptual review were also included in previous empirical reviews in the field, they made a unique contribution by re-examining this literature with a distinct goal. Unlike the reviews that had focused on examining the effectiveness of educational development practices, these authors developed a conceptual framework by identifying and clustering the core characteristics and the key theories that underpinned the design of educational development practices.

Research synthesists can strategically influence principles, practices, policies and public opinions. By generating mid-range theories and principles that are transferable to several contexts, research synthesists can inform policies and practices. By raising public awareness and politicizing or problematizing certain practices, synthesists can influence policy-makers' agendas towards certain directions and influence public perceptions. For instance, a meta-analysis with a large collective sample size may demonstrate that a large proportion of dyslexic students do not feel adequately supported in contemporary school systems. Such a synthesis can communicate to various stakeholders the urgent need to formulate policies that support these students. Interpretive syntheses that provide insights into the general dynamics of various intervention programs for dyslexic students can facilitate informed policy and practice decisions. A deconstructive synthesis may problematize some of the assumptions underlying various intervention programs that 'otherize' dyslexic students. A participatory synthesis may engage groups representing interests of dyslexic students to identify programs that may be particularly useful for these students.

## Pragmatic constraints

A rigorous research synthesis makes much more demands on time and resources when compared with ad hoc reviews. Just as the perfect primary research study has never been conducted, neither has the perfect synthesis. The issue that confronts a synthesist is often 'how to maximize the quality of the synthesis within the available resources' rather than 'how to do the most rigorous synthesis'. Research synthesists are often bound by the pragmatic constraints of time, resources and access to information and expertise. Often decision-makers and stakeholders want 'relevant, understandable, and accurate' information which they can use soon. In many practical situations, synthesists may find that a highly rigorous approach is 'overly formalistic, too time consuming, and unnecessarily expensive' within the available resources and deadlines (Patton 1991, pp. 287-289). Most research syntheses which attract large funding tend to address questions of politicians or other decision-making bodies who can provide adequate funds. Systematic reviewers typically aim for exhaustive sampling and assume sufficient access to financial resources, information and expertise. Unless synthesists strategically design syntheses within various pragmatic constraints, they could inadvertently contribute to silencing of concerns of certain groups of stakeholders who cannot financially afford large-scale syntheses.

### Financial resources

In the current environment of financial cuts to academic research, it is crucial that a synthesist carefully designs the synthesis to ensure its financial viability. One way of improving the financial viability of a synthesis is to apply for funding from a range of sources. However, it is important to ethically consider the pros and cons of accepting funding from a source that is biased in favour of a particular stakeholder. Major sources of expenditure that must be considered in the budget of a research synthesis include costs associated with personnel weighted by the total number of hours and the monetary rate appropriate for the desired level of expertise; photocopying; printing; inter-library loans; basic infrastructure such as office space and computer hardware and software; and any costs associated with appropriate access to various databases for abstracts and full reports of research.

### Time

Structured and strategic planning of time is just as pertinent in a research synthesis as it is in primary research. The synthesist must allocate approximate time required for each phase of the synthesis. In a team situation, each member's domain of expertise and availability of time can be tabulated to allocate tasks strategically. For instance, more seasoned researchers may be allocated tasks that require higher levels of interpretation while allocating less abstract tasks, such as collecting copies of primary research reports, to research assistants. All this information may be tabulated along with the tentative deadlines for each task and a schedule for team meetings. During the planning, appropriate fractions of time ought to be apportioned to different phases of the synthesis in a way that reflects the importance of that phase. The gravity of time-pressure in a research synthesis is compounded by the fact that often audiences are interested in syntheses that include the latest primary research reports in the field (Paterson et al. 2001).

### Access to information

Published research literature is the primary source of evidence in a research synthesis. This requires access to libraries with sufficient resources in terms of subscriptions to relevant journals and electronic databases. Limited access to well resourced libraries can be a serious constraint in developing nations or in smaller nations where government support for educational resources is limited. Another access issue relates to reports in languages other than English which may not be held in the library collections to which the synthesist has access. Building strategic alliances with colleagues working in the same field with access to literature from different geographical locations and in different languages can help to overcome this constraint to some extent. When the synthesis involves government policies or areas in which governments (or corporate organizations) have commissioned research, access to reports of that research may be restricted. A synthesist may lobby or negotiate to gain an access to such reports. When such reports are inaccessible, the synthesist must clearly mention those primary research reports which could not be included in the synthesis due to limited access. At times, the synthesist may even abandon the synthesis if those primary research reports are critical for the comprehensiveness of the synthesis.

### Access to expertise

Two forms of expertise are crucial in a research synthesis: methodological expertise and knowledge of the substantive domain. Advice from experts, in primary research methods and/or research synthesis methods, on methodological issues associated with evaluating and interpreting the information presented in the primary research reports can sensitize a synthesists to specific methodological issues associated with the field. A synthesis can also be enriched with the input from members of groups whose concerns the synthesis is intended to address (Carr and Coren 2007). When synthesizing studies from different countries, 'any evaluative aspect is reflective of the cultural authorship of the study' (Clarke 2003, p. 178). The same data set is interpreted differently by researchers from different countries as each researcher grounds the data in their own cultural context. Authentic inclusion of studies from another country is best enacted by collaborating with an expert who is familiar with the educational context of that country. By creating a team, or drawing on the experts' knowledge from diverse cultural perspectives, a synthesis is likely to better represent an international view.

## Ethical considerations: Whose representations?

Unlike primary research, a research synthesist does not have to worry about the ethical dilemmas associated with accessing deeply personal information as the evidence for a research synthesis comes from publicly available documents. However, research syntheses play a powerful role in shaping further research, practice, policy and public perceptions. They tend to be read and cited frequently (Cooper and Hedges 2009). Accordingly, the ethical issues associated with how different groups are represented become more imperative and complex in a research synthesis report than in a primary research report. The synthesist has an obligation to state clearly and optimally the caveats, subjectivities and assumptions associated with the synthesis findings such that anyone who uses them beyond their intended domain is clearly seen to be doing so. When synthesizing a wide spectrum of layered representations, it is crucial to identify any dominance or absences of the relevant representations that have been missing from the published literature.

---

Ethical considerations in a research synthesis are often refracted through the overarching epistemological orientation of the synthesis. For example,

- postpositivist ethics would prioritize reducing any potential biases,
- interpretivist ethics would prioritize honouring representations of the participants of primary research studies,
- participatory ethics would priorities rich learning experiences for those participating in the synthesis process, and
- critical ethics would prioritize paying attention to issues of power.

---

## Authors of included studies: What status?

Every research synthesis inherently involves three layers of interpretation, selection and representation. First, the participants in primary research studies selectively interpret and represent their perceptions, attitudes, aptitudes, experiences and abilities. This layer of interpretation might not be explicitly acknowledged in non-constructivist epistemologies. Second, this evidence is selectively interpreted and represented, after it has been refracted through the interpretive frameworks of the authors, in the primary research reports. Finally, the research synthesist selects, interprets and represents evidence presented in primary research reports.

---

### Key questions to consider

- Who are the authors of the relevant primary research reports?
- What are their theoretical and disciplinary orientations?
- How are the primary researchers in the field typically related to the participants in their studies? How may this have influenced the interpretations represented in the primary research reports?
- How do the interests of the authors of the primary research reports relate to the diverse interests of different stakeholders?

Scrutinizing the relationship of the authors of the primary research reports with the substantive topic of research, a synthesist can shed some light on how some themes may have become dominant in the field as against some others that have been relatively silenced. Sometimes synthesists can strategically highlight the reports by authors who are from relatively silenced groups in the field. Being sensitive to potential subjectivities of authors of the primary research reports can add depth to the synthetic findings. However, these subjectivities should not essentially be perceived as undesirable sources of error (Patton 1991). Often the authors of primary research reports have a more holistic view of the phenomenon as compared to the view of any single group included in the primary research study.

Synthesists should also be wary of 'othering' the 'researched' by implying an 'invisibility of the researcher', which creates a 'conceptual distance between the observer and the observed, as well as the reader and the observed' where the 'reader and the researcher stand together' (Meacham 1998, pp. 402-403). Recognizing that '*concrete language* is an oxymoron' since 'language is always an abstraction of experience' (Popkewitz 1999, p. 403, emphasis in original), synthesists should contest the naïve assumption of an absolute congruence between the interpretations represented in the primary research reports with those of the participants of the original studies (Elmore 1991). As an illustration, Wideen et al. (1998) problematize the notion of the neutral representation of the authors of reported research and speculate on how their role as teacher educators could have influenced their interpretations and findings.

### Participants of the primary research reports: Whose viewpoints?

Primary research in education typically represents behaviours, perspectives and experiences of students, their parents, teachers or institutions, curriculum developers, administrators and global decision-makers. Not all members of these groups have their perspectives equally represented in research reports. For instance, there is widespread belief that working class parents are frequently silenced stakeholders when compared with middle class parents who are relatively more assertive and more inclined to participate in research studies. Also, different members of these groups may be influenced differentially by a synthesis.

In a rigorous research synthesis, potential misrepresentation of practice should be avoided by empathetically and critically attending to the viewpoints of the participants of the primary research studies to the extent that this is possible through the filtering of the primary researcher. Eastabrooks and her colleagues stress that synthesists 'must examine each theme or category carefully to determine if they have been well rooted in the original data' (1994, p. 508). However, such grounding is often not possible, considering the frequently imposed limits on the length of journal articles that restrict primary researchers from presenting details of their raw data. It is worth considering the option of getting on the team a key stakeholder who belongs to the group whose perspective is predominantly presented in the primary research studies. Such a team member can act as a rich informant and refine the connected understandings emerging from the synthesis. Synthesists can also benefit from collaborating with members of the groups whose viewpoints have been typically silenced in the published literature.

### Funded syntheses: Whose agenda?

Many research synthesists apply for funding to sustain the financial viability of a synthesis. However, research grants that allow the synthesist high degrees of control are often highly competitive and are restricted to high profile scholars in the field. Even though research syntheses could 'provide profound and insightful interpretations to help us better understand what we sometimes take for granted' (Gordon 1999, p. 409), their status in academia was often marginalized in terms of their probability of attracting research funding and in their contribution to the university's overall research quantum (Apple 1999). This has been changing in recent years. For instance, consistent with the OECD's broad notion of research and experimental development, the Australian Research Council has also included synthesis in their recent definitions of research for funding applications:

> Research is defined as the creation of new knowledge and/or the use of existing knowledge in a new and creative way so as to generate new concepts, methodologies and understandings. This could include synthesis and analysis of previous research to the extent that it is new and creative.
>
> (ARC 2011)

Another source of funding that synthesists can tap into are the funds available for commissioned syntheses. In recent years, several government, corporate and philanthropic organizations have started supporting the movement of systematic reviews (EPPI-Centre 2009, CRD 2011). A wide range of research syntheses may be commissioned by different stakeholders to pursue their respective interests (see Table 7.2 for illustrations). A synthesist must take into consideration any real or perceived biases that might compromise the trustworthiness of the synthesis due to any potentially vested interests of a funding agency. Recognizing the seriousness of the issue of conflict of interest, several organizations have policies against taking direct funding from sources with a vested interest in the results of the review (e.g. The Cochrane Collaboration 2011). Issues associated with intellectual autonomy and research funding can be complex and must be addressed sensitively and ethically.

---

### Key considerations in a commissioned synthesis

- What are the interests of the commissioning agency that are relevant to the synthesis?
- What is the relative match between the intended purpose of the synthesist and that of the funding agency? What are the constraints introduced by a degree of mismatch between the interests of the two?
- Who will control the nature of the synthesis? How much control will the synthesists have?
- What is the potential for negotiating any differences of agenda?
- How much control will other stakeholders have?
- How will the interests of other stakeholders be represented?

---

### Politics of publishing: Who/what gets published?

Politics is an inherent part of educational research, practice, praxis and knowledge production. Research syntheses are no exception to this (MacLure 2005, Gallagher 2004). Research synthesists ought to acknowledge that there is an inevitable politics involved in who or what gets published. Synthesists should reflect on the issues associated with the possible biases introduced by the politics of publishing at the level of primary research as well as research synthesis. The next chapter describes a variety of potential biases that can influence funding, publishing and retrieval of certain types of primary research reports. Examples of these biases include confirmatory bias, bias against small-N studies, bias against insignificant difference, funding bias, methodological bias, database bias, citation bias, availability bias, language bias and country bias. Analogous biases are also possible at the level of publishing research syntheses. All these issues, arising from who/what is more likely to get published, must be taken into account when reflecting on the appropriateness and viability of a research synthesis.

## Synthesist's contextual positioning

In Figure 7.1, the synthesist's contextual positioning has been marked by an all-pervasive shaded background to emphasize that all key decisions associated with identifying an appropriate purpose for the synthesis will be inevitably influenced by the synthesist's contextual positioning. This is to highlight how crucial it is for the synthesist to reflect on one's own contextual positioning.

---

**Key questions to consider**

- What is my stake in the synthesis? How might this influence the synthesis?
- How is my own thinking and positioning changing during the synthesis?

---

### Multiple and shifting identities

A research synthesist can have multiple and/or shifting identities within the same synthesis. In the context of a particular synthesis, a synthesist may have one or more overlapping and/or conflicting stakes. For instance, consider a synthesis in the substantive domain of online learning where the synthesist may commence with multiple identities by simultaneously engaging in more than one of the following activities: being enrolled in an online course; teaching in another online course; and conducting primary research in the area of online learning. The synthesist may commence the synthesis with all these multiple frames of reference, any of which may be relinquished during the synthesis. As the synthesis progresses, the synthesist may gain more expertise in the area of online learning and actively engage in policy-making by becoming a member of several decision-making bodies at the institutional level. Thus, the synthesist may have shifting identities within the course of the same synthesis.

Synthesists must reflect on their relative identities with respect to the various groups participating in the study of the phenomenon of interest: students, teaching staff, primary researchers or decision-making bodies. For instance, in their award-winning synthesis, Wideen et al. recognized that a white Anglo-Saxon male is likely to have a different identity from that of a coloured female in the context of a synthesis on multi-cultural education. Accordingly, they described their gender, ethnicity and professional identity at the outset of the synthesis (1998). This self-awareness and perhaps self-disclosure is an inherent responsibility that any synthesist ought to consider. Trying to untangle the aspect of our own positioning that may influence our choice in a synthesis is not an easy task.

---

**Key questions to consider**

- Does who I am, and what my experiences have been, interact with this topic? How? Why?
- Does my sex, race, language background, socio-economic context, heritage, culture, sexuality, education, professional identity or life experiences provide me with insights, or conversely restrictive vision, in this area?
- In what ways might my perspective be partial because of my personal subjectivities?
- What personal values do I hold that interact with this synthesis topic or domain?

---

## Methodological Expertise

Research synthesis is emerging as a methodology in its own right. For example, the EPPI-centre offers several courses about research synthesis methods, some of which contribute to the university's postgraduate programs (EPPI-Centre 2009). Exclusive expertise in a single primary research method does not equip anyone to be a good research synthesis. A research synthesist must be well-versed with the specific issues relevant to a research synthesis as well as methodological assumptions associated with a variety of primary research methods.

---

**Considerations for a potential team of research synthesists**

- Do we have expertise in relation to a variety of methodological issues specific to a research synthesis?
- Can we identify inherent assumptions that are built into primary research coming from a range of methodologies?
- Do we have expertise in the several types of methodologies that are likely to be employed in the primary studies conducted in this field?
- Do we have expertise to recognize the aspects of the phenomenon that have not been understood because few primary research studies have employed the particular methodologies that are likely to shed light on those aspects of the phenomenon?

---

## Synthesist's authority: Learner versus learned

The 'poststructuralist feminist' standpoint contests any 'reviewer's position as 'the one who knows,' the 'expert in the field,' in favour of more situated, partial, and perspectival knowing that, while not knowing everything, does know something' (Lather 1999, p. 4). From this perspective, 'vulnerability is not a position of weakness, but one from which to attempt change and social fellowship' (Tierney 2000, p. 551). Drawing on such a critical perspective, one may assume that inevitably all team members undertaking a research synthesis are learners in a sense; and all team members have an opportunity to learn through the process of a research synthesis by constructing knowledge pertinent to their personal and professional selves.

A synthesist may view himself or herself and each collaborator anywhere on the continuum from the status of a novice to an expert in relation to different domains of expertise at different points of the synthesis. The learner as well as the learned, both have the potential to make worthy contributions in a rigorous synthesis and all team members are likely to take on either role at different times. The learned can contribute by sharing their expert insights. The learners can contribute by seeing the field from a novice's viewpoint that makes explicit several taken-for-granted assumptions in the field. Juxtaposition of the learner and the learned perspective may be achieved in a synthesis by a team of collaborators or by an individual synthesist who draws upon both the perspectives, using each to iteratively refine the other.

## Summary

An emphasis on purposefully informed selective inclusivity necessitates that synthesists carefully identify a purpose that takes into account potential stakes and collaborations; nature of the substantive area; intended audience and utility; pragmatic constraints; and ethical considerations. All these factors will essentially influence, and be influenced by, the synthesist's contextual positioning and the overarching epistemological, theoretical and political orientation of the synthesis.

# Chapter 8

# Searching for relevant literature

What issues should be considered when identifying suitable approaches and techniques to search and retrieve relevant research literature?

Research synthesists draw their evidence from the primary research reported in a field. There is no single 'right' way of searching for relevant evidence in all syntheses. Research syntheses on the same topic conducted for different purposes can have different sampling strategies, each being equally legitimate but tailored to serve the different purposes. Synthesists must strategically search for the relevant evidence to efficiently meet the synthesis purpose within the available resources and pragmatic constraints. This chapter explores different approaches to sampling and searching for relevant studies that are suitable for diverse purposes.

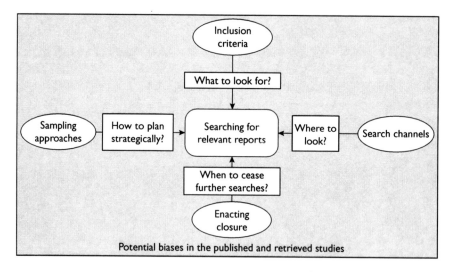

Figure 8.1 Searching for relevant literature

In Figure 8.1, an all-pervasive shaded background is used to emphasize that potential biases specific to the nature of evidence in a research synthesis must be considered when searching for relevant studies. This chapter begins by describing some of these biases followed by a discussion of the four major decisions within this phase of a synthesis: framing an appropriate set of inclusion criteria; strategically utilizing relevant sampling approaches; pursuing suitable search channels and identifying the rationale for enacting closure. All these decisions must:

- be mutually coherent;
- be in alignment with the synthesis purpose;
- strategically take into account relevant pragmatic constraints to ensure the feasibility and timely completion of the synthesis.

---

**Key questions to consider**

- What are some of the issues specifically associated with the evidence of a research synthesis (e.g. potential biases and layered nature of interpretations)?
- What inclusion criteria will be employed to search for primary research reports?
- What sampling logic is amenable for the intended purpose?
- What logic will guide the decision to cease searches for further evidence?
- What is an efficient combination of search channels for locating relevant literature to adequately address the synthesis purpose?
- What are the justifications for and implications of each of these decisions?

---

## Potential biases in the published and retrieved studies

Several biases can influence funding and publishing of certain types of primary research reports as well as research synthesis. Biases are also introduced when searching for relevant studies. These biases can systematically skew the synthesis findings in certain directions (Petticrew and Roberts 2006). Synthesists must not only consider reflexively how these biases influence their synthesis but also how their synthesis may contribute towards reinforcing these biases.

## Publication biases

A publication bias exists when the chances of a study being published depends on the nature of its theoretical premise, methodological orientation and/or findings; with an increased likelihood of some types of research in attracting research funding, being conducted, being submitted for publishing and getting published. Common forms of publication bias include a funding bias, methodological bias, confirmatory bias and outcome bias.

*Funding bias.* Often educational researchers have to seek external funding to make their research financially viable. A bias may be introduced at this stage if some types of primary research are more likely to be funded than others. As noted earlier in Chapter 2, many funding agencies, especially in the USA, are favouring quantitative studies with RCTs as gold standard (Howe 2005, Slavin 2008b). Funding agencies hesitate to fund projects that aspire to study variables that are 'difficult-to-define and difficult-to-measure' (Kennedy 2010). Such a prejudice among funding agencies can increase the likelihood of studies with certain methodological features of getting funded, being conducted and being published. Funding agencies in education, sometimes also prioritize projects that examine innovative approaches to teaching and learning. Embracing innovative approaches iteratively could lead to continual change in policies leading to a dissatisfaction among practitioners for always having to catch up with the latest changes. With the growing push for 'open-access' to publicly funded research, reputed publishers are shifting the cost of publishing to potential authors. This could further introduce a bias where research conducted by well-funded groups is more likely to get published. Another form of a funding bias is introduced with a frequent embargo on commissioned research, especially that funded by government agencies, from being published.

*Methodological bias.* Studies with certain methodological designs, especially with large samples, are more likely to get published (Finfgeld-Connett and Johnson 2012). Sometimes restrictions on length of the articles can influence qualitative researchers' decisions to publish in different outlets. Studies with different research designs and theoretical orientations have different likelihood of being published, or not published, in different journals depending on the methodological preferences of their editorial boards.

*Outcome bias.* Research that does not report marked differences between individual groups or sub-groups examined within a study is less likely to be published. 'Subgroup reporting bias' exists when several subgroups are compared but only comparisons with interesting or statistically significant findings get published. Similarly, 'time-lag bias may exist if research with large effect sizes or significant results is published more quickly that that with small effect sizes or insignificant results' (Sutton 2009). There is some evidence of a bias towards reports of successful innovations. Catchy terms like 'breakthrough', 'radical', 'new' and even 'innovative' tend to have a popular political and public appeal associated with the thinking that 'doing something is better than doing nothing'

(Dixon-Woods et al. 2011). However, implementation of most innovative approaches requires more resources and professional development for practitioners. With an expectation that innovations must be successful to be published, at times researchers consciously or inadvertently invest extra resources in the sites of primary research. It is possible that policy decisions are made based on a synthesis of this published research. However, in real life often these policy decisions are not supplemented with the provision of adequate funding required for effective implementation of these policies (Schoenfeld 2006).

*Confirmatory bias.* Research that is at odds with the current prevailing beliefs or theories is less likely to be conducted or published (Miller and Pollock 1994). Clandinin and Connelly describe tensions between teachers' 'secret, sacred, and cover stories' (1996, p. 24). An analogous tension also exists between the secret, sacred and cover stories of researchers. The 'secret stories' include the tensions, struggles, dilemmas, ambiguities, complexities and uncertainties experienced by researchers and are shared in secret places. The 'sacred stories' are the texts on research methods and theories that dominate the prevalent conception of what ought to be regarded as quality criteria for educational research and practice. The 'cover stories' are the stories that are reported in the published literature and are heavily influenced by the subtext of the sacred stories. The evidence of a research synthesis is often the primary researchers' cover stories of the research participants' cover stories. Another layer is added to this evidence as the readers of a research synthesis get access to the cover stories of the research synthesist. At each layer of representation, certain biases are inherent. However, what is worrying is that all these biases are likely to be in the direction of the prevalent sacred stories.

### Including unpublished reports in a research synthesis

Research synthesists use the terms 'grey literature' or 'fugitive literature' to refer to reports that are typically published by agencies other than commercial publishers, such as government reports, and that are often not included in common indexes and databases (Rothstein and Hopewell 2009). Sometimes published literature can become difficult to find because it is not easily available from the libraries to which the research synthesist has access. Often, unpublished primary research is hard to find.

Research synthesists are divided on the question of whether to include unpublished research or not. Some argue in favour of including only published research on four grounds. First, research that is of high quality is more likely to be published. Including only published research can ensure that the evidence for the synthesis is of a high quality and includes standardized information on samples and results. The logic is that if a study is of high quality, then it would be published anyway. For example, Gijbels et al. (2005) found that all the studies reported in their retrieved set of *unpublished* reports were also reported in their retrieved set of *published* reports. Second, published research tends to be more accessible. Third, most researchers tend to present their findings in their theses or conference papers before submitting them for publishing. Including unpublished research can raise the number of multiple reports of the same set of findings, thus violating the assumption of independence of individual data-points. Excluding unpublished research can reduce the problem of double-counting as authors are less likely to publish the same finding in different published sources. Fourth, sometimes it can be difficult to reliably define and set boundaries of unpublished literature (La Paro and Pianta 2000).

Another concern is the potential incomparability of evidence from journal articles and dissertations or theses. It might be speculated that combining findings from dissertations and journal reports could introduce a potential bias in favour of the dissertations or theses. In dissertations and theses, researchers can show extensive links between the findings and the original evidence. Due to space restrictions in journal articles, it is relatively more difficult to clearly establish the links between the findings and the evidence. At times, this might give an impression of enhanced credibility in favour of dissertation findings. It can be easier to extract the relevant information from dissertations because of the detailed nature of reporting. This might also be associated with higher emphasis or weight being attached to the findings from dissertations. On the other hand, sometimes it might be easier to identify weaknesses in the study designs of theses because of the detailed reporting involved. In that case, these reports may not be given the benefit of the doubt that some other studies reported in journal articles might be given.

Many other research synthesists caution against excluding all unpublished reports for several reasons. First, they argue that some unpublished research is, at least, of comparable quality to much published research. For instance, many unpublished government reports tend to be conducted by seasoned researchers in the field even if the reports do not always undergo formal peer review. Theses and dissertations are another example of unpublished research that go through the rigorous reviewing processes of the university academic committees. Second, excluding unpublished research could make the synthesis vulnerable towards the potential consequences of various publication biases. Third, including quality unpublished research can facilitate a relatively more comprehensive coverage of the field (Glass 2000). Fourth, some qualitative research synthesists point out that the tight word limits which apply to many journal articles restrict authors from presenting a rich description of their study design, context and observations. In this respect, unpublished research such as theses and dissertations can be particularly good sources of evidence for a research synthesis because they can provide the rich descriptions that are crucial for a context-sensitive synthesis of qualitative research (Lloyd Jones 2004). Fifth, peer-reviewed journals typically publish manuscripts authored by researchers from the academy. To include research and perspectives of stakeholders from outside the academy, it is crucial that synthesists are inclusive of reports that are reported in venues other than peer-reviewed journals (Kennedy 2007). Sixth, to understand research in its appropriate context, many research synthesists recognize the merit of including key policy documents and government reports in the synthesis (EPPI-Centre 2009).

There is no right answer in relation to all research syntheses as to whether to include only published research. Also, different research synthesists have different conceptions on the demarcation between what constitutes published research and what constitutes unpublished research. A synthesist ought to conduct a careful cost-benefit analysis when making decisions in relation to inclusion of unpublished research.

### Search biases

In the last three decades, numerous competing databases have entered the market and what one finds depends largely on where one looks. Synthesists should carefully examine their search strategies to take into account any biases introduced by their search techniques such as the following.

*Database bias.* Reports included in popular databases are more likely to be retrieved. Strategies to minimize a database bias include searching in several databases and complementing database searches with other search channels (Papaioannou et al. 2010).

*Citation bias or reference bias.* Reports that are frequently cited are more likely to be retrieved. Even from the retrieved reports, synthesists are more likely to draw on views that are similar to their own (Rothstein et al. 2004). This further reinforces a confirmatory bias.

*Availability bias.* Synthesists often include reports that are easily accessible at relatively low costs (Matt and Cook 1994). Establishing open access to more and more research journals will hopefully reduce this bias in the future (Willinsky 2005). However, as noted in the discussion of funding biases, transferring the cost of publishing to authors could also introduce further biases.

*Language and country biases.* Often, synthesists include reports published in international English language journals that may not be representative of all the studies conducted on the topic. This is of particular concern to meta-analysts in some fields where studies reported in English language journals appear to be associated with larger effect sizes. Limiting our searches to English language journals also limits our access to research with theoretical underpinnings more common in non-English speaking countries. To reduce this bias, synthesists can collaborate with international scholars, especially from non-English speaking nations, as they are more likely to know of research reported in their own language (Booth et al. 2013).

*Familiarity bias.* Often synthesists are more likely to include studies from their own disciplines with which they are familiar (Rothstein et al. 2004). Collaborating with and seeking feedback from colleagues with different disciplinary backgrounds can provide useful insights that may have been overlooked otherwise.

*Multiple publication bias.* With the current environment of 'publish or perish', it is not always clear when multiple reports have been published based on the same study. When synthesists are unsure about the independence of studies reported by the same group of authors in multiple reports, they should contact the authors of the original reports.

## Inclusion criteria

The inclusion criteria set out what the synthesist looks for during the searches for the relevant studies and focus a research synthesis by setting up and defining the scope of the synthesis. The inclusion criteria must be carefully designed to yield the most relevant, trustworthy and comprehensive evidence within the constraints of the available resources. Meta-analysts and systematic reviewers assert that it is crucial to tightly define the outer limits or appropriate boundaries of the research domain that will be included in the synthesis as the success of a synthesis largely depends on the ability of the synthesist to be precise. They often state explicit inclusion and exclusion criteria (Hammerstrøm et al. 2010).

The degree of sharpness between inclusion and exclusion criteria that is feasible in a meta-analysis may not always be feasible in an interpretive research synthesis. A primary research study can be either included or excluded from a meta-analysis, the decision being a dichotomous one. However, the boundaries between inclusion and exclusion may be relatively fuzzy in an interpretive synthesis because even if the findings of a primary research study are not explicitly represented in the report, they could have informed the synthesist's tacit understanding of the phenomenon. Individual reports might be emphasized to different levels in the synthesis report, depending on how typical or atypical they are in relation to a broad spectrum of relevant studies, some of which may not be included in the formal analysis and synthesis. In other words, what and how a synthesist reports some studies can be influenced by a number of studies that may not be explicitly reported in the synthesis (Dixon-Woods et al. 2006a). Maintaining 'an interpretive trail of the different ways in which studies have been used or omitted' (Pawson et al. 2005, p. 31) can improve the reliability, transferability and confirmability of synthesis findings.

### Scope of substantive domain and contextual coverage

In general, all synthesists must clearly describe the meanings that they have attributed to key terms especially those terms that tend to be associated with varied connotations. Delineation of conceptual and operational definitions of all key constructs, independent variables and dependent variables is crucial for reducing ambiguity in a meta-analysis. For example, in their exemplary meta-analysis, Greenwald, Hedges and Laine conceptually defined education production function as 'the relation between school inputs and student outcomes', restricted the breadth of the dependent variable, i.e. student outcome, to indicators of academic achievement only and operationalized the variable student achievement as 'the results of standardized achievement tests' (1996, p. 364).

However, operationalization of key constructs in terms of observable behaviour may not always be feasible or desirable in all syntheses, especially constructivist and non-behaviourist syntheses. For instance, in an interpretive synthesis of different meanings attributed to key aspects of a phenomenon by different stakeholders, a synthesist may deliberately maintain a 'penumbra of ambiguity' (Layton 1994, p. 32) in defining the phenomenon to avoid privileging any particular group's meaning (e.g. Dixon-Woods et al. 2006b).

The scope of substantive domain covered by the definitions of the key constructs, the criteria for inclusion/exclusion of studies, and the selected collection of relevant studies should be carefully matched with the generalizations being inferred about the population of studies. A broad substantive domain is suitable for examining a particular aspect of the phenomenon across its numerous manifestations (Ogawa and Malen 1991). However, a relatively narrow scope for the substantive domain is suited when constructing an holistic understanding of a phenomenon with careful attention to the dynamics between the interacting aspects of the phenomenon.

Synthesists must delineate and substantiate the contextual scope of their synthesis by attending to contextual features, such as: subject matter or tasks being learnt by students; time frame, publication year, demographic details of the samples or participants; and geographical, cultural and temporal boundaries of primary research covered by their inclusion criteria.

The degree of specificity associated with the selection criteria at different stages may vary across syntheses. Most research-synthesists start with broad definitions and selection criteria to reduce exclusion of possibly relevant studies. As the searches continue and they get a clearer idea of the key themes and the variations in the field, they revisit, refine and focus progressively their selection criteria (Abrami et al. 1988). Sometimes, as in a meta-ethnography with purposeful-sampling, synthesists begin with a particularly interesting primary research report or collection of reports and then find more reports that illuminate the key themes emerging out of their initially selected reports. Many synthesists use a combination of both the approaches, i.e. general to specific as well as specific to general at different stages of their synthesis.

It is crucial that the synthesist maintains a record of the emerging selection criteria as this is closely associated with the themes that the synthesist perceives as being important at the time. Reflecting on the emerging selection criteria and their mutual relationship with the synthesist's emerging conception of the phenomenon is likely to facilitate reflexivity, depth and openness to unexpected findings in a synthesis process.

### Including methodologically diverse primary research

Every research synthesis must be characterized by purposefully informed selective inclusivity while refraining from any claims at comprehensive coverage (Pope et al. 2007). Any attempt to be comprehensive would be theoretically flawed because it would presume that all purposes might be served by the same synthesis.

If the purpose of the synthesis is to facilitate an understanding of a broad phenomenon, as in many exemplary educational research syntheses, then it can be useful to synthesize primary research employing diverse methods as each type of research would shed light on a different aspect of the phenomenon. For example, Engberg included quantitative, qualitative and mixed-methods research in his synthesis as large-N studies facilitate generalizability and 'offer an illuminating perspective on both the predictive and the absolute nature of change effects'; qualitative studies offer 'important insights into the theoretical underpinnings of various interventions'; and mixed-methods studies offer 'an in-depth exploration of how the various interventions influence different aspects of' a phenomenon (2004, p. 502). When synthesizing methodologically diverse studies, it can be useful to first synthesize groups of studies with similar designs and then compare them across groups.

On the other hand, meta-analysts often exclude all primary research in which the findings cannot be converted into an effect-size. Many qualitative research synthesists also caution against synthesizing quantitative and qualitative studies because of their incommensurate epistemologies. Even within qualitative research, while some synthesists suggest that including methodologically diverse qualitative research can enrich the synthesis (e.g. Lloyd Jones 2004), others recommend that only primary research with similar methodologies ought to be synthesized (e.g. Jensen and Allen 1996). In synthesizing research that employs different qualitative methods, it is crucial to pay attention to the implications of different philosophical underpinnings across methods (Zimmer 2006). This issue becomes more complex as different qualitative researchers frequently use different terms to describe similar methods, or vice-versa, and embrace diverse epistemology, ontology, methodology and quality criteria.

Methodological and theoretical orientations of primary research studies included in the synthesis are often guided by the purpose of the synthesis and the overarching orientation of the synthesis. Even after the studies are included, the status attributed to them is likely to be influenced by the purpose and the overarching orientation of the synthesis. For instance, even when meta-analysts recommend the inclusion of qualitative information (e.g. Slavin 2008a), they assume that non-quantitative information would play a supplementary role: by helping in defining an intervention precisely; by developing valid research questions; by identifying appropriate outcome measures; by interpreting heterogeneous findings (Campbell Collaboration 2001); or by using Bayesian approaches for identifying potential moderator variables and quantifying qualitative evidence (Kastner et al. 2012).

## Strategic sampling

Identifying an appropriate sampling approach involves making decisions about what to look for, why, and how to approach it strategically within available time and resources. This section discusses how different sampling strategies are suitable for research syntheses with different goals. Depending on the purpose of the synthesis, the sampling logic may also change at different stages of the synthesis. For instance, synthesists could draw upon the logic of exhaustive sampling to get a broad overview of the field. Then, they could draw upon the logic of purposeful sampling to structure their synthesis around key research reports. This could be enriched by drawing supplementary information from additional confirming and disconfirming studies to construct a more nuanced understanding (e.g. Yeager and Walton 2011).

---

**Key questions to consider**

- What combination of sampling strategies is conceptually aligned with the synthesis purpose, feasible within the pragmatic constraints, ethical and efficient for locating the most relevant and trustworthy reports?
- What are main caveats associated with this combination of sampling strategies?
- How might these caveats impact upon the synthesis findings?

---

### Exhaustive sampling

Meta-analyses and systematic reviews typically employ the logic of exhaustive sampling to locate every relevant research report. Many exemplary qualitative research syntheses also employ exhaustive sampling (e.g. Kennedy 2008). The goal here is to provide generalizable conclusions or to construct a comprehensive understanding based on most of the research conducted on the topic. Exhaustive sampling involves searching through a wide range of search channels that are described later in this chapter. When drawing upon the logic of exhaustive sampling, it is crucial to think carefully about the conceptual underpinnings, coverage and the boundaries of the selected search terms and search channels.

### Purposeful sampling

Many qualitative research synthesists have questioned the viability of holistically synthesizing a large number of qualitative reports in a way that adequately attends to how the findings, contexts and methodologies of individual studies interact. They recommend that an in-depth synthesis of purposefully selected studies is more desirable than a superficial synthesis of a large number of studies (Finfgeld-Connett and Johnson 2012).

In the literature on primary research methods, Patton has provided a comprehensive discussion of purposeful sampling for constructing an insightful understanding of a phenomenon by studying in-depth a small number of 'information-rich cases' (Patton 2002, p. 230). Patton has suggested 16 strategies for purposeful sampling in qualitative research, each of which is intended to serve a different purpose. This section explores potential adaptation of the different purposeful sampling strategies to synthesize research for facilitating understanding, participation, emancipation and/or deconstruction. The subheadings used in this section are the verbatim terms that Patton (2002) has used to distinguish between the 16 strategies under the broad umbrella of purposeful sampling. Also, Patton's ideas are deliberately extrapolated to the context of a research synthesis.

### Extreme or deviant case sampling

This involves selecting studies that exemplify contexts where an innovation was perceived notably as a success or a failure. The main weakness of extreme case sampling is its lack of generalizability through representativeness. This weakness is of less concern for synthesists who focus on *how things should be* rather than *how things are*. This strategy is particularly suitable for a realist synthesis (Pawson 2006) that investigates how a program is likely to work under particular circumstances by examining successful as well as unsuccessful implementations of the program.

### Intensity sampling

This involves selecting studies where the phenomenon has been manifested with sufficient intensity. To develop a comprehensive understanding of many educational changes, it is crucial to examine cases where these changes have been embedded thoroughly in the system over a sufficient period of time. However, such intense manifestation of an innovation can be cost-intensive and/or associated with high-risk factors. As a result, the innovation might be implemented with sufficient intensity in only a few studies. Many other studies might examine the implementation of the innovation over short durations of time with minimal interventions. For example, a large number of studies have been conducted to investigate how students learn in collaborative environments. Given the individualistic nature of most high stake testing, most studies use collaborative learning strategies as an add-on to the regular teaching and learning activities. Many students in these studies might engage with collaborative tasks superficially. In a small number of studies, the learning activities as well as the assessment tasks have been revised intensely to reward collaboration. An in-depth synthesis of the latter type of studies would be particularly useful to illuminate a range of opportunities, challenges, advantages and disadvantages associated with curricula driven by an ethos of collaborative learning.

### Maximum variation (heterogeneity) sampling

This involves identifying key dimensions of variations and then finding cases that vary from each other as much as possible. This allows identification of unique features of different types of cases as well as commonalities across different categories. It is particularly useful for identifying essential features and variable features of a phenomenon as experienced by diverse stakeholders among varied contexts to facilitate informed global decision-making. Presuming that different study designs illuminate different aspects of a phenomenon, maximum variation sampling can be utilized to construct an holistic understanding of the phenomenon by synthesizing studies that differ in their study designs along several dimensions. In conceptualizing the MIRS framework, maximum variation sampling was used to deliberately draw ideas from methods of primary research and research synthesis that were markedly different along key dimensions.

## Homogenous sample

This involves an holistic synthesis of a subgroup of studies that are relatively similar in their study designs and conceptual scope. Homogenous samples are particularly suitable for a *participatory synthesis* in which the synthesist co-synthesizes research with practitioners about a phenomenon that has direct implications for their practice examined in settings similar to their own.

## Typical case sampling

Research synthesists can consult with key researchers in the field to identify typical studies being conducted in the field. A synthesis of typical studies can be particularly useful for providing an overview to those who are unfamiliar with the specific domain of the research. When employing typical case sampling, it is crucial 'to attempt to get broad consensus about which cases are typical – and what criteria are being used to define typicality' (Patton 2002, p. 236). This sampling could be particularly useful for studying how common themes recurring in the published literature might be related to the relative strengths and weaknesses of the typical methodologies or theories employed in typical studies.

## Critical case sampling

Critical case sampling can facilitate 'logical generalizations' with the reasoning 'that "if it happens there, it will happen anywhere," or, vice versa, "if it doesn't happen there, it won't happen anywhere"' (Patton 2002, p. 236). Critical case sampling in a research synthesis might be employed to assist stakeholders in making informed decisions about the viability of an educational program. For example, consider an innovation that produces desirable outcomes but is being rejected by many practitioners as they believe that its implementation requires substantial resources. A synthesis of primary research studies that describe in detail successful implementation of the innovation with minimal resources might be useful to alleviate the practitioners' resistance towards that innovation. Alternatively, consider an innovation that requires substantial financial resources but for which the proponents of the innovation assert that the innovation is cost-effective provided sufficient resources are invested in its implementation. In such an instance, a research synthesist can selectively synthesize cases reported in primary research studies that were sufficiently endowed with resources to logically verify, or challenge, the claims made by those advocating the innovation.

### Snowball or chain sampling

Snowball sampling involves seeking information from key informants about details of other 'information-rich cases' in the field (Patton 2002, p. 237). One approach to this is to identify primary research reports that are frequently referred to by various stakeholder groups who are interested in the phenomenon. It is particularly useful for capitalizing on expert wisdom, identifying articles that are highly valued by different stakeholders, and identifying studies that may lie outside of academic mainstream. Another way of adapting snowball sampling is to identify the most cited primary research reports by searching the citation indices or by browsing through the bibliographies of previous research syntheses, primary research reports, policy documents, reports written by practitioners, and reports written for practitioners. However, this approach can reinforce confirmatory bias where studies that agree with the prevalent wisdom are more likely to be published and cited while studies that contest the conventional wisdom are less likely to be published or cited. Another adaptation of snowball sampling is to draw upon retrieved studies to locate further studies or keywords for pursuing further electronic searches (Booth et al. 2013).

### Criterion sampling

This involves including all the studies that meet a priori inclusion criteria. Most synthesists draw on the logic of criterion sampling even though the degree of specificity of a priori inclusion criteria varies depending on the overarching orientation of a synthesis.

### Theoretical sampling

Grounded-theorists define theoretical sampling as the sampling that is based on the concepts emerging from the data for the purpose of exploring 'the dimensional range or varied conditions along which the properties of concepts vary' (Strauss and Corbin 1998, p. 73). Many qualitative research synthesists draw upon the logic of theoretical sampling in their syntheses (e.g. Dixon-Woods et al. 2006b).

### Confirming and disconfirming cases

Seeking studies that confirm the emerging understanding in a synthesis can elaborate and add 'richness, depth, and credibility' (Patton 2002, p. 239) to the synthesis findings. Confirmatory studies may be sought in an openly ideological synthesis when the synthesist wishes to advocate a particular stance for ethical, moral and/or political reasons. A synthesist may also seek confirming cases in order to validate the perceptions of a particular group of stakeholders. To shake our complacent acceptance of popular myths and/or generalizations in a field, synthesists can exclusively seek primary research studies that disconfirm generalizations proposed in policy documents, previous syntheses or primary research studies. Seeking studies that disconfirm the emerging understanding in a synthesis can offer rival interpretations and place boundaries around the key findings of the synthesis. Strategically seeking disconfirming cases in searching for relevant literature, interpreting and distilling evidence from selected studies and constructing a connected understanding enhances rigour and richness of a synthesis (Booth et al. 2013).

## Stratified purposeful sampling

'Stratified samples are samples within samples' where each stratum is 'fairly homogenous' (Patton 2002, p. 240). Many research reviewers tacitly draw on the logic of stratified purposeful sampling by clustering studies according to a key dimension of variation and then discussing each cluster in-depth. A practical example of this approach is the meta-narrative review method where the first phase of literature searching involves seeking input from key researchers and stakeholders in the field in order to identify key traditions and the relevant theoretical papers that have been critical in advancing the field. This is followed by retrieving key empirical studies within each tradition for constructing a storyline that depicts progress within the tradition (Greenhalgh et al. 2005).

## Emergent sampling

Emergent sampling is particularly suitable for an exploratory synthesis in a field that is rapidly evolving or where the synthesist does not have an emic or insider status. It is also suitable for a participatory synthesis where the synthesis purpose evolves in response to the changing needs of the participant co-synthesists.

## Purposeful random sampling

In theory, research synthesists can employ exhaustive searches to locate most of the primary research reported on a topic and from this pool of reports randomly select a few for in-depth discussion. However, given the resources required for locating all primary research reports on a topic, it would not be cost-effective to randomly discard studies from further consideration. Hence, this sampling has little appeal in practice.

### Sampling politically important cases

A synthesist might consciously select politically important reports so that the synthesis gains the attention of different stakeholders and the synthesis findings make the desired impact. For instance, in a synthesis of key criticisms of educational research published in the 1990s, Oancea (2005) illustrated her key observations through a detailed analysis of three politically important documents that were frequently cited in the newspapers. Syntheses of hot topics, in which several stakeholders are interested, are also likely to attract appropriate funding and have more impact (Elmore 1991).

### Convenience sampling

This involves synthesizing only those reports that are easily accessible. Even though convenience sampling is used in many research reviews, it should be avoided as it is prone to several unacknowledged biases. If convenience sampling has been employed in a research synthesis, the nature of its use and associated caveats must be clearly described.

### Combination or mixed purposeful sampling

Synthesists often employ a combination of two or more sampling strategies to select evidence that adequately addresses their purpose. Mixed purposeful sampling can facilitate triangulation and flexibility in meeting the needs of multiple stakeholders (Patton 2002). For example, many synthesists utilize exhaustive sampling to draw generalizations at a higher level of abstraction. Then, they strategically employ typical case sampling to provide readers with an immediacy of typical studies that contributed towards informing the more abstract generalizations. When selecting a combination of sampling strategies, synthesists must reflect on how those strategies complement each other.

## Sample size and enacting closure to searches

Data saturation and data sufficiency are two main logics that guide the decision to enact closure in a research synthesis. Most research synthesists refrain from prescribing a rigid range of sample size appropriate for a research synthesis (Booth et al. 2013). Although many scholars recommend small samples for qualitative research syntheses (e.g. Noblit and Hare 1988, Paterson et al. 2001), many methodologically diverse exemplary reviews have included a large number of studies. For example, La Paro and Pianta (2000) included 70 studies, Wideen et al. (1998) included 93 studies, Kasworm (1990) included 96 documents and Greenwald et al. (1996) included 60 studies. Proponents of several research synthesis methods have suggested that their method could be used for synthesizing even a small number of studies. For example, three in a meta-ethnography (Noblit and Hare 1988), four in an aggregated analysis (Eastabrooks et al. 1994), seven in a meta-analysis (Cooper and Rosenthal 1980), eight in a thematic synthesis (Thomas and Harden 2008) and twelve in a meta-study (Paterson et al. 2001).

Data redundancy or data saturation can be interpreted in different ways depending on the purpose of the synthesis. Data saturation may be associated with the stage when further collection of evidence provides little in terms of:

- new references if the synthesist claims 'exhaustive' searches of all the references that meet the inclusion/exclusion criteria;
- further themes, insights, perspectives or information in a qualitative research synthesis.

The concept of data saturation is dependent on the nature of the data source as well as the synthesis question. There is a higher likelihood of reaching data saturation if the data collection is purposeful. The more precise a question, the quicker it tends to reach data saturation. Progressive refinement of synthesis question is likely to bring an earlier stage of data saturation. With open-ended questions, every new report is likely to have something different to offer. A broad question like 'what does research tell us about virtual classrooms?' is not likely to bring about a sense of closure or data saturation. On the other hand, the synthesist is likely to reach the data saturation stage earlier with a focused question like 'what is the correlation between gender differences and mathematics achievement on standardized tests among middle school students?'

The logic of data sufficiency is guided by the synthesist's perception of what constitutes sufficient evidence for achieving the synthesis purpose. Critically reflecting on how the synthesis purpose, sampling logic and the synthesis findings are mutually influencing, intersecting and evolving can enhance the credibility and trustworthiness of the synthesis.

---

**Key questions to consider**

- Is each claim made in the synthesis sufficiently grounded in the evidence from included studies?
- Does this sample of studies represent a good spread of theoretical, methodological, conceptual and contextual variations relevant to the synthesis purpose?

---

## Search channels

The terms 'exhaustive' and 'expansive' are sometimes used to distinguish between two approaches to search for suitable studies (Finfgeld-Connett and Johnson 2012). Exhaustive searches are more suitable for integrative syntheses aimed at producing generalizable findings. Expansive searches are more suitable for syntheses with emergent designs, where the search criteria evolve as the synthesis progresses. The synthesist must strategically choose and sequence the use of appropriate search channels in a way that is aligned with the sampling logic and yields the most relevant, trustworthy and comprehensive evidence within the available resources.

---

**Key questions to consider for each search channel**

- Is the entry of the study into this channel dependent on the judgement of someone other than the authors of the study, such as editors of the journals and the books?
- How specific or general does the synthesist have to be to seek primary research studies from this channel?
- What are the biases likely to be associated with the literature retrieved through this channel?
- How does this search technique complement the other search techniques being employed?

---

As each search technique is associated with its strengths and limitations, it is essential to search the literature through multiple techniques that complement one another (Papaioannou et al. 2010). If the primary research study enters the channel without mediation from an independent reviewer, then it is less likely to be affected by a publication bias. However, this might also be associated with a relatively less rigorous study design. The second question is related to the critical trade-off between breadth versus depth. Some search channels, such as database searches, require a high degree of specificity. Other channels, such as personal contacts, are more general in nature. Early on in the synthesis, a synthesist can benefit from general searches that might be followed later by more specific searches.

Synthesists often identify primary research conducted by colleagues, supervisors, students and/or friends. Studies found through personal contacts are prone to the methodological and theoretical biases of the synthesist's professional network. A traditional 'invisible college' involves a group of central figures investigating a particular field along with the numerous researchers who are in touch with any of these key researchers. Research retrieved through this channel is likely to be biased towards the beliefs prevalent among these key researchers (Rosenthal 1994).

Most research synthesists search the suitable reference databases available in their field. The most commonly used USA, UK or Australia-based reference databases in education include Education Resources Information Centre (ERIC), PsychINFO, Education Research Complete (EBSCO), Academic Search Elite,

British Education Index (BEI) and Australian Education Index (AEI). As most database searches require a high degree of specificity, it is crucial to think of an optimal combination of search terms, Boolean operators and scope of various fields to yield the most relevant literature. This will vary depending on the stage and the purpose of the synthesis. At later stages, a more comprehensive selection of search-terms is necessary to ensure that the coverage is genuinely reflective of the scope of the synthesis. The search techniques, selection criteria and bibliographic references described in the previous research syntheses can be a rich source of information for defining and refining the process of selecting evidence for the current synthesis. One strategy for locating such reviews is to restrict the searches to records which include 'review* OR meta* OR synthesi*' in their abstracts or 'literature review' OR 'state of the art review' or 'meta analysis' or 'synthesis' in the subject. Using research bibliographies, annotated bibliographies, bibliographies of previous research reviews and research studies can speed up the searches with a high precision level yielding studies with methodological rigour (Papaioannou et al. 2010). However, the selection of references into these bibliographies is likely to be affected by the biases of the authors of the particular bibliography (White 2009).

Chasing bibliographic references also excludes the most recent research in the field. This approach should be complemented with a more forward-looking approach by using suitable citation indexes, such as the Social Sciences Citation Index (SSCI), or Google Scholar to locate papers that cite a key paper that was published earlier. Most research synthesists also use suitable search engines, such as Google Scholar, to locate current or frequently cited reports. When synthesizing research on some intervention programs, synthesists can browse through the web pages of developers of those intervention programs, and they can even contact these developers, to get initial lists of research studies on their particular programs. This technique is sometimes used to find additional studies reported after completion of initial exhaustive searches. Browsing through the websites of main professional bodies, e.g. *Higher Education Academy* on issues related to teaching and learning in higher education, can help in locating key researchers and most recent research in the field. Another essential strategy for locating most recent research is to skim through the Table of Contents of key journals and conference programs in the field.

'Electronic invisible colleges' include listservs or newsgroups, some of which might be focused on research while some others might be focused on contemporary practices. Listservs that have a research focus can be useful in identifying primary research studies or previous syntheses. Practice-focused listservs can be useful in identifying reports that are particularly valued among practitioners or in identifying the synthesis questions that might be of particular interest to practitioners. Browsing through listservs can also help in identifying researchers and practitioners who have an expertise in the substantive domain of interest. The synthesist can later contact these experts directly to request for references to the specific studies on which their claims and opinions are based.

Library information scientists frequently use 'recall' and 'precision' as two measures for evaluating literature searches (White 2009). 'Recall' refers to the ratio of retrieved documents that satisfy the inclusion criteria to the universe of all the documents which would satisfy the inclusion criteria. Most research synthesists aim for a high recall by conducting extensive searches to enhance the representativeness of the sample by retrieving as many relevant documents as possible. Extensive searches through several channels can reduce the subjectivity introduced by the synthesist's personal biases and make the sample more representative. High recall may be associated with casting one's net wide enough to reduce the chances of missing any eligible studies. This may be achieved by keeping the searches sufficiently broad, especially during the early stages. Recall is a hypothetical construct since it is likely that there will be many studies from the universe of all the eligible studies of which the synthesist will not be aware (White 2009). Practical considerations, such as cost and time, set pragmatic bounds on the degree of recall achievable in any synthesis.

'Precision' refers to the ratio of documents that satisfy the eligibility criteria to the total number of documents retrieved from the searches. High precision can be achieved by reducing the number of false hits. In other words, to achieve high precision the synthesist must only pursue the search channels that are likely to yield a high proportion of relevant documents. Another way of achieving a high precision is to construct sharp and focused search strategies. Extensive and broad searches can reduce the precision and hence cost-effectiveness of searches (White 2009).

The synthesist ought to maintain the financial viability of the synthesis while refraining from compromising on the representativeness of the evidence. Often the synthesist might settle for a middle ground between sometimes competing demands of recall and precision. One way of achieving reasonable levels of recall and precision might be to conduct sharp and focused searches on several search channels. Even though some strategies for conducting focused searches for meta-analyses (e.g. White 2009) and qualitative syntheses (e.g. Wilczynski et al. 2007) have been suggested, this is an area which requires further streamlining as substantial effort is wasted in sifting through irrelevant records.

## Summary

This chapter discussed critical considerations in searching for relevant literature for inclusion in a synthesis. A research synthesist must bear in mind how might potential publication biases and search biases influence the synthesis product. A clear set of inclusion criteria defines the scope of the synthesis. The level of specificity associated with the inclusion criteria at different stages of the synthesis would vary in accordance with the synthesis purpose. A synthesist must identify an appropriate combination of sampling strategies and search channels that will yield most relevant and trustworthy evidence within the constraints of available resources. Decisions related to the sample size and enacting closure to further searches can be guided by the notions of data redundancy or data sufficiency.

**Key questions to consider in searching for relevant literature**

- How is the primary research literature positioned in relation to:
  - the key aspects of the phenomenon being examined in the synthesis?
  - the various contexts in which the phenomenon occurs?
  - the suitable methods and theories for examining the phenomenon?
- How are the selected reports positioned in relation to the trends of all the primary research studies conducted on the topic (e.g. specific to one context or population, or oriented along a particular theory or methodology)?

# Chapter 9

# Evaluating, interpreting and distilling evidence from selected studies

What issues should be considered when evaluating the retrieved research reports for inclusion into a research synthesis? What issues should be considered when interpreting and distilling relevant and trustworthy information from the selected primary research reports?

The previous chapter discussed issues for consideration in retrieving a sample of research reports for a synthesis. This chapter discusses issues that are worth considering when evaluating these retrieved reports, interpreting evidence from selected individual reports and distilling evidence from each selected report. Research synthesists often evaluate the methodological quality of each study from the sample of retrieved studies in order to make decisions about its inclusion in, or exclusion from, further analysis and synthesis. The chapter begins with a discussion of this finer-grained selection process of individual studies. The next section emphasizes the interpretive nature of the process of making sense of the evidence reported in individual primary research reports. The notion that the data is 'out there', lying in a research report of which the synthesist can make sense objectively, is contested here. The underlying premise here is that it is through the synthesist's interpretations that the evidence presented in a research report comes to life for the purpose of the synthesis. This is followed by a discussion of issues associated with distilling relevant and trustworthy information from individual reports. This chapter concludes by discussing procedures for enhancing rigour in sifting trustworthy and relevant information from the sample of retrieved reports.

As illustrated in Figure 9.1, each layer of evaluation, interpretation and distillation is associated with some form of data-concentration. There are no sharp boundaries between these layers of data-concentration. The synthesist progresses through each layer of data concentration towards the central core of the evidence that intensely focuses on the synthesis purpose. The arrow from a corner of this figure to its centre indicates the direction of progressive refinement and data concentration.

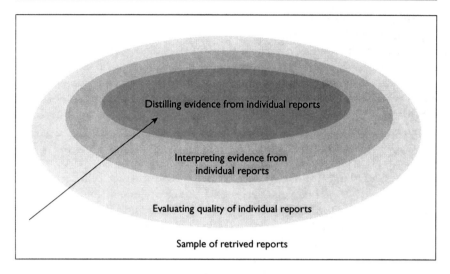

Sample of retrived reports

*Figure 9.1* Evaluating, interpreting and distilling evidence from retrieved reports

## Evaluating quality of individual reports

Some synthesists prefer the term appraisal to evaluation as appraisal more explicitly 'encompasses understanding in addition to estimating value' (Sandelowski and Barroso 2002, p. 10). To stress the need for evaluating as well as interpreting the reported evidence, these two inseparable aspects of appraisal are discussed separately in this section and the next section respectively. This section discusses issues associated with evaluating methodological quality and relevance of individual studies for inclusion in, or exclusion from, further analysis and synthesis. This selection process of individual studies is more fine-tuned than that elaborated in the previous chapter.

While some synthesists argue that all research reports which meet the substantive selection criteria ought to be included in the synthesis (e.g. Jensen and Allen 1996, Glass 2000), others insist that studies that have relatively weak study designs ought to be excluded (e.g. Eastabrooks et al. 1994, Slavin 2008). Instead of discarding the primary research studies on grounds of poor methodology, some meta-analysts include all relevant primary research reports, code them for their study design features and empirically examine how different study design features moderate the effect-size (Bowman 2010). These meta-analysts argue that if there is no significant correlation between the average effects and the study design features, it suggests that the overall findings are robust. In such a case, as in Smith and Glass's (1977) meta-analysis, including all the studies for further analysis would provide the analyst with a larger database of studies. This in turn could facilitate an identification of potential moderator variables that might not have been possible with a smaller set of only well-designed studies. Significant moderation of the average effect by study design features might provide a plausible explanation for some unexplained variation across the findings of individual primary research studies. In such cases, as in Glass and Smith's (1979) meta-analysis on class-size, further analysis could involve integrating findings from only the studies with strong study designs. However, some research synthesists argue that studies with relatively weak designs should be included in a synthesis only when there is a paucity of studies with strong designs. Synthesists should be cautious not to apply so stringent criteria for methodological rigour that they throw out studies with potentially useful insights (MacLure 2005, Briggs 2008).

All synthesists agree that findings from primary research that have stronger study designs should be given more weight in constructing collective understandings. These methodologically 'sound' studies represent information-rich cases that provide more trustworthy information. Excluding a large proportion of research on the grounds of poor methodology can raise serious questions about the validity and generalizability of the synthesis findings (Dynarski 2008). Often, studies with minor shortcomings can also provide useful insights for identifying transcendental patterns across studies (Valentine 2009). Rather than asking 'is this a perfect study?', a synthesist ought to ask 'how do methodological features of this study impact upon the trustworthiness of its findings in ways that are relevant to my synthesis purpose?' In a field that has a paucity of rigorous research, one of the purposes of a synthesis could be to identify common shortcomings across these studies. This could lead to the formulation of a set of methodological guidelines for further research in the field.

Over the past three decades, numerous publications have noted the inadequacy of quantitative criteria for rigour when used to evaluate qualitative research and proposed alternative criteria for evaluating qualitative research. Amongst qualitative researchers also, there are diverse views on what should be the criteria for evaluating qualitative research (Cassell 2010). The wide range of methodologies employed in educational research tends to be associated with diverse philosophies, ideologies, and techniques. Consequently, the notion of rigour and quality also varies across individual methodologies. For example, Teddlie and Tashakkori illustrate how there are at least 35 types of 'validity' that have been proposed by different methodologists (2003, p. 13). Such diversity in criteria for evaluating primary research poses complex issues for research synthesists.

Research synthesists can usefully adapt published discussions of quality criteria in primary research literature for the purpose of their syntheses (e.g. Seale 1999). However, most published discussions on quality criteria are written for primary researchers about ways of enhancing rigour of their own studies. When adapting these criteria, it is crucial to distinguish between the research report and the research study that the report represents (Hammersley 2001). Synthesists must distinguish between the 'data quality' and 'inference quality' in primary research as well as research synthesis (Tashakkori and Teddlie 2003, p. 694). The research report is an 'after-the-fact reconstruction of the method' which is the sanitized version of the messy process that is followed in practice (Sandelowski et al. 2012,

p. 321). Synthesists must closely examine each report for a coherence between its theoretical background, intended purpose, context and/or nature of intervention being studied, methods for collecting, analyzing and interpreting evidence, results and conclusions. Equally important is the relevance of the report for the synthesis purpose (Dixon-Woods et al. 2006).

In a rigorous synthesis, the set of evaluation criteria for individual studies is essentially guided by the overarching teleological and theoretical orientation of the synthesis. For example, studies with representative samples are suitable for generating global generalizations. However, issues of how views and voices of different stakeholders are represented become critical in an emancipatory synthesis. The same study could be evaluated differently in syntheses with distinct epistemological orientations. For instance, research that is discounted as anecdotal in a meta-analysis may be considered a rich and authentic piece of narrative inquiry in a participatory synthesis.

Many formally proposed methods of research synthesis have tended to include reports based on similar methodologies. For instance, meta-ethnography was proposed to synthesize ethnographic reports and meta-analysis was proposed to synthesize quantitative studies with comparative designs. In each of these methods, theoretical orientations of the majority of primary research studies included in the synthesis tend to be in alignment with the overarching teleological and theoretical orientation of the synthesis. Accordingly, there has been a tendency to recommend 'a' set of criteria that is aligned with the spirit of the dominant methodology evident in the included primary research studies.

---

### Key questions to consider

- How will reports with relatively weak study design be treated within this synthesis?
- What criteria will be used to evaluate the trustworthiness of individual primary research reports?
- Would different sets of criteria be used for evaluating paradigmatically distinct reports?
- How different can these selection criteria be?
- Would they lead to inclusion or exclusion of different primary research reports?

---

In a synthesis which includes research that stems from various methodologies, what criteria should be used to decide inclusion or exclusion of a report based on its methodological quality? The answer to this question is rather complex. Often, research synthesists address this by adopting a multi-step evaluation process. For instance, in their synthesis, Wideen et al. (1998) first evaluated each report from within the theoretical positioning of that particular report in the light of the reported evidence. Then, they evaluated each report for its relevance to the synthesis purpose. Another common approach is to include all relevant reports of reasonable methodological quality (Dixon-Woods et al. 2006). The rest of this section illustrates how specific evaluation criteria may vary in accordance with the overarching orientation of the synthesis. This list is illustrative not comprehensive. The purpose of this section is to illuminate differences and similarities between quality criteria appropriate for different paradigmatic positions.

### Evaluation criteria for postpositivist research

While all meta-analysts converge on general criteria for judging the quality of primary research studies, there is no universal agreement about the relative emphasis which ought to be attached to individual criterion (Valentine 2009). Sometimes randomized blind trials are regarded as the gold standard of rigour. However, often such trials are difficult to conduct in educational settings and are commonly associated with three biases: 'lack of blinding, attrition bias and inadequate randomization' (Petticrew and Roberts 2006, p. 126).

Postpositivists frequently utilize Cook and Campbell's (1979) conceptualization of four types of validity (internal validity, construct validity, external validity and statistical conclusion validity) for evaluating research. 'Internal validity' refers to the truthfulness 'with which statements can be made about whether there is a causal relationship from one variable to another in the form in which the variables were manipulated or measured'. 'Construct validity' refers to the approximate truthfulness with which one 'can make generalizations about higher-order constructs from research operations'. 'External validity' refers to the approximate truthfulness 'that the presumed causal relationship can be generalized...across different types of persons, settings, and times'. 'Statistical conclusion validity' refers to the truthfulness of 'conclusions about covariation' between presumed independent and dependent variables (Cook and Campbell 1979, pp. 38-41). Often, there is a trade-off between internal validity and external validity of individual study designs. Synthesists can usefully draw on various published evaluation criteria for different types of quantitative research (e.g. Valentine 2009, CRD 2009).

### Evaluation criteria for interpretive research

LeCompte and Goetz (1993) redefined the constructs of 'reliability and validity' and proposed the following techniques for enhancing the 'credibility' of ethnographic research: delineating the major factors contributing to the uniqueness of an inquiry, such as 'researcher status position, informant choices, social situations and conditions, analytic constructs and premises, and methods of data collection and analysis' for improving external reliability; 'low-inference descriptors, multiple researchers, participant researchers, peer examination, and mechanically recorded data' for improving internal reliability; recognizing researchers' own influences on participants' responses; meticulously describing variations among their subjects; and refraining from drawing 'spurious conclusions' for improving internal validity; and addressing 'selection effects, setting effects, history effects, and construct effects' for improving external validity (LeCompte and Preissle 1993, pp. 322-56).

Analogous to the constructs of internal validity, external validity, reliability, and objectivity of rationalistic inquiry, Lincoln and Guba proposed 'truth value', 'applicability', 'consistency' and 'neutrality' as the more generic terms for all inquiries and 'credibility', 'transferability', 'dependability', and 'confirmability' as the terms specifically suited for naturalistic inquiry (1985, pp. 290-300) and recommended the following techniques: prolonged engagement at a site, persistent observation, peer debriefing, triangulation, referential adequacy of materials and member checks for improving credibility; 'purposive sampling to maximize the range of information' and 'providing thick description' to enable informed decisions about the extent to which findings may be adapted from one context to another for improving transferability; overlap methods, stepwise replication and maintaining a dependability audit for improving dependability; and triangulation, maintaining a reflexive journal and confirmability audit to ascertain that every finding is sufficiently supported with appropriate documentation for improving confirmability (Guba and Lincoln 1999, pp. 147-8).

Interpretive synthesists recommend that all reports should be evaluated by the extent to which the reported evidence is sufficient to warrant the reported findings. They recommend evaluating each qualitative research report for evidence of privileging lay views over 'constructs brought in from professional discourse' to 'illuminate the subjective meaning, actions, and context of those being researched'; 'adaptation and responsiveness of the research design to the circumstances and issues of real-life social settings'; purposeful sampling to adequately understand the 'structures and processes within which the individuals or situations are located'; adequate description to assist the reader in interpreting the meaning and context of what is being studied; transparency and reflexivity in processes through which data have been collected, analysed, and presented; potential for logical generalizations; and clear implications for policy and practice (Popay et al. 1998, pp. 345-6). Several quality appraisal forms for qualitative research have been developed by research synthesists from health care. See Hannes, Lockwood and Pearson (2010) for a comparison of three such appraisal forms that are available online for free.

### Evaluation criteria for participatory research

Many action researchers assert that the 'credibility, validity, and reliability in action research' should be measured in terms of the extent to which local stakeholders are willing to act on the study findings (e.g. Greenwood and Levin 2000, p. 96). However, Kemmis (1999) observes that major 'shortcomings of contemporary advocacies for action research' arise when proponents of action research fail to appreciate the dialectical connections between various elements of action research. For instance:

- dichotomizing the individual and the social can focus too much on the individual practitioner's progress without due recognition to the social context in which the individual works;
- dichotomizing 'the cognitive (practitioners' ideas) and the theoretical (formal discourses)' fails to acknowledge that an individual's thinking is informed by the prevalent 'language and formal discourse';
- dichotomizing 'theory and method in action research' ignores the implicit axioms of action research (Kemmis 1999, pp. 157-8).

In general, participatory research reports should be evaluated in terms of the efforts taken by the authors to see beyond these dichotomies by engaging in reflexive participation throughout the study. Participatory research can be evaluated by the degree of 'congruence of experiential, presentational, propositional, and practical knowings' where practical knowing is facilitated through 'critical subjectivity', which involves 'a self-reflexive attention to the ground on which one is standing'; 'epistemic participation', which involves grounding the research findings in the researchers' own 'experiential knowledge'; and 'political participation', which involves participation of 'research subjects' in designing the research (Heron and Reason 1997, pp. 284-90).

### Evaluation criteria for critically oriented research

Criteria for evaluating critically oriented research include its substantive contribution, aesthetic merit, reflexivity and impact, the degree to which it expresses a reality (Richardson 2000a, p. 254) and imagination (Bochner 2000, p. 267). The following four criteria identified by Lather (1986) are useful for evaluating emancipatory research:

- triangulation of *methods, data sources, and theories;*
- reflexive subjectivity (some documentation of how the researcher's assumptions have been affected by the logic of the data);
- face validity (established by recycling categories, emerging analysis, and conclusions back through at least a subsample of respondents);
- catalytic validity (some documentation that the research process has led to insight and, ideally, activism on the part of the respondents)

(Lather 1986, p. 78, emphasis in original).

The ethical and ideological issues can be further addressed by the following five 'authenticity' criteria: *'fairness'* to ensure that all stakeholders have an equal chance of expressing their views and negotiating recommendations and subsequent actions; *'ontological authentication'* to combat *'false consciousness'* dialectically so that all participants 'can achieve a more sophisticated and enriched construction'; '*educative authentication*' to promote 'increased understanding of (including possibly a sharing, or sympathy with) the whats and whys of various expressed constructions' among different stakeholders; '*catalytic authentication*' to 'facilitate and stimulate action'; and '*tactical authenticity*' to engage all stakeholders, especially those typically silenced, to collaboratively control the course of further action (Lincoln and Guba 1986, pp. 78-83, emphasis in original).

Contesting the pursuit of a single truth, postmodern critical scholars seek 'a deepened, complex, thoroughly partial, understanding of the topic' through the process of 'crystallization' (Richardson 2000b, p. 934), where the same phenomenon is observed and represented from different points of views. Recognizing validity as 'multiple, partial, endlessly deferred', postmodern studies lend themselves to 'validity of transgression' rather than 'validity of correspondence'. Various notions of validity held by postmodern critical scholars include 'ironic validity', which involves problematizing representation by dispersing, circulating and proliferating forms and 'creating analytic practices which are doubled without being paralyzed'; 'paralogical validity', which is 'concerned with undecidables, limits, paradoxes, discontinuities, complexities'; 'rhizomatic validity', which 'proliferates open-ended and context-sensitive criteria; works against reinscription of some new regime, some new systematicity' by unsettling from within; and 'voluptuous validity' which 'embodies a situated, partial, positioned, explicit tentativeness' and 'constructs authority via practices of engagement and self-reflexivity' (Lather, 1993, pp. 685-686).

## Interpreting evidence from individual reports

Research synthesis can be a triple hermeneutic process. A synthesis report is often the synthesist's interpretation of the primary researcher's interpretation of the interpretations of the participants in the primary research study. The relationships between different accounts must be examined carefully. A certain level of interpretation is inevitable in every synthesis regardless of it being quantitative or qualitative (Schwandt 1998). Synthesists inevitably and appropriately apply their own theoretical framework while interpreting any evidence. Ongoing reflexive engagement with the selected studies is crucial to reduce unaccounted or unacknowledged biases. Recognizing that 'every way of seeing is also a way of not seeing' (Silverman 2000, p. 825), synthesists must contemplate on how the evidence reported from individual studies is influenced by the author's methodological and theoretical orientation, prevalent theories and socio-cultural context current at the time.

A synthesist should clearly distinguish between low inference interpretations and high inference interpretations, both in the primary studies and in the synthesis, to explicitly share the level of abstraction involved in interpreting different aspects of the primary research reports. Coded items that require higher levels of interpretation may be assigned 'confidence ratings' along with the logic or justification for that interpretation (Stock 1994, p. 128). Low inference codes tend to have a high internal reliability, but often give a bland description of the phenomenon. High inference codes tend to have low reliability, but often provide useful insights into a phenomenon with high interpretive validity.

Different degrees of interpretation are required according to the conceptual distance between the primary research study and the purpose of the synthesis. The higher this conceptual distance is, the higher the level of abstraction (in the sense of distillation) and interpretation will be. For example, high degrees of interpretation, bordering on transformation, are required in a synthesis that addresses a question different from the focus of the included primary research studies. The higher the degree of correspondence between the purpose of a selected primary research study with the purpose of the research synthesis, the lesser is the interpretive (in the sense of 'transformative') role of the synthesist. For instance, consider a study that compares the effectiveness of cooperative learning on mathematics achievement scores using a quasi-experimental design. The findings of such a study will require relatively low degrees of interpretation to be included in a meta-analysis on the effectiveness of cooperative learning on mathematics achievement scores. On the other hand, a high degree of interpretation is necessary in a critical interpretive synthesis where the synthesist deliberately moves beyond a thematic analysis to construct new ways of understanding a phenomenon (Dixon-Woods et al. 2006).

When a synthesis includes studies that are methodologically, theoretically and/or contextually diverse, the interpretive task of extracting comparative information from individual studies becomes more complex. The more diverse the primary research studies included in the synthesis, the more complex the interpretive task of comparing these diverse accounts becomes. This complexity is accentuated by a proliferation of methodological and theoretical vocabulary where different researchers frequently use the same term differently. Paying attention to methodological and theoretical citations of individual reports can facilitate a more informed interpretation of the connotations attached to different terms by the original authors (Paterson et al. 2001). Diversity within the contexts of individual studies also necessitates higher degrees of interpretation. For example, synthesizing studies across cultures adds another layer of complexity to the interpretive task (Clarke 2003).

The overarching orientation of the synthesis will further influence the level of interpretation involved in a synthesis. As an illustration, minor interpretations might be involved in a meta-analysis of relatively homogenous studies on effectiveness where synthesists may differ in their approaches to handle differences in methods, precision levels and reporting conventions of primary research included in the synthesis. Interpretations might be involved in assumptions about the missing information which may not structurally influence the synthesis product (Orwin and Vevea 2009). However, in an interpretive synthesis like a meta-ethnography, the synthesis commences with the synthesist's assumption about the relationship between individual studies. The greater the variations between individual studies, the more sophisticated and demanding becomes the interpretive task of comparing diverse accounts of a similar phenomenon (Noblit and Hare 1988). Synthesis of qualitative research often necessitates higher degrees of interpretation where 'concepts and ideas are invented (rather than discovered)' leading to 'differing levels of abstractness versus concreteness' and 'differing labels' used to describe a phenomenon in individual reports (Jensen and Allen 1996, p. 554-558). Synthesists' interpretive role is maximized in deconstructive syntheses which recognize 'multiple and contradictory readings' of each text 'some of which may be contrary to the writer's intentions' (Marshall and Peters 1999, p. 246).

---

### Key questions to consider

- How might the author's, and the prevalent, theoretical, methodological and socio-cultural context have influenced this finding?
- What criteria will be used to evaluate the trustworthiness of individual findings or accounts?
- What degree of trust may be accorded to different accounts or findings?

---

### Missing information and bias associated with specific findings

At times there is a possibility that specific findings of individual studies might be biased in a particular direction. By bias, I mean an inclination to select data, studies, findings, contexts or theories in a way that is non-representative or constrains the synthesist to a restricted set of possible interpretations. Such an intentional or inadvertent bias might arise due to numerous factors associated with the primary research study, such as the nature of the evidence, characteristics of the original sample, positioning of the primary researcher or varied interests of different stakeholders interested in the phenomenon being researched. For example, a synthesis of research studies employing a culturally biased IQ test could lead to conclusions that inappropriately associate race and academic ability. Equally, a synthesis of studies employing culturally neutral IQ tests might still produce biased conclusions if only ethnicity were considered as an explanatory variable rather than socio-economic status. In their meta-analysis, Borman and his colleagues (2003) found that studies conducted by the developer of a comprehensive school reform intervention programs reported higher effects than studies conducted by other researchers. Such a finding makes one question if, to some extent, the effectiveness could be accorded to the narrow focus of a test. If the test itself privileges performances emphasized in instruction, then instructional effectiveness may be exaggerated (Schoenfeld 2006).

Error and bias are an inherent part of every report. However degrees and types of errors and biases in relation to specific findings within the selected primary research reports tend to vary. A research synthesist must be sensitive to the possible unintended selectivity and errors in the reporting of findings by primary researchers. This sensitivity should guide which specific findings from within selected reports should be included or excluded. Only those findings that have relatively less bias, or those for which the influence of the associated bias can be accounted for in the synthesis, may be included. At times the decision to include or exclude a study may be graduated rather than binary. The synthesist may attach graduated weights or levels of trust, expressed numerically or by qualitative annotations, to different findings within the same study. One approach is to code all findings as 'unequivocal (findings supported with clear and compelling evidence), credible (findings that are plausible given the weight of evidence) and unsupported (findings that are suggested but not supported by data)' (Major and Savin-Baden 2010, p. 61).

Individual findings within each report must be checked against any potential logical error, lack of rigour, or poor grounding in the reported evidence. If the lack of rigour in the procedures employed to yield the finding is obvious from the report, then this specific finding ought to be omitted from the synthesis. Given the current variety in reporting styles of educational research, especially of qualitative research, this is rather a complex task. At times synthesists may find no explicit discussion of methods in a report even though rigorous methods are evident through other parts of the report. Sometimes, a synthesist may not notice a certain piece of information because it is located in parts of the report where the synthesist does not expect it to be (Sandelowski and Barroso 2002, Orwin and Vevea 2009). Some reports may include a well-described methods section with little evidence of rigorous implementation of those methods in the study. Carefully noting the details of the sampling, methods, designs, procedures and contexts of every finding included in their synthesis, synthesists must avoid the following two common errors in reviews that lead to misclassification of findings.

> In some cases, the reports reviewed are about parts of larger projects and contain descriptions of the larger projects as well as the relevant parts. Details of the whole are sometimes thought to apply to the part when, in fact, they do not. In other cases, the reviewer accepts an opening statement of sample size without recognizing that attrition occurred and that the data actually came from a smaller sample.
>
> (Dunkin 1996, p. 90)

Synthesists must carefully distinguish between the reporting quality and methodological quality of individual studies (Valentine 2009). Often synthesists find that information crucial for pursuing the synthesis purpose, such as information about the individual study's context, methods or results, is missing from several individual reports. Meta-analysts refer to this as 'the problem of missing data' and identify three categories of potential reasons for missing information which must be taken into account when determining a suitable strategy for dealing with this problem: random reasons unrelated to the study; reasons related to other variables of the study such as the author's theoretical orientation; and reasons related to the missing variables themselves such as insignificant differences (Pigott 2009). As synthesists can never be sure about the reasons for missing information, they must clearly delineate their assumptions about these reasons.

Many of the strategies suggested by meta-analysts for dealing with the problem of missing information can be adapted to a research synthesis process in general. First, the synthesist can contact the authors of the original reports to solicit further information (e.g. Lloyd Jones 2004). However, this requires substantial time and resources, especially when the number of selected primary research reports is large, and is often not practicable and cost-effective. It is possible only if the original authors can be contacted, have collected and saved the relevant information and are willing to share that information (Orwin and Vevea 2009). Second, the synthesist can include only those studies which report all the relevant information. However, this can greatly reduce the number of studies and synthesists could miss out on opportunities to reveal some potentially useful connections, which might have been possible with a larger number of included studies. Further, if the reasons for missing information are related to some aspect of the study itself, then excluding reports with the missing information would yield a biased sample (Pigott 2009). Third, the synthesist can make an educated guess about the missing information guided by the information available within the relevant research report, rest of the selected primary research reports and the related external literature (Bushman and Wang 2009). Examples of such methods available to meta-analysts include imputing a single value according to the assumed reason for the missing information; Buck's method of regression imputation which assumes that the missing variables are linearly related to other variables in the data; and Little and Rubin's model-based procedures (Pigott 2009). Fourth, the synthesist can give the author the benefit of doubt and assume that the finding is well founded even if it is not clear from the report (Sandelowski and Barroso 2002). The synthesist can include this finding with caution by attaching to it relatively less weight, a lower level of trust or confidence rating. Fifth, the synthesist may collect some new evidence to make an educated guess about the missing variable (Hedges et al. 1989).

Sometimes the synthesist can follow more than one of these five options to construct multiple collective understandings. Comparing these collective understandings would be similar to the process of sensitivity analysis, which meta-analysts sometimes employ. Sensitivity analysis is conducted to examine the robustness of the findings against the assumptions made by the synthesist about the evidence at hand (Greenhouse and Iyengar 2009).

Synthesists must carefully scrutinize groups of primary research reports with similar study designs reported by the same group of authors. Often, synthesists find multiple reports of the same project reporting on different aspects of the project findings. A cluster of such reports represents a single study rather than multiple discrete studies. Treating each of these reports as a discrete study, particularly when these findings are based on the same sample and study design, could wrongly attach more weight to the findings of that particular study when constructing connected understandings (Dunkin 1996). The decision regarding which reports are discrete accounts of distinct studies becomes more complex when different reports are based on the same project, but examine different constructs or aspects of the phenomenon; use different methods of collecting evidence; analyze evidence collected from different sub-samples, some of which may not be mutually exclusive; and/or analyze evidence collected at different stages of the project (Borman et al. 2003, Lipsey 2009). Disproportionate representation of any particular set of findings in a research synthesis is a matter of concern.

The synthesist should reflect not only on the potential biases introduced by the primary researcher's positioning, but also on the potential biases introduced by the synthesist's own positioning. For example, consider a study that reports three test scores on the effectiveness of cooperative learning. These three scores are from tests based on Intelligence Quotient, mathematical ability and reading ability. A synthesist who is a disbeliever of Intelligence Quotient may choose to include the findings based on the latter two tests but exclude the findings based on Intelligence Quotient. It is crucial that synthesists are explicit about the potential implications of such exclusions of findings based on the relative mismatch between their own positioning with that of the primary researcher. Readers should be alerted to such considerations. When there is a silence, a reader can ask to what effect has the issue been ignored.

### Familiarity with the substantive topic: Emic versus etic

How familiar should a research synthesist be with the substantive topic (such as online learning, educational leadership or cooperative learning) to be synthesized? This question is analogous to the emic (an insider within a culture) versus etic (an outsider from a culture) debate in anthropological research methods.

An emic-like familiarity with the substantive domain of research can sensitize the synthesist to the key themes, explicit and implicit, in the field. Knowledge of the substantive domain can help synthesists to make informed decisions about which aspects of the research reports they should focus on (Stock et al. 1996). Frequently, research synthesists need to make informed decisions when dealing with the problem of missing or insufficient data in primary research reports. Judgements can also become complex when there is access to detailed information, as there is more information to be considered in making a decision (Orwin and Vevea 2009). Making informed choices that facilitate such high levels of abstraction require the synthesist to have a sophisticated understanding about the common editorial policies in the relevant field, 'such as page limitations and journal and disciplinary conventions concerning what needs to be explicitly said, what can be implied, and what can be omitted' (Sandelowski and Barroso 2002, p. 13). It is generally agreed that some members of the research synthesis team must be familiar with the substantive topic of the synthesis (e.g. Orwin 1994, Thorne 2001, Eastabrooks et al. 1994).

On the other hand, etics have the potential to make the familiar strange and reveal the implicit assumptions in a field. They can speculate from a fresh and distanced perspective the impact of these assumptions in shaping the field. An etic has the advantage of not having the emic's 'blinkers' towards taken-for-granted meaning and understanding in the field. To minimize biases involved in judging the quality of primary research reports, some meta-analysts recommend the technique of 'blinding papers by blotting out the sources and disguising the results' (Chalmers and Lau 1993, p. 163). Most emic synthesists are likely to be familiar with the key research reports in the field and hence the reports cannot be truly blinded for them. At times, meta-analysts achieve this distancing by employing graduate students, who are relatively new to the field, for such blinded coding since.

It is impossible for researchers to approach their work without some theoretical frame of reference. Even formulating a question involves some theorizing (Popper 1965). A balanced team including both an etic as well as an emic perspective is ideal for a research synthesis as they provide complementary perspectives (Oliver et al. 2012). Etics can problematize and ask questions to make the familiar strange. Emics can construct informed interpretations based on a thorough understanding of some implicit and explicit ideas within the field.

## Distilling evidence from individual reports

Common synonyms of the verb 'distil' are 'condense', 'purify' and 'refine'. The distillation process in a synthesis is not a process of unique purification. Rather, it is a process of fractional or selective distillation in which the relevant information is condensed differently for different purposes. This involves capturing a selective essence of the report for the synthesis purpose through an interpretive process of filtering, sorting, coding, classifying and transforming.

---

### Key questions to consider

- What features of each report will be focused on?
- Why would these, and not other, features be focused on?
- What strategies will be used for encoding the selected information from individual reports?

### Focus of the synthesis

The synthesis purpose is enacted repeatedly throughout the synthesis process. It is notable at the points of selection of relevant primary research reports and interpretive distillation of information for these selected reports. Most synthesists focus on one or more of the following aspects of selected reports: 'research outcomes, research methods, theories, and practices or applications' (Cooper 1988, p. 108).

Research outcomes tend to be the most common focus of syntheses that appeal to a variety of audiences and address questions, such as: What does research say on this topic? How similar or dissimilar are different research outcomes? Which aspects of the phenomenon are well understood in the research literature? What are some of the gaps in our understanding about the phenomenon?

Research synthesists can not only examine 'what is' but also reflexively search for 'what should be' (Zhao 1991, p. 379). Sometimes synthesists exclusively focus on research methods (e.g. Shimpuku and Norr 2012). Audiences who are likely to be interested in such syntheses include specialized scholars with an expertise or particular interest in the substantive or methodological topic covered, general scholars with peripheral interest in the area, funding agencies, policy-makers and editorial boards or other regulatory bodies of research. Questions addressed by syntheses focusing on research methods include the following: What are the common methodologies utilized to study the relevant phenomenon? How may this have influenced the prevalent understandings about the phenomenon? What are some methodological variations that may be potentially influencing the research outcomes of individual studies? What are some common methodological strengths and caveats of the primary research studies in the field? What are some methodological issues that further studies in the field must consider?

Policy-makers, practitioners and specialized scholars are among the various groups with an interest in syntheses that identify the key theories that have informed research and practice in a field. One way of identifying key theories informing a field of practice is to identify the key theorists cited in the selected studies (e.g. Amundsen and Wilson 2012). By inspecting the conceptual and theoretical orientations of selected studies, a synthesist can address several useful questions including the following (Lucas and Beresford 2010): What are the prevalent theoretical premises of the research studies in the field? How are these theories commensurate or incommensurate? How may these theoretical viewpoints have potentially influenced prevalent understandings about the phenomenon? How may variations in theoretical allegiances have influenced the research outcomes of individual studies? What are the key theories or principles about the phenomenon that are supported by the relevant research? What are some potentially useful theories that are seldom utilized in researching the phenomenon? (e.g. Bransford and Schwartz 1999).

Syntheses that focus on how an educational strategy is applied in practice, or how an educational phenomenon is actually manifested in different contexts, are likely to appeal to practitioners and other practical decision-makers (e.g. Hofer and Pintrich 1997). Questions that may be addressed by such syntheses include (Lipsey 2009): What are the various contexts in which a particular educational strategy or phenomenon worked or did not work? What are the contextual variables that may potentially moderate the effectiveness of a program? What are some practical guidelines for effective implementation of an educational strategy in different real-life teaching and learning situations? What are the levels of acceptance with respect to a particular educational practice among various stakeholders?

Syntheses that examine the interactions between theories, methods and findings of individual studies to generate a sophisticated understanding about how a phenomenon works in different settings can be particularly useful. Often synthesists focus on research methods in conjunction with research outcomes (e.g. Warschauer and Matuchniak 2010). Synthesists that identify core characteristics and theoretical underpinnings of common practices in a field are also useful for advancing theory, practice and policy (e.g. Amundsen and Wilson 2012).

## Strategies for encoding selected information

Bibliographic summaries, coding schemes, statistical summaries, narrative summaries, reflective remarks, highlighted texts, marginal remarks and analytic memos constitute a formal, retrievable database that synthesists can 'readily reference, repeatedly scrutinize, and regularly reclaim to check for omissions and distortions' when constructing connected understandings (Ogawa and Malen 1991, p. 281). Utilizing multiple tools for distilling information from individual reports can stimulate 'complexity and subtlety of insight' (Faulkner 1982, p. 81) in a research synthesis. Synthesists should refrain from "*over*reducing' data [as it] can obscure understanding' (Miles and Huberman 1994, p. 100, emphasis in original).

Bibliographic summaries include bibliographic information from each selected report: the title of the report; author(s), country, source, and year of publication; authors' disciplinary and theoretical orientations and other aspects of authors' positioning which are likely to intersect with the interests of the participants of original study. Most synthesists use bibliographic referencing software, such as Endnote, RefWorks or Procite for managing bibliographic information, documenting reasons for inclusion or exclusion of individual studies, and encoding key features of individual studies. Some synthesists also use spreadsheets, like Excel, for tabulating such information (e.g. Amundsen and Wilson 2012). Some synthesists use software specifically designed for managing information for the purpose of a research synthesis, such as EPPI-Reviewer (EPPI-Centre 2011). From the outset, it is important to identify appropriate strategies for managing the masses of information that are collected during a synthesis.

Coding can facilitate construction of 'categories that organize and characterize' the information distilled from individual reports 'to identify "partitions" that make seemingly disparate and unwieldy literatures more manageable and more discernible' (Ogawa and Malen 1991, p. 277). Using different colours to code different aspects of each study can facilitate a 'quick visual impression' of each study (Stock 1994, p. 136). To ensure consistency in coding, it is essential to operationally define each code. All the codes should structurally relate to each other while being purposefully distinct. Metaphorical coding can be particularly effective for synthesizing 'large blocks of data in a single trope' (Miles and Huberman 1994, p. 302). Yet we must also remember the problematics of coding as 'codification is the concept, captured on paper, in the dirt, on the chalkboard, on the wall. It is the thought, painted. It is the symbol, symbolized.' (Wink 1997, p. 33). Deliberate reflection on the metaphors or codes chosen to categorize the data can frequently unveil the synthesist's assumptions about the synthesis topic.

While refined coding can be more cost-intensive at the stage of initial coding, coarse coding can become more cost-intensive if the coders have to go back to recode the finer details. The decision to code categories from broad to specific or vice-versa should be largely guided by several factors including the scope, purpose, focus and theoretical orientation of the synthesis (Lipsey 2009). An exploratory synthesis is more amenable to an initial refined, emergent, coding scheme while a confirmatory synthesis lends itself to an itemized a priori coding scheme that matches the synthesis conjecture. A structured approach to coding where codes 'relate to one another in coherent' ways reduces the probability of 'purely opportunistic analysis' (Miles and Huberman 1994, p. 62). When synthesists have limited time and resources they can adopt a framework synthesis approach where they can start coding with themes which are derived initially from a conceptual framework from the literature, which are then modified and refined as further relevant themes emerge from the literature (Carroll et al. 2011, Dixon-woods 2011).

Synthesists may begin with broad coding to identify overarching themes and categories followed by refined coding to preserve the integrity and uniqueness of each report as the synthesis progresses. Refined coding may involve looking for specific illustrations of confirming and disconfirming cases to illuminate and define the parameters of the broad codes. Alternatively, synthesists can employ a grounded-theory like approach that involves an initial open coding followed by clustering of these refined codes into meaningful broad categories and themes (Strauss and Corbin 1998). Finer codes can then be collapsed into broad codes using computer programs (e.g. Thomas and Harden 2008). Most synthesists use a combination of these two approaches to coding and iteratively modify their appraisal tool as their synthesis progresses to encapsulate important features of all the studies included in the synthesis (L'Hommedieu et al. 1988).

Some syntheses, such as meta-analyses, lend themselves primarily to variable-oriented analyses. Some others, such as meta-ethnographies, are more amenable to study-oriented analyses. Most syntheses use a combination of variable-oriented and study-oriented analyses. In a variable-oriented quantitative synthesis, coding 'represents an attempt to reduce a complex, messy, context-laden, and quantification-resistant reality to a matrix of numbers' (Orwin 1994, p. 140). Useful practical guidelines have been published for improving replicability and transparency of coding protocols in quantitative syntheses (e.g. Wilson 2009). Coding too many details can become cost-intensive and also increase the probability of identifying significant correlations between variables by chance. On the other hand, omitting to code some important variables can reduce the scope and utility of the synthesis. Interesting characteristics of interventions to code include information about research design, setting, details about the treatment, intervention or program being examined, sample, unit of analysis; resources; staffing, stage of development of the intervention, retention rate, implicit logic about how the intervention would work, and relevant findings (Petticrew and Roberts 2006). For an example of a variable-oriented coding sheet, see CRD (2009).

Many interpretive synthesists assert the need to maintain the integrity and holism of individual studies. It involves iterative reading of individual accounts with a focus on 'metaphors, themes, concepts, or organizers' (Noblit and Hare 1988, p. 39) to understand and represent their respective contexts and essence in a condensed form. Recognizing that some contextual configurations are more likely to be efficient than others, study-oriented analyses focus on these complex combinations rather than seeking variable-oriented causal links. Study-oriented distillation is more amenable to open-ended, emergent, coding sheets with some key areas of interest. For an example of such a coding sheet, see Sandelowski and Borosso (2002, pp. 31-43).

Synthesists often prepare summaries of individual research reports by distilling information that is particularly relevant, trustworthy and interesting for the synthesis purpose. In these summary sheets, the synthesist should not only include the coded information about the study, such as key categories, features, themes and effect-sizes, but also information justifying the encoding. This facilitates quick revisiting of data at different stages of the synthesis process. When the evidence is relatively heterogeneous, standard coding sheets are of little use. In such syntheses, as in a realist synthesis, synthesists assimilate 'information more by note-taking and annotation than by extracting data as such' (Pawson et al. 2005, p. 30).

Reflective remarks, highlighted texts and marginal remarks noted while reading individual reports facilitate active reading. Reflective remarks include conjectures about potential relationships between individual reports, judgements about the reported information, mental notes to pursue certain issues in further readings, cross-references to information in other reports, elaboration or clarification of emerging understandings (Miles and Huberman 1994) and notes on what is missing from the report. Highlighted texts and marginal notes, written in the margins of individual reports in the form of tentative codes, facilitate a quick glimpse of important parts of the report.

## Rigour in evaluating, interpreting and distilling evidence

Depending on the purpose and the overarching orientation of the synthesis, rigour in evaluating, interpreting and distilling evidence from individual studies can be enhanced by striving for objectivity, neutrality and consistency; by being reflexive; and/or by collaborating to enhance trustworthiness.

### Objectivity, neutrality and consistency

Various strategies, many of which have been suggested by meta-analysts, can be employed to improve objectivity, neutrality and consistency throughout a synthesis process, such as: blinding information from reports; employing multiple coders; maintaining a detailed code-book; and monitoring coder fatigue.

Synthesists must be wary of their own biases. This is not an easy task as even experienced researchers are prone to spot inadequacies in studies that do not agree with their own thinking. To reduce such a bias, some meta-analysts recommend that each primary research report should be selectively blinded before any relevant information is extracted from it. Blinding involves hiding any information that may trigger a bias, such as study results, reference to the author and source of publication (Chalmers and Lau 1993). However, 'several studies have found that masking author, institution, journal name and study results is of limited value in study selection' (CRD 2009). Given the costs involved in blinding the studies, educational research synthesists seldom employ the technique of blinding.

To minimize subjective biases, some synthesists recommend that at least two coders should separately code each report on subjective items such as methodological quality of the report (e.g. Bowman 2010). Many meta-analysts stress the need to assess the levels of inter-rater reliability (IRR) by employing multiple coders to code items that require judgement calls in at least a fraction of the total number of selected reports. Meta-analysts have proposed numerous indices for IRR, such as the 'agreement rate (AR)', 'Cohen's kappa and weighted kappa', 'intercoder correlation' and 'intraclass correlation' (Orwin 1994, pp. 147-150).

To improve consistency and reduce unstated ambiguity, synthesists should maintain code-books with detailed notes describing the development of the coding protocol. The coding protocol should be thoroughly tested with all the coders before commencing full-scale coding. Synthesists should 'become more aware, and take deliberate account, of the multiple sources of uncertainty in reading, understanding, and interpreting research reports'. The code-book should include the 'rationale for each judgement'. Intercoder agreement may also be enhanced by devising a 'guessing convention…to standardize decisions under uncertainty'. However, a guessing convention may '*bias*' the overall results as any associated errors are not likely to be randomly distributed (Orwin 1994, pp. 140-159, emphasis in original).

As in any coding process, coders in a synthesis may also erroneously punch wrong keys while entering data electronically. To improve coder consistency, coder fatigue should be carefully monitored by randomly checking coding decisions at regular periods of time (Wilson 2009).

## Reflexivity

Openly ideological scholars argue that 'scientific "neutrality" and "objectivity" serve to mystify the inherently ideological nature of research in the human science and to legitimate privilege based on class, race, and gender' (Lather 1986, p. 64). They argue that all research is 'shaped by its political and social context, and this should be recognized explicitly instead of being hidden away behind a veil of scientific objectivity and political neutrality' (Gaskell 1988, p. 405). Hence, synthesists should aspire for reflexivity rather than objectivity.

As a process progresses, the rules, variables, and relationships between variables, all change. This requires the synthesist to reflexively respond to the change rather than rigidly follow the a priori protocol (Pawson et al. 2005, Zhao 1991). Reflexivity requires one to reflect on how one's own positioning intersects with what one sees, i.e., contemplating about how we see influences what we see, and vice-versa. It involves reflecting critically while being cautious that the critical framework itself doesn't become the 'container into which the data are poured' (Anderson 1989, p. 254). A reflexive stance not only values 'clarity, countability and accountability' but also 'intertextual connectivity, critique, interest, expertise, independence, tacit knowledge, chance encounters with new ideas, and dialogic interactions between researcher, '"literature" and "data"' (MacLure 2005, p. 394).

## Collaborating to enhance trustworthiness

Many synthesists recommend that each primary research report should be first reviewed independently by more than one co-synthesist to unfold multiple interpretive possibilities. Then, interpretations of individual co-synthesists should be compared to identify differences between individual interpretations. These differences should next be resolved through negotiated construction of meaning or through expert interpretation.

Several experts recommend that the complexity of a research synthesis process requires collaborative efforts to ensure a certain level of trustworthiness (see Table 9.1). Meta-analysts and systematic reviewers tend to employ more than one coder for each paper to measure and reduce the levels of subjective judgements. Synthesists employing exploratory case study method can work in teams to 'develop analytic memos, air interpretations, and engage in a process of deliberate, adversarial critique' so that fellow team-members can detect and check individual biases (Ogawa and Malen 1991, p. 282). Qualitative research synthesists who are interested in mid-range substantive theory generation

*Table 9.1* Enhancing trustworthiness through collaboration

| Research synthesis form | Trustworthiness criteria enhanced by collaboration |
| --- | --- |
| Meta-analysis | Reliability by reducing subjective biases (Chalmers and Lau 1993) |
| Systematic review | Comparison and resolution of differences (Evans and Benefield 2001) |
| Exploratory case-study method | Reduce error and bias by delineating and debating rival interpretations (Ogawa and Malen 1991) |
| Qualitative synthesis for mid-range substantive theory generation | Triangulation, cross-validation of interpretations, comprehensiveness (Eastabrooks et al. 1994) |
| Meta-study | Dialogic consensus to make synthesists conscious of their own theoretical and perceptual leanings (Paterson et al. 2001) |
| Critical analysis of research | Reflexivity through critical dialogue (Wideen et al. 1998) |

recommend synthesists to work in teams as a form of triangulation to improve rigour (Eastabrooks et al. 1994). Proponents of meta-study work in teams to alert themselves of their own 'theoretical and perceptual leanings' and arrive at 'consensus' in a 'dialogical climate' (Paterson et al. 2001, p. 47). Research synthesists drawing from a critical theory framework can collaborate to enhance reflexivity by bringing together team members 'for multiple sessions of extended reflexive discourse and writing' with the purpose of discussing and negotiating their collective interpretations (Wideen et al. 1998, p. 135).

As noted earlier, synthesists can enrich their synthesis by collaborating with different stakeholders. Systematic reviewers routinely engage the members of key stakeholder groups in refining their synthesis protocols (EPPI-Centre 2009). Seeking feedback on coding sheets and summary reports from authors of original studies, and/or members of the groups represented in the original studies, serves as a form of member-checking. This facilitates authenticity while evaluating, interpreting and distilling information from the selected reports.

## Summary

This chapter discussed issues and strategies associated with interpreting, evaluating and fractionally distilling relevant and trustworthy information from individual reports for the synthesis purpose. The next chapter will discuss issues and strategies associated with constructing connected understandings from this distilled information. As analysis is an inherent aspect of synthesis, decisions associated with these two phases of a synthesis are intertwined and mutually informing.

# Chapter 10

# Constructing connected surroundings

What issues should be considered when constructing understandings by connecting the information distilled from individual research reports?

When evaluating, interpreting and distilling evidence, a synthesist inevitably makes some implicit and explicit connections between information reported in individual research reports. The emphasis in Chapter 9 was on understanding each report in its entirety. The emphasis in this chapter is on constructing a collective account of evidence across individual reports. This chapter describes the process of making explicit connections between the information presented in individual reports for the synthesis purpose.

The chapter begins with a general discussion of variable-oriented, study-oriented, inductive and deductive constructions of connected understandings. Then, some techniques for constructing connections across individual primary research reports are discussed. Following this, some strategies for improving the quality of these connections across studies are discussed. The final section of this chapter illustrates diverse criteria for evaluating connected understandings stemming from different theoretical positions.

## Nature of connections

Inductive and deductive connections complement each other, as do variable-oriented and study-oriented connections. The principle reasoning in a research synthesis may be deductive, inductive or a dialectical combination of both. Deductive reasoning begins with a preliminary proposition while inductive reasoning results in a preliminary proposition. These categories are not mutually exclusive and synthesists often utilize them in conjunction.

Like hypothetico-deductive research, a deductive synthesis would begin with a hypothesis that is empirically tested on specifics as the synthesis proceeds. Deductive reasoning progresses from generally accepted theories to understanding particular instances of the phenomenon. Confirmatory syntheses with the purpose of testing or refining generalizable theories are particularly amenable to deductive reasoning (Ogawa and Malen 1991b). A good example of this is a framework synthesis approach to a synthesis that starts with a conceptual framework from the literature that gets refined during the synthesis (e.g. Carroll et al. 2011).

Inductive reasoning proceeds from particular observations grounded in the evidence towards more general inferences. Interpretive syntheses lend themselves to inductive reasoning, where the connections are constructed from the pieces of evidence reported in individual studies. Inductive reasoning is particularly suited for exploratory syntheses to generate insights that are 'suggestive and instructive, not definitive or conclusive' (Ogawa and Malen 1991b, p. 271).

In variable-oriented connections, the variations in the effects, implementations, manifestations, meanings, understandings or conceptions of a phenomenon are the prime focus of a synthesis. The synthesist is less interested in the uniqueness and dynamics of individual accounts. Each account is examined to the extent that it contributes to explaining the relationships between the target variables. When several individual studies examine a particular intervention, concept or phenomenon using similar methodologies, the findings may be aggregated to increase size and variations of the overall sample. These findings could then be used to make generalizations, provide plausible explanations, and predict patterns of human behaviour as in a meta-analysis or an aggregated-analysis (Eastabrooks et al. 1994). The focus is on variables, and their relationships, with little interest in examining if the picture fits any particular case. The goal of this reductionist approach is to simplify the chaos and messiness of collective evidence distilled from individual accounts and provide a sense of clarity (Miles and Huberman 1994). The next section will describe several comparative techniques such as content-analysis, statistical techniques and visual displays, which are commonly employed for constructing variable-oriented connections.

Study-oriented connections are amenable for constructing holistic and complex understandings with an attempt to retain the contextual integrity of individual accounts, as in Noblit and Hare's (1988) meta-ethnography. Here, the synthesist attempts to reconcile the findings of each study with those of the other studies. The process is 'good at finding specific, concrete, historically-grounded patterns common to small sets of cases, but its findings often remain particularistic' (Miles and Huberman 1994, p. 174). This process is 'expansionistic, in that it seeks to compare and analyze many studies together in a constructivist way, allowing interpretive themes or key metaphors to emerge and build from the synthesis' (Bair 1999, p. 4). The synthesist tries to determine the relations and tensions between individual accounts through a 'dialectic' process of 'comparing and contrasting' (Jensen and Allen 1996, p. 555) by juxtaposing 'the key metaphors, phrases, ideas, and/or concepts (and their relations) used in each account' (Noblit and Hare 1988, p. 28) as interpreted by each co-synthesist.

When the individual reports are addressing similar issues, they are amenable to a reciprocal translational synthesis to generate 'a new construction on which there is consensus' (Jensen and Allen 1996, p. 555) and which 'accurately portrays the shared and unique findings of the included research studies'

(Paterson et al. 2001, p. 65). The findings of each report are tested for their abilities to translate the findings of the other reports. Those terms or findings are selected that can more succinctly describe the findings of all the reports within the subset. At times, the terms employed in individual reports may not be suitable to portray concisely all the reports. In those cases, new terms may be introduced that adequately describe the major findings from all the reports (Noblit and Hare 1988). When the synthesist has limited resources, the synthesist can select an exemplary study and examine other studies for the extent to which they demonstrate or add to the description of the phenomenon in the exemplar study (Miles and Huberman 1994).

When individual reports give conflicting representations of the same phenomenon, they lend themselves to a 'refutational synthesis' (Noblit & Hare, 1988, p. 47) where the relationships between individual studies and the refutations become focus of the synthesis process. The contradictions between individual reports may be explicit or implicit. The implicit refutations are made explicit using an interpretive approach. This is followed by an attempt to explain the refutation.

If the individual reports examine different aspects of the same phenomenon, a 'lines-of-argument' synthesis could be used to make inferences (Noblit & Hare, 1988). In this method, findings from individual reports are used as pixels to get a fuller picture of the phenomenon at hand. It involves a grounded-theory like approach for open-coding and identifying the categories emerging from the data. The key categories that are more powerful in representing the entire data-set are identified by constant comparisons between individual accounts. These categories are then linked interpretively to create an holistic account of the phenomenon.

When synthesizing methodologically diverse reports, a synthesist can begin by constructing collective understandings from clusters of studies with similar designs and then synthesize collective understandings across clusters (Suri 1999, Greenhalgh et al. 2005). For example, in their synthesis on concepts of wellness and illness, Jensen and Allen (1994) constructed collective understandings about the process from studies using a grounded-theory approach, about meaning and experience from phenomenological studies, and about context from ethnographic and descriptive studies. In the next phase, they synthesized these complementary accounts to construct an holistic understanding about wellness and illness. There are numerous ways of clustering data. The synthesist must decide the degree of variation that would be imposed within individual subsets. Study-oriented cluster-analysis (by hand) can help the reader to get a local as well as an external perspective. Rather than simplistically clustering based on a single variable, study-oriented clustering involves grouping studies in different subsets on the basis of their findings and certain contextual configurations (Miles and Huberman 1994).

Study-oriented connections can also be implemented, as in Pawson's realist synthesis, by inferring theory from each study and examining its transferability to other cases to refine the initial theory. In a realist synthesis, this process is repeated with every study of successful and unsuccessful implementation to develop a more sophisticated and comprehensive theory that can explain many cases (Pawson et al. 2005).

## Techniques to facilitate connections

A synthesist must judiciously choose from various tools and techniques to conceptualize and express connections across individual reports by covering 'many possibilities and alternative interpretations, casting a wide net, quickly identifying and abandoning those measures that show nothing, and moving lightly to avoid being buried in data' (Dabbs 1982, p. 60). Drafts and re-drafts of coding-schemes, narratives, matrices and concept-maps can help in organizing, and leaving a trail of, the synthesist's own emerging thinking. This section illustrates how synthesists can draw on various techniques from primary research methods to construct meaningful and rigorous connections across studies.

### Content-analysis

Research synthesists often use content-analysis broadly to identify frequently occurring concepts, themes and characteristics across all studies without pondering over which individual studies the information came from (Mays et al. 2005a). Content-analysis is particularly useful at the early stages of a synthesis to partition literature and to tease out prevalent dimensions of variations collectively across studies (e.g. Engberg 2004, Kasworm 1990).

However, simple frequency counts of key themes or variables are not sufficient in most syntheses. Often, synthesists augment a content-analysis with more complex techniques for constructing connections as merely counting occurrences of certain themes tells us little about how they may be related. Understanding relationships between individual themes requires attending to complex configurations and local dynamics within individual studies to identify meaningful transcendental patterns across studies (Dixon-Woods et al. 2005). It also requires being mindful of the wider context in which the studies were published. A good example of this approach is Haggis' (2009) content analysis of the titles of articles published in three leading non-American journals on higher education to identify common themes recurring in the literature on student learning in the last four decades.

### Statistical techniques

The *Handbook of Research Synthesis and Meta-analysis* (2009) includes sophisticated discussions on how to analyze and combine estimates of effect-sizes across studies. This section briefly describes commonly-used techniques for statistically integrating findings across studies. In general, the choice of statistical techniques should be guided by the purpose of the synthesis and the nature of studies included in the synthesis (Hedges 2009).

Often, bringing all comparable quantitative findings to a common metric, like an effect-size, can facilitate meaningful comparisons even if there is no intention to statistically integrate these effect-sizes for further analysis. Every finding included in a meta-analysis must be converted into an effect-size. Meta-analysts frequently define effect-size as the difference of means between the experimental and control groups divided by the standard deviation. Algebraically:

$$( M_e - M_c ) / SD$$

where $M_e$ is the mean of the experimental group, $M_c$ is the mean of the control group and SD is the standard deviation (Glass 2006). This SD could be that of the experimental group, the control group, or the pooled standard deviation (PSD). Each choice of SD has its advantages and disadvantages. The main argument against the experimental group SD and the PSD is that different treatments may alter the experimental group SD, and hence the PSD, resulting in comparisons being made on different metrics. At times, an educational strategy can reduce the SD of the experimental group, and hence the PSD resulting in artificially inflating the magnitude of the effect-size (Glass et al. 1981). However, in practice often the variances of the control group and the experimental group do not vary significantly and it is more accurate to use the PSD for several other reasons. First, using the PSD reduces the sampling error of the SD by about half as the total number of sample units is about twice the number of sample units in the control group alone. Second, effect-sizes based on incomplete results, such as those based on t-values, F-values, ANOVA tables, or p-levels, are more readily comparable to effect-sizes calculated using PSD. Finally, at times, comparisons are made between different conditions of a particular treatment. For instance, different teaching styles used in web-based courses might be compared to find the more effective teaching style. In these cases, it is not clear which is the control condition and hence it is more appropriate to take the PSD (Lou et al. 1996).

The PSD is given by

$$PSD = \{ [ ( n_E - 1 ) ( s_E )^2 + ( n_C - 1 ) ( s_C )^2 ] / ( n_E + n_C - 2 ) \}^{1/2}$$

where $n_E$ and $n_C$ are the number of sample units, and $s_E$ and $s_C$ are the standard deviations of the experimental and control group respectively. In studies that do not report means or standard deviations, the effect-size can be estimated from other indicators of treatment effects using appropriate transformations (Borenstein 2009, Fleiss and Berlin 2009, Bushman and Wang 2009). To avoid any spurious inflation of effect-size estimates by the use of aggregated data, the SDs used should be always from the individual-level scores rather than the class or school means (e.g. Veenman 1995). For studies that provide pre-test data, the effect-size is computed as the difference between the experimental and the control gain scores divided by the gain score SD. At times, in the original study, the reported effect-size ignores the initial differences between the experimental group and the control group. To take these differences into account, the effect-sizes for all these studies are computed again using raw gain scores. For studies that statistically adjusted post-test scores for one or more covariates, the difference in adjusted scores is divided by the unadjusted SD (Slavin 1986).

Some research reports do not provide sufficient data for an accurate calculation of an effect-size. In these studies, if the author has reported an effect-size, then it can be considered for further analysis. These effect-sizes, referred to as g-statistics, often give a biased estimation of population effect-size, especially for studies with small samples. Each g-statistic must be converted to a d-statistic using the appropriate formula (Hedges and Olkin 1985).

With multiple reports of the same empirical study or with multiple effect-sizes within the same report, taking each effect-size as an individual observation gives more weight to that study and violates the assumption of independence of data points. Many meta-analysts use Cooper's 'shifting unit of analysis' (1998, p. 100) in which first an effect-size is computed independently, based on each statistical summary. In computing the cumulative effect across studies, effect-sizes within individual studies are averaged so that each study contributes only one effect-size towards the cumulative effect. At the same time, each study can contribute an effect-size to each category when examining potential moderator variables (e.g. Sirin 2005).

Synthesists can also draw from published discussions on computing effect-sizes from qualitative evidence. For instance, Onwuegbuzie and Teddlie define nine different types of effect-sizes for mixed-methods and categorize them into three categories: 'manifest effect-size', which includes 'frequency effect-size, intensity effect-size, cumulative intensity effect-size and raw intensity effect-size'; 'adjusted effect-size', which includes 'fixed-interval effect-size, fixed-interval intensity effect-size, fixed-response frequency effect-size and fixed-response intensity effect-size'; and 'latent effect-size', which includes 'variance-explained latent effect-size' (2003, p. 357).

When pooling conceptually similar effect-sizes across studies, some synthesists recommend using the median effect-size as a measure of the central tendency to overcome the effect of anomalous outliers (e.g. Slavin 1986). However, this approach gives equal weight to the findings of each study regardless of their sample sizes. Many other meta-analysts recommend that the mean of the appropriately weighted effect-sizes should be taken as the pooled effect-size. Reasoning that findings from studies with large samples are more precise, often meta-analysts compute the composite effect by averaging the relevant d-statistics weighted by the reciprocal of their respective variances (Hedges and Olkin 1985).

Within each category of conceptually similar effect-sizes, the homogeneity statistic between the studies ($Q_B$) is estimated by assuming that $Q_B$ has an approximate chi-square distribution with m-1 degrees of freedom, where m is the number of studies within each category. In rare cases, when $Q_B$ value is non-significant indicating a consistency of outcomes across studies, the composite effect-size is taken as a conclusive result representative of the within category findings. However, often the $Q_B$ value is significant, which indicates a considerable inconsistency across findings. In these cases, the composite effect-size does not adequately describe the studies since the magnitudes and perhaps the directions of the findings are very different from each other. These categories are analyzed further to account for the differences in individual outcomes (e.g. Gijbels et al. 2005).

At this stage of the analysis, an outlier diagnosis is performed by identifying the study which reduces the homogeneity statistic, $Q_B$, by the largest amount. If the study design of the outlier markedly differs from the remaining studies, then the outlier is isolated and the difference noted. This isolation procedure is continued until major differences are observed in the designs of the isolated studies from the remaining studies.

The remaining studies are subjected to categorical model testing, which is analogous to analysis of variance (ANOVA), to account for the heterogeneity of outcomes of different studies by identifying potential moderators of the effect. The studies are divided into subgroups based on a study characteristic. Within each class, composite effect-size and within group homogeneity statistic, $Q_W$, is estimated by assuming $Q_W$ to have an approximate chi-square distribution with k-1 degrees of freedom, where k is the number of studies within each subgroup. A non-significant $Q_W$ value indicates consistency of outcomes within a class. The between group homogeneity statistic ($Q_B$) is also estimated where a significant $Q_B$ indicates that the study characteristic under consideration significantly moderates the effect-size (Hedges and Olkin 1985).

There are several useful and cost-effective software programs for meta-analysis which offer many features including user-friendly menus for synthesists: to input information about individual study's characteristics and data for computing effect-sizes; to compute and transform individual effect-sizes; to calculate cumulative effect-sizes after appropriately adjusting relevant effect-sizes; to conduct homogeneity analyses, outlier diagnoses and categorical testing for identifying moderator variables; and to conduct sensitivity analyses for comparing results based on different assumptions and analytic paths. See Shadish (n.d.) for a list of commonly used software for meta-analysis.

### Interpretive techniques

In the literature on research synthesis methods, the term interpretive is often used to highlight the inherent subjectivity in any process of constructing new meanings which 'attends to words and ideas, going well beyond a counting of occurrences of specific findings' (Bair 1999, p. 7). Interpretive techniques in a synthesis involve consciously constructing understandings by connecting subjective insights gained from individual studies. Synthesists can adapt interpretive techniques from a range of qualitative methods. Given that there are blurred boundaries and overlaps between several qualitative methods, it is not my intention to exhaustively discuss adaptation of all interpretive techniques from primary research. The previous section described Noblit and Hare's (1988) adaptation of ethnographic techniques to the process of a research synthesis. This subsection briefly illustrates adaptation of some common interpretive techniques from traditional qualitative methods. The next subsection will describe adaptation of interpretive techniques typically employed by educational historians.

Some qualitative research synthesists assert that a rigorous interpretive synthesis is essentially hermeneutic (e.g. Jensen and Allen 1996, Zimmer 2006). Hermeneutics broadly refers to recurrent cyclic interpretation, where one feeds back one's interpretation and sees how it affects other pieces of information. It emphasizes the inherently cumulative nature of reading, where 'each new reading builds upon preceding readings of this and other texts' (Sandelowski and Barroso 2002, p. 6). Drawing on the notion of a dialectic hermeneutic circle (Ödman and Kerdeman 1999), synthesists begin with reading each selected report to construct a pre-understanding about different aspects of the phenomenon. This pre-understanding enhances their understanding of individual reports that further facilitates their synthetic interpretation of all the reports. An holistic understanding of the phenomenon is constructed by iteratively pursuing an hermeneutic circle of pre-understanding-and-understanding of parts-and-whole until a stage of data-saturation or data-sufficiency is reached.

Research synthesists can adapt techniques from case-study research: to bound their object of study; to select the phenomena, themes or issues to focus; to seek patterns of data to develop the selected issues; to triangulate key observations and bases for interpretation; to select rival interpretations to pursue; and to develop generalizations across cases (Stake 1998). For a good discussion of case-study based approach for synthesizing educational research, see Ogawa and Malen's (1991b) discussion, and its critiques (Patton 1991, Yin 1991), on the topic.

Interpretive synthesists often conduct 'thematic analysis' to identify key themes emerging from the literature, which is similar to a content-analysis of themes. Thematic analysis can also be 'theory driven' to evaluate particular themes by interrogating the literature. In the analysis, the emphasis may be given according to the relative frequency of the themes or according to their explanatory power. The latter approach can facilitate development of higher order thematic categories (Dixon-Woods et al. 2005, p. 47).

Several qualitative research synthesists have drawn on techniques and ideas from grounded-theory approach (e.g. Fitzgerald 1995). A purist grounded-theory approach which seeks to 'generate a rich, tightly woven, explanatory theory that closely approximates the reality it represents' is difficult to achieve in a research synthesis as the evidence of a research synthesis is often 'fragmented and fragile' (Ogawa and Malen 1991a, p. 311). The evidence reported in primary research reports is inevitably preconceived. As the synthesis is restricted to the evidence reported in original studies, saturation of thematic categories is often difficult to achieve. Nevertheless, sometimes synthesists adapt a grounded-theory like approach to generate theory grounded in themes emerging from primary research reports rather than seek evidence to support their preconceived theories (Yin 1991). When using a grounded-theory like approach, synthesists should refrain from clustering categories into overarching themes until at least two-thirds of the analysis is complete, to avoid projecting their own preconceived themes on the data; look for 'both typical and atypical elements of the theory, interpretations, and descriptions of the phenomenon located in the primary research' (Paterson et al. 2001, p. 53); and subsume particulars into general by noting 'regularities, patterns, explanations, possible configurations, causal flows, and propositions... [while] maintaining openness and skepticism' (Miles and Huberman 1984, p. 26). Beginning with open-coding, in this approach, the synthesist progresses to axial-coding followed by theory-building when permissible within the constraints of available evidence and resources. Through constant comparisons, the synthesist discovers similarities and differences between individual studies to construct an 'integrating scheme' of categories that fit the relevant evidence rather than being forced upon them; work to meaningfully explain the phenomenon being studied; are parsimonious; have adequate scope; and are theoretically saturated (Glaser and Strauss 1967, p. 41). For a list of practical examples of grounded-theory approach in research synthesis, see Finfgeld (2003).

Contrasting with the grounded-theory like approach is the framework synthesis approach where synthesists begin coding with themes from a preconceived conceptual framework. This framework is tested, modified and refined iteratively against the evidence reported in individual studies as well as collective evidence reported across studies. This approach is particularly suitable for syntheses that have to be conducted within limited time and resources (Carroll et al. 2011, Dixon-woods 2011).

In general, within each report, synthesists must pay particular attention to information that helps in identifying new leads of importance; by extending the area of information, relating or bridging pre-existing elements, reinforcing main trends; by accounting for other information already in hand; by exemplifying or providing more evidence for an important theme; and by qualifying or refuting existing information. A careful balance must be maintained between immersing in sufficient detail to maintain the integrity of each study while refraining from drowning in so much detail that it interferes with identification of overarching themes. A good practical example in which such a balanced approach is adopted is a 'thematic synthesis' with the following three stages, with some overlaps: 'the free line-by-line coding of the findings of primary studies; the organisation of these "freecodes" into related areas to construct "descriptive" themes; and the development of "analytical" themes' (Thomas and Harden 2008, p. 48).

As noted earlier in Chapter 3, several common methodological features implicit in most exemplary interpretive syntheses include the following: conceptually substantiated and well-bound coverage of the substantive topic; inductive approaches to identify common assumptions, theories, methods and findings emerging from extant research; critical analyses of extant research; coherent structuring of the report along meaningful themes; providing a unique conceptual framework or perspective to think about the topic; and providing clear implications for intended audience who often include fellow researchers, teachers and professional developers.

### Historical methods

This subsection is informed by personal communication with three well-known Australian educational historians, Marjorie Theobald, Bob Bessant and Allyson Holbrook, who generously shared their perspectives and key references on historical methods in education. Techniques discussed here come under the broad umbrella of social history.

Traditional historiography looks for the origins, meanings and evolution of past events (Franklin 1999). Educational historians can also contribute to contemporary policy and practice by engaging with the historical roots of various current issues (Donato and Lazerson 2000). Like research synthesists, historians often synthesize disparate, fragmented and diverse documents. It can be fruitful to explore adaptation of techniques employed by historians for synthesizing methodologically diverse educational research on a topic (Yin 1991, p. 304).

Historians vary in their rationale for doing historical research; in methods for collecting, analyzing, interpreting and reporting evidence; and in their criteria for judging the quality of an historical piece of research (Henry 2006). Social historians emphasize the interpretive nature of historical research and stress that history is shaped not only by the factual evidence, but also by the historian's values and perspective. For instance, a statement like 'religious schooling was a good awakening for the moral values in children' raises several questions with a reasonable degree of interpretation: What is 'good'? Whose story are we telling? What evidence do we collect or reject? How do we make sense of that evidence? (Kaestle 1997, Tuchman 1998).

When judging the merit of an historical piece of research, historians often inspect its references. Thorough referencing is also essential in all syntheses. Like historians, synthesists must ask themselves the following questions: Have all likely sources been covered? What databases were searched? How is the credibility of information from key sources established? How valid are the references to illuminate the main argument? Is the way of referencing specific and clear? Are the biases in the evidential material critically examined, made explicit and accounted for? Have the motives of informant studies been verified? Has the evidence from related topics, which could have had an impact on the main idea, been considered? Has the evidence relevant to the key question been compared with the evidence from the other similar locations and time-periods? Have some unestablished ideas been taken for granted or generalizations made beyond the scope of the evidence in hand? Is the narrative interesting? Does it go beyond a mere presentation of factual data with a coherent story supported by evidence from interviews with different stakeholders, current literature and other sources? (B. Bessant, personal communication, July 6, 2000).

Like historians, research synthesists must clearly distinguish between primary and secondary sources; discern patterns with an openness using quantitative and qualitative comparative techniques; clearly distinguish between the intent and the consequences of actions by comparing all available evidence; try to understand the motivation of participants and authors of primary research within their historical contexts without making any timeless moral judgements; reflect on what definition of education is implicit in their work, which in turn, depends upon the questions being asked; familiarize themselves with major theoretical positions and background information in related disciplines and reflect on how these theories shape their own convictions and hunches; clearly distinguish between correlation and causality; precisely define key terms; avoid presentism, or assuming that terms had present-day connotations in the past, by scrutinizing etymological origins of key terms; not simplistically assume that people did as they were told by distinguishing between the evidence on how people should have behaved from the evidence on how people actually behaved; and avoid inferring intent from consequences by clearly distinguishing between intent and consequences (Tuchman 1998, Kaestle 1999).

## Visual displays

Most synthesists use visual displays for condensing and connecting information reported in individual primary research reports. Often, each display is modified several times until it encapsulates the salient features and highlights the gaps within the relevant evidence. For examples of a variety of visual displays in research synthesis, see also Pope, Mays and Popay (2007).

Most synthesists use matrices with each row representing an individual study and different columns representing different aspects of those studies to illuminate patterns of variation across studies. In different tables, synthesists can tabulate different aspects across studies. Visual displays facilitate analysis techniques like partitioning, clustering, counting, noting patterns, themes and making 'if-then' tests. Covariations or interactions between two or more variables across studies can be examined often by crossing these variables in a matrix. In the early stages of a synthesis, matrices are useful for stacking comparable information from individual studies. Eventually, depending on the synthesis purpose, this information can be ordered along different sources and time of publishing; contextual features; methodological characteristics; perspectives of different stakeholders; themes; concepts and diverse outcomes. These outcomes can be long-term or short-term; numerical indices or summarized phrases; positive or negative; at the level of students, teachers or schools; direct effects, meta-effects or side-effects. Synthesists can construct a 'contrast table' to examine a key variable in selected studies 'where the variable is present in high or low form, and contrast several attributes of the basic variable' (Miles and Huberman 1994,

p. 195). Matrices allow synthesists 'to incorporate strategies designed to test emergent interpretations'; 'continuously interrogate the data'; 'deliberately seek, directly locate, and systematically examine evidence' which supports, negates or confounds their emerging interpretations (Ogawa and Malen 1991b, p. 279).

Synthesists can employ a range of graphic displays to focus on different aspects of their cumulative evidence, such as: pie-charts and column-graphs for comparative prevalence of different features; scatterplots for spreads of individual features; line-graphs for variations in individual features; and stem-and-leaf plots for typical and atypical study outcomes (e.g. Borman et al. 2003). Some meta-analysts plot study sample sizes against their effect-sizes to examine potential publication biases in the literature by examining the funnel plot (Sutton 2009). The implicit assumption here is that studies with smaller samples sizes are likely to show more variable effects. A symmetrical inverted funnel plot suggests an absence of any publication bias (Sirin 2005).

Synthesists can refine their evolving understandings through displays like Venn diagrams, flow-charts, concept-maps and networks. For an example of a review with simple user-friendly visual displays, see the website of Te Manatu Taonga Ministry for Culture and Heritage (2005). Venn diagrams are useful for clustering various elements of a phenomenon and illuminating overlaps between these individual clusters. Flow-charts can succinctly represent sequential shifts and developments across several primary research reports. Concept-maps and networks can concisely represent interactions and relationships between different concepts, variables, themes and characteristics. Concept-maps and networks need not be constrained by the rigidly planar (and orthogonal) nature of matrix representations (Lawson 1997). Different types of variables and relationships can be visually distinguished by using different shapes and colours of nodes and links.

### Narrative methods

In primary research, a variety of approaches are being used under the broad umbrella of narrative inquiry (Chase 2011). Riessman described three commonly used frameworks for narrative analysis: Labov's approach, Burke's approach, and Gee's approach. In Labov's approach, representative narratives are reduced under six elements: abstract, orientation, complicating action, evaluation, resolution, and coda. Burke's approach draws on dramatism and grammatical resources to reduce narratives through the use of questions identifying the act, scene, agent, agency, and purpose. Gee's approach focuses on how the story is told by analyzing the changes in pitch, pauses, and other features that punctuate speech (Riessman 1993). Labov's and Burke's approach can be adapted to some extent for synthesizing research. However, the narratives of primary research reports do not provide the kind of information required for Gee's approach. Any synthesis based on Gee's approach would have to identify the meta-level analogues of pitch, pauses, silences, and so on.

Meta-narrative review (Greenhalgh et al. 2005) is a good example of a research synthesis method that draws on narrative methods for synthesizing heterogeneous bodies of literature. This method involves partitioning the literature along key traditions. For each tradition, a storyline is constructed to portray how the core knowledge advanced in that tradition. Using each storyline as a unit of analysis, a rich meta-narrative is constructed by systematically examining the tensions between individual storylines.

In counselling and therapy sessions, narratives are used as tools to hear people's stories of how they understand their experiences. Then the counsellor helps people in rewriting or retelling their stories in ways that help them to come to terms with their difficult experiences. Synthesists can also adapt this technique to empower different stakeholder groups by assisting them in constructing their own synthetic meta-narratives in research domains where they have been inadvertently disempowered.

Teachers tend to share stories about their practice through their own narratives in understandable and actionable genres (Connelly and Clandinin 1999). Often these reports get tagged as being anecdotal and are excluded from research synthesis. Sometimes synthesists can purposefully co-synthesize practitioners' tales in the field to construct a meta-narrative for practitioners.

Synthesists can draw on Richardson's notion of writing as a 'method of inquiry' (2001, p. 35) to write copious personal, methodological, and substantive memos about their hunches, critical decisions, ambiguities and tensions throughout the synthesis process. Through writing, synthesists can become conscious of their own understandings and the gaps in their understandings (Lather 1999). New insights and understandings can develop through an iterative process of refining drafts and redrafts of generated text (Wink 1997). Traditional narratives encourage linear thinking. They provide a sense of sequence to our thoughts. Experimenting with new genres of writing which are multi-layered and multi-geared can facilitate multi-dimensional connections by juxtaposing diverse stances.

### Critical sensibilities

Research synthesists can draw upon various critical sensibilities, such as genealogy, analytics of interpretive practice and postmodernism. Drawing on genealogy, synthesists can clarify present understandings by studying the 'lineage or lines of descent', 'differences and discontinuities in our discourse' to uncover the 'linkage between knowledge and power' (Franklin 1999, p. 350) with an awareness 'that the very act of bringing together the research literature nuances, shifts and scrambles the conceptual and historiographical contours and investments, embedded in the bodies of knowledge under review' (Livingston 1999, p. 15). For a good example of genealogical construction of connected understandings, see Franklin (1999).

Informed by 'the analytics of interpretive practice', synthesists can focus on 'the *interplay*, not the synthesis, of discursive practice and discourses-in-practice', which privileges neither practice. This 'dynamic relationship' can be achieved through constant 'analytic bracketing' that involves 'alternately focusing' on one practice while remaining temporarily indifferent towards the other practice (Gubrium and Holstein 2000, pp. 497-505). They can 'zoom in' and 'zoom out' of selected reports to demonstrate how they are constituted by, and constituting, the dominant discourse (Keogh and Garrick 2011).

'Using the concept of REDO (reveal, examine, dismantle, open)', synthesists can contest prevalent 'hierarchies of knowledge' (Kress 2011, p. 263) by revealing their own standpoint and vulnerabilities; by examining their own perspectives with different lenses; by dismantling the prevalent hierarchies of knowledge and allowing others to dismantle their tendencies toward reproducing those hierarchies; and by opening themselves up by engaging in genuine dialogues with those with different life experiences (Kress 2011).

In a deconstructive synthesis, the synthesist can temporarily bracket individual influences to scrutinize each study for the extent to which its theory, methods and findings have influenced, and been influenced by, prevalent understandings. Drawing on 'a deconstructive problematic that aims not to govern a practice but to theorize it, deprive it of its innocence, disrupt the ideological effects by which it reproduces itself, pose as a problem what has been offered as a solution', synthesists can seek possibilities that lie 'between the no longer and the not yet' (Lather 1993, p.683). Subscribing to the 'law of paradox rather than of consistency' (Baker 1999, p. 376), synthesists can go beyond interpreting primary research reports to adapt, interrogate and/or distort what is given in order to create spaces for different perspectives.

Informed by postmodernism, synthesists would '*doubt* that any method of theory, discourse or genre, tradition or novelty, has a universal and general claim as the 'right' or the privileged form of authoritative knowledge'; suspect 'all truth claims of masking and serving particular interests in local, cultural and political struggles' (Richardson 2001, p. 35, emphasis in original); and address a 'question via dispersion, circulation, and proliferation of counter-practices of authority that take the crisis of representation into account' (Lather 1993, p. 674). Recognizing 'the situational limitations of the knower', postmodern synthesists can regard every text as being 'partial, temporal knowledge'. Abandoning any attempt to write a single comprehensive text, synthesists can reflexively construct multiple, nuanced texts for different audiences from 'particular positions at specific times' (Richardson 2001, p. 35).

Using multiple frames of reference, synthesists can highlight disconnections between current theory, policy and practice and propose ways of strengthening their nexus. For example, in an excellent theoretical analysis of 'constructivism in practice', Windschitl first explicated relevant 'conceptual dilemmas', 'pedagogical dilemmas', 'cultural dilemmas' and 'political dilemmas' (p. 132) experienced by teachers and he then re-interpreted these conditions as 'conceptual understanding, pedagogical expertise, cultural consciousness, and political acumen' (Windschitl 2002).

## Arts-based methods

When appropriate, synthesists can use 'arts-based educational research' methods to incorporate one or more of the following 'design elements': 'contextualised and vernacular "everyday" forms of language, as opposed to speech that is abstract, technical, or removed from the primary qualities of experience'; 'expressive rhetorical strategies and devices'; 'the capacity of the text to entice the reader or recipient through the particular physical realities it evokes into an alternative reality'; or 'the presence of a heightened degree of ambiguity' (Barone 2001, p. 25). Utilizing art-based methods, synthesists can 'produce interesting, innovative, and evocative texts, works that seek to nurture the imagination not kill it' (Bochner 2000, p. 268).

Synthesists can evoke meanings metaphorically through image, gesture and sound using techniques like concrete poetry, collage, musical interpretation, dramatic movement, role-playing and playbuilding. Using different colours and fonts to signal different types of themes, synthesists can construct connected understandings by rearranging them in different symmetries, artistic patterns or literary forms. Multiple copies of key themes can be made to mark their different connotations. Synthesists can also engage different stakeholders in these creative meaning making processes. An insightful poem with a compelling flow can deeply engage audience with a condensed set of data. By arranging and rearranging themes in a collage, new meanings and understandings can emerge to signal the creation of a product without necessarily representing the product as representation becomes an ambiguous concept. Reflecting on each arrangement, with its empty spaces, choice of colours and fonts, repetition and omission of themes, can reveal and fine-tune associated beliefs and understandings. Musical interpretation can involve assigning a note or a sound to each theme and a percussive instrument or a jazz instrument to each perspective, which are then simultaneously played to create music. Interpreting such music can provide new, connected understandings. Dance movements and dramatic movements can facilitate embodied knowing through creativity, balance, risk and surrender. Through role-playing and play-building co-synthesists can collectively develop complex understandings of how different perspectives intersect. Working with an audience, synthesists can recursively use arts-based methods of constructing synthetic insights (Norris 2003).

Arts-based methods require synthesists to think in terms of criteria such as: power, elegance and aesthetic quality with appropriate level of discourse, precision and evocative value of metaphor to stimulate and provoke; creativity to open the world in new ways by revealing new understandings, meanings and questions; interpretive vitality and openness to problematics and reinterpretations; independence from the given frames with an evidence of intellectual wrestling during the synthesis; emotional and intellectual craftsmanship with courage to go beyond the safe limits by flowing from self with a voice that is distinct and expressive; egalitarianism especially in relation to informants of primary research in ways that feel true, authentic or true; and ability to connect with and move with audience (Patton 2002, Barone and Eisner 2006).

### Computer-assisted connections

Depending on the synthesis purpose and synthesis techniques, synthesists often use appropriate software for data retrieval, data searching, data indexing and data editing. The previous chapter described some advantages of using bibliographic referencing software, for referencing and coarse partitioning of literature according to individual fields or a combination of fields. Earlier, the subsection on statistical techniques described the utility of meta-analytic software for managing information and conducting sophisticated statistical analyses.

Most research journals and search databases are available electronically, which allows synthesists to download easily electronic copies of entire research reports, citation details and abstracts. To conduct a fine-grained analysis of a small number of research reports, synthesists sometimes highlight and encode key features and findings on electronic copies of individual reports. These reports or summaries of reports can be subjected to sophisticated analyses using qualitative data-analysis software such as NVivo (e.g. Thomas and Harden 2008), which allow operations like Boolean searches, data indexing and visual displays. Synthesists can also use software specifically designed for managing, assessing and reviewing information in a research synthesis, such as EPPI-Reviewer 4 (EPPI-Centre 2011) or SUMARI (JBI n.d.).

Various features of word-processing software can also be utilized to construct and reconstruct collective understandings. For example, the 'outline-view' feature of Microsoft Word can be used with multiple-levels of headings to organize, re-organize, edit and refine evolving understandings. Advanced search operations can be used to find particular pieces of information within and across electronic copies of selected summaries and complete articles of individual references. Storyboarding software, like Inspiration or Text Block Writer, can help in visualizing potential connections between different pieces of information distilled from individual studies. Such software allow users to build, edit, arrange and rearrange virtual index cards which help in clarifying connections between individual narrative blocks.

## Strategies for enhancing the quality of connections

Strategies for enhancing plausibility, authenticity, utility, robustness and validity of synthesis findings include reflexivity; collaborative sense-making; eliciting feedback from key stakeholders; identifying disconfirming cases and exploring rival connections; sensitivity analyses and using multiple lenses.

### Reflexivity

Being reflexive involves being 'more self-conscious about claims of authorship, authority, truth, validity, and reliability' as well as 'some of the complex political/ideological agendas hidden in our writing' (Richardson 2000, pp. 253-4). It involves reflecting on how the evidence and the synthesist 'bring each other into existence in dialectical fashion' (Hodder 2000, p. 714). One sees different things depending on the frame of reference. Synthesists must explicitly locate themselves in the synthesis (Lather 1999); be 'attentive to the social scripts that are constructed and subordinated by the work of the review as a tool of recasting' (Livingston 1999, p. 16); make judgement calls, acknowledge and live with tensions within their assumptions; and understand their own 'implication in, and the implication of, discourse and/as authority as well as the authority and politics of discoursing others' as they 'work the hyphen between the academy and the field' (Segall 2001, p. 588).

While maintaining a questioning stance and being analytically honest, synthesists should make detailed documentation of the critical decisions, and their justifications, throughout the synthesis process. Systemization is good as it improves transparency of process, thereby improving the transferability of synthesis findings. However, an exclusive focus on systemization can restrict a synthesist's sensitivity to emergent connections and inhibit reflexivity. Maintaining a reflexive stance, synthesists must make the most of serendipitous opportunities offered during the course of the synthesis.

### Collaborative sense-making

The previous chapter described how synthesists can collaborate to unfold multiple interpretive possibilities when distilling evidence. This section stresses that different individuals can see different associations between the distilled evidence. This collaboration is in the benefit of complementarity of perspectives and more sophisticated at a meta-level. Trustworthiness of a synthesis can be enhanced through collaborative sense-making where individual co-synthesists reveal and identify possible connections independently first. This is followed by a process of discussion, debate and negotiation to reach a consensus on the connected understanding reported in the synthesis. Synthesists must seek feedback from critical friends and colleagues who can supportively challenge their taken-for-granted approaches and suggest alternatives.

### Eliciting feedback from key stakeholders

Research synthesists can seek 'collegial and/or informant reviews' on the connected understandings constructed in the synthesis. This can be done formally, or 'informally and serendipitously', by presenting the emerging synthesis findings at conferences, professional development workshops, seminars, electronic forums, and other sites, that are likely to engage the authors of the included reports or members of the groups whose experiences are represented in the reports (Ogawa and Malen 1991b, p. 282). Eliciting feedback from key stakeholders is particularly useful for enhancing the degree of consonance between the synthesis product and the contexts of those whose practices or decisions synthesists wish to inform. For a practical example of this approach, see Bassett and McGibbon (2012) who adopted a participatory approach in their scoping review. They first identified key stakeholders from the relevant literature and professional networks. Then, they used the logic of snowball sampling to identify more key stakeholders. Throughout their review, they sought feedback on their emerging understanding from the key stakeholders through workshops, meetings and through Delphi-method.

### Identifying disconfirming cases and exploring rival connections

Synthesists must put in an effort to identify cases that disconfirm or contest the connected understandings constructed in their syntheses to make their findings more robust. This is particularly important for syntheses where the purpose is to generate generalizations, as in a meta-analysis, or to identify some transcendental patterns, as in an aggregated case-analysis. Seeking rival cases facilitates tightening the boundaries of these generalizations or patterns. To reduce the chances of spurious conclusions, synthesists should examine all plausible explanations of a relationship and verify them by repeatedly going back to the individual reports. By conscientiously exploring rival hypotheses, explanations and connections, synthesists can enhance trustworthiness of their findings. Each alternative explanation must be argued against when feasible within the available resources. As an illustration, in their meta-analysis, when Borman and his colleagues found that schools that had implemented comprehensive school reform (CSR) programs for more than five years tended to report higher effects they explored both plausible explanations. First, they examined if the impact of CSR was potentially cumulative. Second, they examined if schools that did not find significant gains from CSR for a few years discontinued its implementation (2003).

A research synthesis may also be conducted to seek anomalous cases in terms of a few methodologically sound studies that challenge prevalent generalizations in the field. Such an approach could investigate in some depth how these studies, with atypical findings, challenge the commonly assumed generalizations based on several primary research studies.

### Sensitivity analyses and using multiple lenses

Meta-analysts sometimes conduct sensitivity analyses to 'assess robustness and bound uncertainty' (Orwin and Vevea 2009). In this procedure, the synthesist constructs connected understandings from the same data by making different assumptions about the data, including the missing data. The relative match between these constructed understandings demonstrates the degree to which these understandings are dependent on the initial assumptions that the synthesist had made about the data. Alternatively, sensitivity analyses may be conducted by comparing understandings constructed from pursuing different analysis techniques. For instance, meta-analysts often compute inter-rater reliability in terms of multiple measures of inter-rater agreement; isolate outlier cases; isolate variables with low confidence ratings; or use different formulae for computing or transforming effect-sizes (e.g. Borman et al. 2003); compare generalizations to the study sample based on a fixed effects model with generalizations to a large population based on a random effects model (e.g. Sirin 2005); or compare cumulative effects obtained by using weighted and unweighted procedures (e.g. Gijbels et al. 2005). Meta-analysts employ various strategies to examine a potential publication bias, such as: funnel plot method of plotting sample sizes of individual studies against their effect-sizes; computing a fail-safe n (Rosenthal 1980) to estimate the number of studies with insignificant findings that would have to be added to the analysis to make the cumulative effect-size insignificant (e.g.Bowman 2010); and computing correlation between the ranks of standardized effect-sizes and the ranks of their sampling variances (e.g. Sirin 2005). See Sutton (2009) for a comprehensive summary of methods to address publication bias in a meta-analysis.

An outlier diagnosis is performed by systematically excluding extreme accounts to examine how it affects the collective account. Sensitivity analysis can also be performed to examine the extent to which the synthesis product is dependent on the evidence from less rigorous studies (e.g. Thomas and Harden 2008). Examining a phenomenon from multiple perspectives using multiple methods can add depth to our understanding of the phenomenon. Grouping and regrouping evidence in multiple configurations can sensitize synthesists to different aspects of relationships between individual studies (Greenhouse and Iyengar 2009). Sensitivity analyses facilitate ratification and validation of conclusions geared at consensus and convergence.

Synthesists can also use multiple lenses as a means of unfolding multiple connections that are juxtaposed complementarily for a richness of portrayal. Here, synthesists have no compelling reason to advocate one assumption rather than another. Nonetheless, they have an obligation to explore the consequences of adopting one assumption over the other for the synthesis. Use of multiple lenses in a non-convergent framework is an enactment of selective eclecticism. Peshkin (2001) notes 'that although researchers always use one or another lens while engaged in the process of observation, they can learn to see in unexpected but useful ways if they are aware of a range of possible focal points'. He offers alternative lenses which can also be used to enhance perception within every phase of a research synthesis. These include 'patterns, time, emic, positionality, ideology, themes, metaphor, irony, and silence'. By 'consciously using different lenses', synthesists can enhance their 'perceptual efficacy' (Peshkin 2001, pp. 238–42). Synthesists can also conduct multiple analyses of the same set of selected studies to construct complementary accounts.

## Evaluating the construction of connected understandings

There is no universal framework by which the results of all quality syntheses may be evaluated. However, the process by which the synthesis was conducted can be evaluated with respect to its methodological coherence and consistency of alignment with its overarching epistemological orientation. Any notion of rigour is essentially situational and will be guided by the intended purpose and the audience for the synthesis. For instance, 'decision makers and practitioners' are likely to 'apply *truth tests* (whether data are believable and accurate) and *utility tests* (whether data are relevant) in deciding how seriously to pay attention to' synthesis findings (Patton 1991, pp. 288-291, emphasis in original). In general, understandings constructed in a synthesis may be evaluated by the extent to which they are useful and insightful to the intended audience. There are diverse generic criteria for evaluating research reviews and literature reviews which can be usefully adapted to evaluate research syntheses also (e.g. Boote and Beile 2005, Mays et al. 2005b). Criteria commonly used to evaluate primary research from different paradigmatic orientations, as illustrated in the previous chapter, can also be adapted to evaluate construction of connected understandings in research syntheses with similar overarching orientations. Illustrated below are some criteria that may be applied to evaluate syntheses with the relevant orientation.

---

**Key question to consider**

- What criteria will be used to evaluate the quality of connected understandings constructed in the synthesis?

---

### Postpositivist syntheses

Dunkin described and illustrated nine types of errors commonly found in research reviews: '*unexplained selectivity*' by excluding 'research which comes within the declared scope of the review without explaining or justifying the exclusion'; '*lack of discrimination*' between 'good and poor research'; '*erroneous detailing*' of the 'sampling, methods, designs, procedures, and contexts of the studies reviewed' leading to their misclassification; '*double counting*. ... [by] listing different reports from the same project as providing additional confirmation of the same finding'; '*nonrecognition of faulty author conclusions*' when primary researchers do not 'represent their findings fully in their statements of conclusions'; '*unwarranted attributions* ... claiming that studies yield findings or reach conclusions that they do not'; '*suppression of contrary findings*' by not acknowledging 'every single finding that is contrary to a generalization a reviewer intends to make about the findings of the body of research concerned'; '*consequential errors*' by making flawed generalizations as a consequence of above-mentioned errors; and *'failure to marshall all evidence relevant to a generalization'* (1996, pp. 88-94, emphasis in original). All synthesists, in particular postpositivist synthesists, must be wary of all these nine threats to the validity of their syntheses.

Postpositivist synthesists can strategically enhance the 'global quality' of their connected understandings; of 'construct validity' by 'considering competing theories and measures of theoretical constructs'; of 'external validity' by addressing publication bias through extensive literature searches and estimating the extent of potential bias; of 'internal validity' by 'creating strata for design types' and estimating associated biases; and of 'statistical conclusion validity' by carefully 'noting important sources of potential heterogeneity such as study participants, setting, time periods, and reliability of measures' (Wortman 1994, pp. 106-108).

All meta-analysts must take into account the following ten threats to inferences about the existence of a relationship between treatment and outcome classes: unreliability in primary studies; restricted range in primary studies; missing effect-sizes in primary studies; unreliability introduced in coding process; capitalizing on chance during statistical integration; biases in transforming effect-sizes; lack of statistical independence among effect-sizes; a failure to weight study-level effect-sizes proportional to their precision; an unsubstantiated use of fixed or random effects models; and a lack of statistical power. Most of these threats have been discussed in different chapters of this book. For a further discussion of these threats and additional threats to inferences about causal or correlational relationship between treatment and outcome classes as well as threats to generalized inferences, see Matt and Cook (2009). Cooper (2010) has presented a comprehensive checklist of questions related to the validity of research syntheses which is particularly relevant to postpositivist syntheses.

### Interpretive syntheses

In addition to procedural rigour, an interpretive synthesis can be evaluated by its potential to increase our understanding of a research domain; illuminate implications of contextual, theoretical and methodological positioning of individual studies on prevalent understanding of a phenomenon; generate or expand theory; and provide a new way of understanding the phenomenon.

The truth value or the credibility of a synthesis may be the extent to which participants of the relevant primary research can resonate with the synthesis findings or the extent to which the authors of the relevant primary research feel that their findings are faithfully represented. Internal validation in a synthesis may be accomplished by comparing its findings with the quotes of the informants of original research and the metaphors used to describe the phenomenon in individual reports (Jensen and Allen 1994). Strategies that can enhance the truth value, credibility or internal validity of a synthesis include prolonged engagement with the research literature to be synthesized; persistently looking out for the implicit and explicit assumptions in each study; peer-debriefing; triangulation;

referential adequacy of materials; member-checking; reflexivity; exploring rival connections; and identifying disconfirming cases.

External validation of synthesis findings is possible by comparing them with the related theoretical literature (Jensen and Allen 1996). A major threat to external validity is the 'observer-setting' effect. A synthesist who is novice to the field may not be able to grasp all the implicit assumptions and understandings of the field. On the other hand, synthesists who are experts in the field are likely to encounter the problem of 'oversaturation', where their prior knowledge of the field prejudices their findings and processes in certain ways. A synthesis that was valid a decade ago may not be valid any more because of the recent changes that have occurred in the field. These are referred to as 'history effects'. 'Construct effects' can be reduced by techniques such as peer examination, triangulation and self-monitoring (LeCompte and Goetz 1982, p. 51). 'Applicability' or 'transferability' may be described as the extent to which connected understandings constructed in the synthesis can be adapted to similar real-life contexts. Transferability can be enhanced by using purposeful sampling to maximize the range of information; by selecting reports from diverse theoretical perspectives, research foci and contexts; and by providing thick description of the synthesis process as well as the contexts covered by the original studies.

Internal reliability, consistency, dependability or auditability may be the extent to which similar conclusions would be made by following the reported synthesis process. It can be enhanced by using strategies such as: collaborative sense-making; low-inference descriptors; peer examination; 'overlap methods'; and 'stepwise replication' (Guba and Lincoln 1999, p. 148). Synthesists can employ a range of strategies to 'develop more accurate, dependable inferences and to produce more replicable and, consequently, more reliable analyses', such as: constructing a formal, retrievable database of distilled evidence; clearly defining emergent constructs and delineating 'the manner in which evidence is being used to examine the constructs (or their relations)'; 'systematically seeking contrary findings and alternative interpretations'; and seeking 'collegial and/or informant reviews' (Ogawa and Malen 1991b, pp. 280-282).

Given the inherent subjectivity involved in an interpretive process, an interpretive synthesis may approach rather than attain external reliability. Interpretive synthesists should clearly describe factors which contribute to the uniqueness of their synthesis, such as: the synthesist's identity; inclusion-exclusion criteria; sources of primary research reports; units of analysis, major foci and salient assumptions; and strategies employed for distilling and connecting information. An interpretive synthesis 'meets the criterion of fittingness when the findings can fit into contexts outside the studies and when the findings are grounded in the life experiences studied and reflect their typical and atypical elements' (Jensen and Allen 1996, p. 556). Neutrality, objectivity or confirmability may be enhanced by strategies such as triangulation, maintaining a reflexive journal and maintaining a confirmability audit to ascertain that every claim is substantiated with appropriate documentation.

'*Credibility* is a complex notion that includes the perceived accuracy, fairness, and believability' which can be enhanced by 'report clarity, full and frank disclosure of data strengths and weaknesses, balanced reporting, defensible information sources, valid measurement, and justified conclusions'. However, the 'issues of credibility and validity also have critical interpersonal dimensions' where the synthesist's perceived 'personal credibility and integrity will override all other methodological concerns' (Patton 1999, pp. 289-290, emphasis in original).

## Participatory syntheses

Value and validity of a participatory synthesis lies in providing 'effective support for the stakeholders' actions, organizations, and/or communities in their processes of self-determining social change' (Greenwood and Levin 2000, p. 94). Issues related to the positioning of practitioner co-synthesists in the process and product of a participatory synthesis become critical (Yu 2011). Political participation can be facilitated by active engagement of all co-synthesists in making key decisions throughout the synthesis process.

Participatory syntheses can be evaluated in terms of the degree to which co-synthesists have been equally 'integrated' rather than being 'distanced' or merely 'related' on the following issues: 'motivation for involvement, depth of participation, quality of dialogue, authority for decision making and meaning making' (Shulha and Wilson 2003, p. 665). The goal of a participatory synthesis is to accomplish holistic and ecological progress in thinking and contexts of the individuals and the communities of those engaged in the synthesis process. The synthesis process and product must facilitate the realization that 'we are part of the whole rather than separated' and make us conscious of the related 'rights and obligations' (Heron and Reason 1997, pp. 275-6). Participatory syntheses should 'connect the local and the global' by transforming '*both* practitioners' theories and their practices *and* the theories and practices of others whose perspectives and practices may help to shape the conditions of life and work in particular local settings' (Kemmis and McTaggart 2000, p. 598, emphasis in original).

'Epistemic participation' can be accomplished through 'critical-subjectivity' (Heron and Reason 1997, p. 284), where the relevant research literature, and the synthesis process, serve as sites for all co-synthesists to reflect critically on their own practices and engage in a process of reciprocal learning about useful strategies for selecting, interpreting, evaluating, distilling, connecting and reflecting upon research relevant to their own practices. When possible, all co-synthesists can participate at a site of the phenomenon and use this experience as a mirror to critically reflect on their own conceptions about the phenomenon. A participatory synthesis would be a product of connected understandings constructed through these experiences.

### Critically oriented syntheses

At every stage of a critically oriented synthesis process, synthesists must see beyond ostensible dichotomies and be reflexive about the dialectical relationship between the synthesis product and the literature to be synthesized; between their own knowledge base and the relevant academic discourse; and between the implicit theories underlying their synthesis process and their synthesis product (Kemmis 1999).

Critical synthesists should be conscious of how 'reviews *contain silences*' and 'expressions' that privilege some discourses over others, thus becoming 'the bearer of truth and power effects'. At the same time they should also be wary that 'voice and silence do not operate in antithesis and that appeals to 'voice' on the basis of fixed 'identity' do not 'represent' inclusion, but may in fact reinvoke the terms on which repression is given ground' (Baker 1999, p. 380, emphasis in original). Quality of these syntheses can be determined by the 'empathy they generate, the exchange of experience they enable, and the social bonds they mediate' (Jackson 1998, p. 180).

Postmodern critical synthesists would 'operate from a premise of the impossibility of satisfactory solutions' by recognizing 'the obduracy of the problems and obstacles as the very way toward producing different knowledge and producing knowledge differently' (Lather 2004, p. 28). In critically oriented syntheses, 'data must be allowed to generate propositions in a dialectical manner that permits use of a priori theoretical frameworks, but which keeps a particular framework from becoming the container into which the data must be poured' (Lather 1986, p. 267). Critical syntheses should be 'tempered by a sense of openness' by constantly watching 'for the interruptive, counter-hegemonic capacity and absent-presence of what James Scott (1990) calls "hidden transcripts"' (Livingston 1999, pp. 15-16).

## Summary

This chapter illustrated how synthesists can adapt ideas, techniques strategies and evaluation criteria from a range of primary research methods to the process of a research synthesis. Rather than trying to comprehensively cover all types of research techniques, the goal has been to illustrate how some commonly-used techniques in primary research may be adapted to the process of research synthesis. It is hoped that this will open spaces for further discussion and debate on strengths and limitations of these adaptations and prospective synthesists will use this discussion as a departure point and explore adaptation of those techniques that have not been discussed here, such as linguistic and semiotic analysis.

# Chapter 11

# Communicating with an audience

How can research synthesists effectively communicate the process and product of their syntheses to diverse audiences?

Some may argue that the phrase 'communicating with an audience' is misleading as it is really the author whose voice gets heard. It is presumptuous to imply an input from the audience when there is none. Drawing from Richardson's (2000) notion of writing as a 'method of inquiry' (p. 923), I believe that by remaining empathetic to the needs of our audience, we are better prepared to look at the same domain of knowledge from a perspective that takes into account the specific audience's needs. Thus both the author and the audience benefit from this shared construction of knowledge. An underlying premise of this phase is that research synthesists have an obligation to communicate their synthetic understandings to appropriate audiences. It is crucial that synthesists carefully select the content, representational style, medium, genre and techniques in alignment with the impact they wish to make on their target audience. They must skilfully share the process and the product of their sense-making in a way that is credible, trustworthy and useful to the intended audience.

## Content of the message

This section describes the conceptual categories of information that are likely to be of interest to the users of a research synthesis. While some synthesists present this information in four discrete sections, others explore alternative structures that are aligned with the overarching orientation of the synthesis.

*Introductory information.* The introductory information provides a background of the synthesis and whets the audience's curiosity to engage with the synthesis. It contextualizes the synthesis with information such as: the broad topic covered; theoretical and practical importance of the topic; the general nature of the primary research in the field; the issues addressed, or not addressed, by previous syntheses in the field; how the current synthesis relates to the previous syntheses; the intended audience and purpose of the synthesis; the synthesist's theoretical and contextual positioning; and the structure of the synthesis report.

*Information about the synthesis process.* Information about various critical decisions, that could influence the synthesis results, should be clearly described and substantiated, including the following: overarching theoretical orientation of the synthesis; feedback or input from different stakeholders in the synthesis process; source of funding, if any; definitions of key terms; meanings and scope associated with each term along with the relevance of particular operationalizations to the synthesis context; sampling strategies and search techniques employed; suitability of the selected techniques, especially complementarity of various techniques, for the intended purpose such as in reducing biases and enhancing representativeness; the appropriateness of the search descriptors and the coverage in terms of the relevant data-bases and years of publication for electronic and manual searches; inclusion/exclusion criteria; coverage and nature of reports selected by reading the retrieved report titles, abstracts and full-reports; techniques employed to evaluate, interpret and distil relevant information from selected studies and constructing connected understandings; and the canons of rigour against which the synthesis process and product may be evaluated.

*Connected understandings constructed across studies.* The heart of the synthesis essentially lies in delineation and substantiation of the synthesist's construction of the connected understandings across studies. Synthesists have an obligation not only to share their collective insights, but also to justify each of these claims to the intended audience in a way that makes sense to them. For example, decision makers and practitioners are often less interested in 'construct validity' and more interested in 'face validity', i.e. 'Are the procedures and findings reasonable from a commonsense point of view?' They 'focus on relevance and applicability rather than procedural rigor in judging the value of findings' (Patton 1991, pp. 290-291). While being explicit about the tensions and ambiguities associated with the synthesis findings, synthesists must carefully articulate boundaries to their claims to minimize the chances of any unjustified extrapolation. Synthesists often find that new research has been reported during the course of their synthesis. While it may be difficult to integrate this information structurally into the synthesis findings, synthesists must demonstrate an awareness of these reports in the discussion of the synthesis findings.

*Implications, recommendations and discussion of connected understandings.* Synthesists ought to 'serve as facilitators of the dialogue between the perspectives of the audience and the perspectives revealed in the synthesis'. An 'audience-appropriate' synthesis enables 'the audience to compare their perspectives with those revealed in the studies and the synthesis' as well as suggest 'implications of such differences in world view'. This can be 'achieved by ensuring that the metaphors and analogies employed reveal the ways in which the world views of audiences are alike and dissimilar from those of the authors of the accounts' (Noblit and Hare 1988, pp. 76-77). In addition to statistical significance of synthesis findings, synthesists should also discuss their practical or educational significance (Kirk 1996). For example, in their meta-analysis of comprehensive school reform programs, Borman and his colleagues presented an excellent discussion of relative costs and benefits of different programs (2003, p. 164).

Encouraging feedback from various stakeholders while formulating recommendations can help in reinforcing their trust in the synthesis product. Recommendations informed by views of key stakeholders are likely to have greater practical viability and utility. Also, involvement of key change agents may improve the likelihood that the recommendations are acted upon.

## Identifying appropriate audiences and their specific needs

The synthesist ought to anticipate an audience and be respectful to their varied needs (Hannes and Lockwood 2011). The potential audience of a synthesis include different stakeholders and individuals with a specific, or general, interest in the synthesis topic. Focusing on the needs of an audience can prevent synthesists from being narcissistic or overindulgent in their writing. Meeting the 'needs of an audience' is not same as asking yourself, 'What do my audience want to hear?' It involves making a value judgement about 'What responses would I like to evoke in my audience from this piece?' For each group of audience, it is worth considering what might they already know, what might be of interest to them and how they might interpret or misinterpret the synthesis findings by remaining sensitive to the politics of how syntheses are 'received and read by audiences' (Hammersley 2003, pp. 8-9).

---

### Key questions to consider

- How can I share my expertise in the field and/or share my partial understanding of the field?
- How can I make explicit some of the patterns and the general nature of methods and findings typically reported in this domain of research and/or make explicit some of the conflicts, tensions and incommensurabilities of findings and methods reported in the field?
- How can I substantiate common sense knowledge and practice with the evidence from the research literature and/or present evidence from research that shakes and agitates the audience from their complacency by provoking them to think in directions they would not normally think along?
- How can I provide a thick description of the synthesis process and product in a way that the audience can relate to my process and adapt the product to their own context?
- How can I encourage the audience to make connections of their own practice, policy, research, methodology and/or beliefs with my synthesis and venture to create new conceptual spaces?'

The synthesist might consider preparing a 'communication plan' by listing groups who may be interested in the topic. With respect to each potential audience, the synthesist must identify 'the specific content of the material that is to be communicated' along with the suitable 'format, timing and setting for the communication' (Posavac 1992, pp. 273-80). A careful balance, guided by the needs of the target audience, must be struck between sharing details of the process and the product. It is essential that the synthesist establishes a relationship of trust with the key stakeholders and is perceived as one who is familiar with their needs and concerns. It would be presumptuous of synthesists to assume that they know what their intended audiences need to know. Synthesists must try to collaborate with members of the intended audience and solicit information about what kind of information they would like to have prior to the presentation of any final report (Patton 1991). This could be achieved through various formal and informal techniques. For instance, the synthesist could arrange a focus group discussion or an electronic forum with the members of intended audience and simply ask the questions that they would like to be addressed in a synthesis report.

At times, synthesists can be tempted to focus exclusively on the flaws of prior research in the field and overlook how this body of research has facilitated an understanding of the phenomenon. This can evoke a defensive response among many academic and non-academic stakeholders. While critiquing prior research, policies and practices in the field, synthesists should sensitively contemplate on how their synthesis could impact upon the feelings of various stakeholders including the authors of prior research and syntheses. While recommending directions for further research, synthesists should give due recognition to the contributions made by prior research, policies and practices in the field (e.g. Engberg 2004, Bransford and Schwartz 1999). Synthesists should try to enrich and enlarge their audiences' discourse through engagement at every stage.

Evidence from the same primary research project can be used to tell different tales from different perspectives for different audiences (Van Maanen 1988, Gaskell et al. 1998). Our representational style colours the story we want to tell. Given that considerable resources and time are invested in a quality research synthesis, efforts should be made to make the synthesis broadly available to a wide range of audiences. When permissible within the pragmatic constraints of the project, synthesists could consider writing multiple tales to communicate the insights gained to various stakeholders and audiences.

## Issues of voice, authority and representation

Considering that reviews represent a 'canonizing genre for summarizing and codifying subfields of educational research, inclusion and censorship have become issues of concern in their framing and writing'. As educational reviews are often seen to represent wider power relations, synthesists should be conscious of a 'review's authorizing or legitimating function' and attempt to ethically address the issues of 'voice, identity, and representation' in a synthesis (Baker 1999, p. 365).

Throughout the synthesis process, the synthesist should remain in touch with the potential tensions between different layers of representation in the triple hermeneutic process of a research synthesis as well as potential biases which might be introduced at individual layers. Sharing these tensions and complexities with the audience of a synthesis can facilitate a more informed reading. Synthesists should be particularly sensitive to the emotional responses evoked by their reports as these reports can impact upon lives, practices and environments of different stakeholders. Synthesists must carefully acknowledge their own 'voice' in the synthesis product. 'Too strong a voice' can lead to 'an autocratic subjectivity', while 'too little voice' can lead to an abdication of authorial *'presence'* (Connelly and Clandinin 1999, p. 138, emphasis in original).

In every synthesis, how we present our narrative is crucial to our and the reader's understanding of the narrative. Numbers and statistical summaries provide a powerful way of representing collective views. When reporting any central tendency, it is crucial to indicate the level of variance associated with it. This allows readers to make an informed decision about the level of homogeneity within the data.

Synthesists can ground their connected understandings in the direct quotes of the authors or participants of original studies. Direct quotes may be used to carry primary meanings as well as illuminate specific points (Ely et al. 1997). Going out of our way to paraphrase in order to demonstrate our understanding of the topic raises questions, such as: 'Whose voice is more powerful?', 'Whose representation is more valid?' At the same time, synthesists should be wary of the romanticized view of giving voice through direct quotes.

While acknowledging that reviews privilege 'some discourses more' than others, Baker questions the unproblematic conception of voice as a 'liberatory or emancipatory strategy in re-viewing reviews'. Through an historical examination, she calls to attention 'the complexities, the multiplicities, and the divergence that give different meaning to voice, identity and representation', which in turn, have different implications for building and circulation of power in our society (Baker 1999, pp. 377-80). Often, quotes need to be abridged in a way to strengthen our argument. 'What we appropriate from others as well as how and where we choose to use it will alter its meaning' (Segall 2001, p. 585). So, claiming a representation of the original speaker using abridged quotes will not be completely honest either. However, abridged quotes do provide a reasonable way of supporting our argument by drawing on our informants' words.

## Finding a suitable medium to reach intended audience

Synthesists generally use traditional paper-based media that allow their audience to read the synthesis product at any time, and are often regarded as having more status. These media include academic journals, practitioner-focused journals, chapters in books, monographs, project reports, executive summaries, memos, newsletters, magazines and newspapers. Often, synthesists share their connected understandings with fellow academics through academic journals, monographs and book chapters. Publishing in peer-reviewed research journals and books also enhances their research profiles. Some journals, such as *RER* and *Educational Research Review*, are specifically geared towards publishing research reviews. An increasing number of high-status journals are regularly publishing rigorous research syntheses (White 2009). Monographs and book chapters tend to be purposefully geared at specific audiences by the publishing companies. Practitioner journals are particularly useful for communicating to key stakeholders how the synthesis findings can inform their practices and decisions. Often, commissioned synthesis products take the form of project reports and executive summaries with an emphasis on implications and recommendations sections.

Digital media can include more details, such as archived appendices and supporting documents, than in the conventional channels for publishing such as scholarly journals, which cannot be included due to space restrictions. Using hypermedia, synthesis products can be made more interactive, allowing users to follow different paths by making different choices and thus taking more control of how they wish to engage with the contents. As electronic publishing tends to be associated with low editing costs, it is particularly useful for syntheses in areas where more primary research is being conducted regularly and hence syntheses need regular updating. For example, Campbell's systematic reviews are published electronically so that they can be amended when the need arises (Campbell Collaboration n.d.). Publishing on the World Wide Web increases the accessibility of the synthesis product amongst audiences who have limited access to diverse print-based forms, especially audiences from developing nations and rural areas. Internet publishing also opens up opportunities for synthesists from developing nations who sometimes do not have equal opportunities in terms of publishing or gaining access to many of the scholarly international journals. However, Internet publishing raises several unresolved issues of copyright. Much of the content on the Internet tends to be unrefereed and hence there tends to be a certain amount of scepticism towards the quality of information published on the Web.

Formal presentation channels include small-group presentations, public speeches and various forms of mass media. Most synthesists share their connected understandings at relevant research-based conferences and professional conferences. Newspapers, magazines, newsletters, public speeches, radio or television can be effective channels for communicating synthesis findings to the wider community.

Interactive presentations may be face-to-face, virtually synchronous or virtually asynchronous. They are particularly useful: as professional development sessions for practitioners; as sessions for decision-making bodies such as policymakers and administrators; and as seminars for colleagues and various stakeholders. Asynchronous interactive sessions via discussion forums or group emails are useful when different participants wish to engage with the synthesis product at different times. Interactive sessions can be adapted to address the interests and reactions of the specific audience; mutually inform the synthesist and the audience; empower audience with an opportunity to air their own views; and engage audience in interpreting the implications of the synthesis to their own contexts. Stakeholders are more likely to accept recommendations and act upon them when they are involved in negotiating the meaning of the reported synthesis as it relates to them.

Synthesists should be wary of the tendency people have to project their own expectations on a report and pay less attention to information that challenges their current understanding. In interactive settings, sometimes the audience can inadvertently, or deliberately, influence the interpretation of the synthesis findings to conserve or justify their own vested interests. Posavac describes a procedure, developed by Raymond G. Carey, for primary researchers that can be usefully employed by synthesists also. First, the audience can be encouraged to document, individually or collectively, their expectations by filling in empty graphs with marked axes or record their hunches in the form of dot points. Only after the audience have documented their expectations, the synthesist might share the synthesis findings with the audience (Posavac 1992). Comparing and contrasting the new knowledge with their existing knowledge can facilitate deeper understanding of the new knowledge. Finally, the audience may be encouraged to reflect on the plausible reasons for discrepancies, if any, between their expectations and the synthesis findings. This may conclude with a discussion of the various implications of the synthesis findings.

## Appropriate genre

Many synthesists, especially meta-analysts, employ the scientific reporting format with four distinct sections, i.e. 'Introduction/Methods/Results/Discussion' (Cooper 1982, p. 300). The synthesists begin with an identification and contextualization of the problem; describe their attempts to find the solutions; then they describe their findings; and finally they interpret and contextualise their findings. This format is particularly suited for hypothetico-deductive syntheses that are reported in the problem-solution format.

Many synthesists use coherent thematic narratives to share their synthetic understandings with their audience. They construct their narrative by organizing into a coherent logical structure the main themes which contextualise and describe the synthesis process and product. These themes, headings and sub-headings may vary purposefully according to intervention types; methodological designs; contextual features (e.g. Engberg 2004); types of descriptive commentaries such as retrospective, prospective or critical (e.g. Bransford and Schwartz 1999); or according to an aspect of the synthesis process being described such as introduction, methods, results and discussion. Scientific reports, thematic narratives and executive summaries are commonly used to communicate with an academic audience and decision-makers. Familiarity of these formats makes it easy for them to pick out the information they are interested in for the purposes of informing and justifying their own research, practices and policy-decisions. Drawing on postmodernism and intertextuality, synthesists can construct multi-layered narratives to juxtapose divergent perspectives.

Synthesists can sometimes reach diverse audiences through stories. 'Stories give a measure of coherence and continuity that was not available at the original moment of experience' (Bochner 2000, p. 270). Different forms of stories are suitable for different purposes. Synthesists can describe the chronological development of key understandings in a research domain through a factual story; various socio-economic and historical factors that could have influenced prevalent conceptions of a phenomenon at different points of time through a critical story; their own interactions with a research topic through an interpretive story of their own process of sense-making in which they scaffold various dimensions of a research topic with their audience; a partial view of the field from their own perspective, rather than a 'God's eye view' of the field, through a reflexive story.

Synthesists can sometimes communicate allegorically with their audience 'to express the lessons of the studies collected as well as to invite a range of readers to pursue them'. Allegories are particularly useful to 'express the interaction of forces in some social or cultural process' and to engage audience in reflective thinking when synthesizing 'studies of educational change and program implementation'. Allegories 'may also be useful for educational purposes in general, providing direction for what is to be learned, while giving the lesson a concrete manifestation' (Noblit and Hare 1988, p. 79).

When appropriate, synthesists can use various artistic genres, such as drama, documentary films, poetry, music and art to reach diverse audiences. Drama can be used skilfully to show how different perspectives are sometimes in consensus, sometimes building on each other's arguments, and sometimes diverging. Dramatic genres should be 'well-plotted, compelling' with 'minimalist narrative'; be 'based on realistic, natural conversation, with a focus on memorable, recognizable characters'; they should 'show, not tell'; and 'enact an enabling' (Denzin 2000, pp. 261–262). Documentary films, poetry, music, art and comedy are useful for reaching wider communities in accessible forms. Artistic genres can engage audiences emotionally as well as intellectually. Given the challenge inherent in communicating procedural rigour of the synthesis through artistic genres, some methodologists are sceptical about suitability artistic genres for research syntheses (e.g. Hammersley 2003).

## Pertinent representational techniques

For each idea, theme or finding, synthesists should identify pertinent techniques for a rich, succinct and audience-friendly representation. Given the vast nature of evidence in research syntheses, descriptive statistics, abridged quotes and visual displays can be particularly useful tools. Synthesists can also choose from a range of narrative techniques and artistic devices.

*Quantitative techniques.* The rhetorical power of summary statistics can be used to succinctly provide the gist of a field. Numerical summaries are used not only in quantitative syntheses, but also in qualitative syntheses. For instance, we rely on numbers when we use adjectives such as 'many', 'most', 'few', 'sparse', 'extensive'. All synthesists can draw usefully from the rich meta-analytic literature to convert findings of quantitative studies into an effect-size or a common metric to facilitate easy comparisons across studies.

*Visual displays.* Systematic visual displays, such as graphs, tables and charts, concept-maps and flow-charts can succinctly represent summarized quantitative and qualitative data. Self-contained charts can be used effectively to communicate key findings especially in face-to-face and electronic presentations. Each chart can highlight a specific synthesis question juxtaposed with the corresponding synthesis finding; essence of the evidence supporting the finding; and its implication or recommendation.

Synthesists can highlight different aspects of their synthetic insights using visual displays like matrices, pie-charts, column-graphs, scatterplots, line-graphs, stem-and-leaf plots, networks, concept-maps, Venn-diagrams and flow-charts. In general, good visual displays should be *'presented in a meaningful way'* by ordering or clustering information meaningfully; *'emphasise the big picture'* so that the readers get the main points clearly before pursuing further details in which they are interested; indicate the level of confidence associate with each finding; *'encourage the eye to compare different pieces of information'* by juxtaposing findings from different samples of studies, or from multiple analyses of the same sample of studies to clarify the impact of different analytic paths; and describe the distribution of main findings across groups of studies (Light et al. 1994, pp. 451–452, emphasis in original). Every visual display should be described adequately in words to ensure that it is noticed and interpreted appropriately by the audience.

*Narrative techniques.* Synthesists can draw on a range of narrative techniques, such as: asking questions; zooming in and out; vignettes and stories; and prologue/epilogue. Often, teachers are encouraged to whet the curiosity of their students by asking questions. A synthesist can also anticipate a set of relevant questions that are likely to rise in their audience's minds. Enhanced curiosity can facilitate active reading rather than passive absorption of information. Sections of the synthesis report can be presented in a 'question and answer' form. Alternatively, all the key findings can be presented as a series of 'Frequently Asked Questions' and their responses. Thus, a dialogue between the reader and the synthesist can be simulated even in the synthesist's absence.

Synthesists can tactfully zoom in or out to highlight particularities or generalizations respectively. They can begin with a typical or atypical specific example and then build their narrative around it. Alternatively, they can build their main narrative around broad themes giving specific illustrations in-between.

A vignette is a short, focused, narrative with a chronological flow. Research synthesists can use typical vignettes and stories that are directly taken out of primary research reports and are tied to the central issues dealt within the synthesis. Through vignettes and stories, synthesists can directly and succinctly communicate the general significance of their synthesis topic; key dilemmas in the synthesis of research in the relevant domain; personal and social importance of their synthesis; the critical incident that prompted the genesis of the synthesis; or an optimistic vision towards which the synthesist hopes to contribute.

In a reflexive synthesis, a synthesist closely attends to a range of influences on the synthesis process as well as the influence that the synthesis process has had on changing the synthesist's own thinking. This shift, between the self that the synthesist brings into the project and the self with which the synthesist enacts closure, can be portrayed skilfully through a prologue or an epilogue.

*Artistic tools.* Sometimes, synthesists can use artistic tools like poetry and cartoons to engage their audience and leave a deep impact upon them. Poetry can be used to 'evoke feelings, prod reflections, act politically, enjoy complexity, use metaphorical thinking, shift gear, and make connections' (Hildebrand 2001, p. 162). The humour and satire of cartoons can make a lasting impression on the audience. Poetry can be use 'to say – paradoxically – what words can never say' (Eisner 1992). Artistic forms of data representation can facilitate 'productive ambiguity' (Eisner 1997, p. 8).

## Rigour in communicating with an audience

A rigorous report is 'convincing, readable, and makes a contribution' (Bogdan and Biklen 1998, p. 205). Synthesists must clearly delineate their synthesis purpose and how their synthesis makes a contribution to the wider discourse. By employing techniques like 'quantification', 'graphical displays', 'conceptual renderings, quotes, and narratives', every synthesist should strive for 'coherence, attractiveness, and economy' (Sandelowski and Barroso 2002, p. 9). Useful criteria for evaluating all syntheses include: '(a) quality of the literature reviewed, (b) significance of the topic, (c) potential impact of the review on research and practice, (d) contribution to the field, (e) appropriate length, (f) clarity of expression, and (g) balance and fairness' (Murray and Raths 1996, p. 417).

Synthesists must critically choose appropriate target audiences and align the content of their message, representation style, medium, genre and techniques to match their audiences' preferences. Synthesists must communicate those aspects of the synthesis process and product that are most likely to be of interest to their intended audience anticipating that the audience will engage in their own act of further selection. A range of interesting, engaging and effective possibilities for communication can arise by embedding various representational tools within diverse structural genres expressed through varied media.

# Epilogue

What are the implications of methodologically inclusive research syntheses for educational research, policy and practice? Are we talking here about the building of bridges or the building of fences?

The development of the MIRS framework itself has been a process of synthesis, which exemplifies a methodologically inclusive interpretive synthesis informed by critical sensibilities. This purposeful synthesis of the immense and diverse literature on research synthesis methods and primary research methods is itself an enactment of key critical considerations discussed in this book. This is a theoretical synthesis, which must be judged by its coherence and logic of argument. Here, theory is generated by using prevalent theories as data. Despite using theories as building blocks, no universal theory, a grand theory or a meta-theory is generated.

My goal in each of the preceding 11 chapters has been to achieve a meticulous logic expressed through a coherent structure. In this Epilogue, I have a different purpose: I want to challenge and confront the reader in the same way that this project has challenged and confronted me. I hope this does not undermine the sense of rigour that I have tried to convey in the preceding chapters. However, an exclusive emphasis on scholastic rigour can mask some of the heated debates that have galvanized discussions about evidence-based education. Expressions like 'paradigm-wars' capture some of the emotive heat associated with inclusive versus exclusive configurations of the methodological territories in education.

Traditionally, this is the place for a concluding chapter. However, it is in the actual chapters of this book that the MIRS framework is constituted. Any attempt at summary would risk trivializing the argument constructed over many pages. In the final section of this book, I would like to emphasize the importance of keeping open conversations about how a research synthesis should be conducted. My conception of the MIRS framework continues to be situated, partial, temporal, tentative and evolving. The principles, practices and primary research methods in education are continually changing and diversifying. Any discussion that is geared towards making sense of such growing complexity, such as that presented in this book, must remain sufficiently fluid to continue to embrace and accommodate these changes.

Challenging prevalent ways of thinking about research synthesis methods has opened spaces for new ways of thinking. Throughout this book, in preference to providing prescriptive answers or conclusions, I have attempted to open spaces, raise questions, explore possibilities and contest taken-for-granted practices. Rather than prescribing how a research synthesis ought to be conducted or evaluated, the goal has been to support critical reflection among producers and users of research syntheses. I have attempted to do this by raising questions to structure and inform critical decision-making throughout a synthesis process. I hope this book will stimulate debate and discussion about numerous aspects of research syntheses from a methodologically inclusive perspective.

Inclusivity is an enabling constraint, which requires us to recognize and honour differences. I hope that each and every chapter of this book incisively encourages producers and users of research syntheses towards informed decision-making. The purpose of this book has been to identify key considerations for undertaking a methodologically inclusive research synthesis critically, purposefully and with informed selectivity.

# Bibliography

Abrami, P. C., Cohen, P. A. and d'Apollonia, S., 1988. 'Implementation Problems in Meta-Analysis'. Review of Educational Research, 58(2), 151–179.

AERA, 2012. Review of Research Award [online]. American Educational Research Association website. Available from: http://www.aera.net/AboutAERA/Awards andHonors/ReviewofResearchAward/tabid/12786/Default.aspx [Accessed 17 October 2012].

Amundsen, C. and Wilson, M., 2012. 'Are We Asking the Right Questions?' Review of Educational Research, 82(1), 90–126.

Anderson, G. L., 1989. 'Critical ethnography in education: Origins, current status, and new directions'. Review of Educational Research, 59(3), 249–270.

Apple, M. W., 1999. 'What counts as legitimate knowledge? The social production and use of reviews'. Review of Educational Research, 69(4), 343–346.

ARC, 2011. Discovery Early Career Researcher Award: Funding Rules for funding commencing in 2012 [online]. Australian Research Council website. Available from: http://www.arc.gov.au/ncgp/decra/fundingrules.htm [Accessed 24 September 2011].

Aronowitz, S. and Giroux, H. A., 1991. Postmodern education: Politics, culture, and social criticism. Minneapolis: University of Minnesota Press.

Bair, C. R., 1999. Meta-synthesis. ed. 24th annual meeting of the Association for the Study of Higher Education, November 18–21 1999, San Antonio, 26.

Baker, B., 1999. 'What is voice? Issues of identity and representation in the framing of reviews'. Review of Educational Research, 69(4), 365–383.

Baldwin, R. G. and Austin, A. E., 1995. 'Toward greater understanding of faculty research collaboration'. Review of Higher Education, 19(1), 45–70.

Barnett-Page, E. and Thomas, J., 2009. 'Methods for the synthesis of qualitative research: a critical review'. BMC Medical Research Methodology, 9(1), 59.

Barone, T., 2001. 'Science, art, and the predispositions of educational researchers'. Educational Researcher, 30(7), 24–28.

Barone, T. and Eisner, E. W., 2006. 'Arts-based educational research' in Green, J. L., Camilli, G. and Elmore, P. B., eds. Handbook of complementary methods in education research. 3rd ed. Washington: American Educational Research Association, 95–109.

Bassett, R. and McGibbon, E., 2012. 'A critical participatory and collaborative method for scoping the literature'. Quality and quantity, (Published online 26 April 2012).

BEE, 2011. Best Evidence Encyclopedia [online]. John Hopkins University website. Available from: http://www.bestevidence.org/ [Accessed 24 June 2011].

Bernstein, R. J., 1986. 'What is the difference that makes a difference?' in Wachterhauser, B. R. ed. Hermeneutics and modern philosophy. New York: State University of New York Press, 343–376.

Bochner, A. P., 2000. 'Criteria against ourselves'. Qualitative Inquiry, 6(2), 266–272.

Bogdan, R. C. and Biklen, S. K., 1998. Qualitative research for education: An introduction to theory and methods. 3rd ed. Boston: Allyn and Bacon.

Boote, D. N. and Beile, P., 2005. 'Scholars before researchers: On the centrality of the dissertation literature review in research preparation'. Educational Researcher, 34(6), 3–15.

Booth, A., Carroll, C., Ilott, I., Low, L. L., and Cooper, K. ., 2013. 'Desperately Seeking Dissonance: Identifying the Disconfirming Case in Qualitative Evidence Synthesis'. Qualitative Health Research, 23(1), 126–141.

Borenstein, M., 2009. 'Effect sizes for continuous data' in Cooper, H. M., Hedges, L. V. and Valentine, J. C. eds. The handbook of research synthesis and meta-analysis. 2nd ed. New York: Sage, 221–235.

Borman, G. D., Hewes, G. M., Overman, L. T., and Brown, S.., 2003. 'Comprehensive school reform and achievement: A meta-analysis'. Review of Educational Research, 73(2), 125–230.

Bowman, N., 2010. 'College Diversity Experiences and Cognitive Development: A Meta-Analysis'. Review of Educational Research, 80(1), 4.

Bransford, J. and Schwartz, D., 1999. 'Rethinking transfer: A simple proposal with multiple implications'. Review of Research in Education, 24, 61–100.

Briggs, D. C., 2008. 'Synthesizing Causal Inferences'. Educational Researcher, 37(1), 15.

Buchanan, E. A. and Ess, C. M., 2009. 'Internet research ethics and the institutional review board: current practices and issues'. SIGCAS Computers and Society, 39(3), 43–49.

Bullough, R. V., Jr and Pinnegar, S., 2001. 'Guidelines for quality in autobiographical forms of self-study research'. Educational Researcher, 30(3), 13–21.

Burbules, N. C. and Warnick, B. R., 2006. 'Philosophical inquiry' in Green, J. L., Camilli, G. and Elmore, P. B. eds. Handbook of complementary methods in education research. 3rd ed. Washington: American Educational Research Association, 489–502.

Bushman, B. J. and Wang, M. C., 2009. 'Vote-counting procedures in meta-analysis' in Cooper, H. M., Hedges, L. V. and Valentine, J. C. eds. The handbook of research synthesis and meta-analysis. 2nd ed. New York: Sage, 207–220.

Campbell Collaboration, 2001. Campbell Collaboration Guidelines (Version 1) [online]. The Campbell Collaboration website. Available from: http://www.campbellcollaboration.org/guidelines.html 2002 [Accessed 29 December 2001].

Campbell Collaboration, n.d. The Campbell Collaboration: What helps? What harms? Based on what evidence? [online]. The Campbell Collaboration website. Available from: http://www.campbellcollaboration.org/ [Accessed 20 September 2011].

Carr, S. and Coren, E., 2007. Collection of examples of service user and carer participation in systematic reviews [online]. London: Social Care Institute for

Excellence website. Available from: http://www.scie.org.uk/publications/ researchresources/rr02.asp [Accessed 24 September 2011].

Carroll, C., Booth, A. and Cooper, K., 2011. 'A worked example of "best fit" framework synthesis: A systematic review of views concerning the taking of some potential chemopreventive agents'. BMC Medical Research Methodology, 11(1), 29.

Cassell, C., 2010. What is good qualitative research? [online]. The University of Manchester website. Available from: http://www.methods.manchester.ac.uk/ methods/qualityinquali/index.shtml [Accessed 20 September 2011].

Chalmers, T. C. and Lau, J., 1993. 'Meta-analytic stimulus for changes in clinical trials'. Statistical methods in medical research, 2, 161–172.

Chase, S. E., 2011. 'Narrative inquiry: Still a field in the making'. in Denzin, N. K. and Lincoln, Y. S. eds. The sage handbook of qualitative research. 4th ed. Thousand Oaks, CA: Sage, 4211–4434.

Chatterji, M., 2008. 'Synthesizing Evidence From Impact Evaluations in Education to Inform Action'. Educational Researcher, 37(1), 23.

Clandinin, D. J. and Connelly, F. M., 1996. 'Teachers' professional knowledge landscapes: Teacher stories – stories of teachers – school stories – stories of schools'. Educational Researcher, 25(3), 24–30.

Clarke, D. J., 2003. 'International comparative studies in mathematics education'. in Bishop, A. J., M. A. Clements, C. Keitel, J. Kilpatrick and F. K. S. Leung. eds. Second international handbook of mathematics education. Dordrecht: Kluwer, 145–186.

Clegg, S., 2005. 'Evidence-based practice in educational research: A critical realist critique of systematic review'. British Journal of Sociology of Education, 26(3), 415–428.

Connelly, F. M. and Clandinin, D. J., 1999. 'Narrative inquiry' in Keeves, J. P. and Lakomski, G. eds. Issues in educational research. New York: Pergamon, 132–140.

Constas, M. A., 1998. 'Deciphering postmodern educational research'. Educational Researcher, 27(9), 36–42.

Cook, T. D. and Campbell, D. T., 1979. Quasi-experimentation: Design & analysis issues for field settings. Chicago: Rand McNally.

Cooper, H. M., 1982. S'cientific guidelines for conducting integrative research reviews'. Review of Educational Research, 52(2), 291–302.

Cooper, H. M., 1988. 'Organising knowledge syntheses: A taxonomy of literature reviews'. Knowledge in society, 1, 104–126.

Cooper, H. M., 1998. Synthesizing research: A guide for literature reviews. 3rd ed. Thousand Oaks, CA: Sage.

Cooper, H. M., 2009. 'Hypotheses and problems in research synthesis' in Cooper, H. M., Hedges, L. V. and Valentine, J. C. eds. The handbook of research synthesis and meta-analysis. 2nd ed. New York: Sage, 19–35.

Cooper, H. M., 2010. Research synthesis and meta-analysis: A step-by-step approach. 4th ed. Los Angeles: Sage.

Cooper, H. M. and Hedges, L. V., 2009. 'Research synthesis as a scientific process' in Cooper, H. M., Hedges, L. V. and Valentine, J. C. eds. The handbook of research synthesis and meta-analysis. 2nd ed. New York: Sage, 3–16.

Cooper, H. M., Hedges, L. V. and Valentine, J. C., eds., 2009. The handbook of research synthesis and meta-analysis. New York: Sage.

Cooper, H. M. and Rosenthal, R., 1980. 'A comparison of statistical and traditional procedures for summarising research'. Evaluation in Education, 4, 33–36.

CRD, 2009. Systematic reviews: CRD's guidance for undertaking reviews in health care [online]. the Centre for Reviews and Dissemination, University of York website. Available from: http://www.york.ac.uk/inst/crd/index_guidance.htm 2011 [Accessed 30 September 2001].

CRD, 2011. Centre for Reviews and Dissemination [online]. the University of York website. Available from: http://www.york.ac.uk/inst/crd/index.htm [Accessed 24 June 2011].

Creswell, J. W., 2013. Qualitative inquiry and research design: Choosing among five approaches. 3rd ed. Thousand Oaks, CA: Sage.

Dabbs, J. M., Jr, 1982. 'Making things visible' in Van Maanen, J., Dabbs, J. M., Jr and Faulkner, R. R. eds. Varieties of qualitative research. Beverly Hills: Sage, 31–63.

Denzin, N. K., 2000. 'Aesthetics and the practices of qualitative inquiry'. Qualitative Inquiry, 6(2), 256–265.

Denzin, N. K., 2008. 'The new paradigm dialogs and qualitative inquiry'. International Journal of Qualitative Studies in Education 21(4), 315–325.

Denzin, N. K. and Lincoln, Y. S., 2011a. 'Introduction: The discipline and practice of qualitative research' in Denzin, N. K. and Lincoln, Y. S. eds. The sage handbook of qualitative research. 4th ed. Thousand Oaks, CA: Sage, 1–32.

Denzin, N. K. and Lincoln, Y. S., 2011b. The Sage handbook of qualitative research. 4th ed. Thousand Oaks, CA: Sage.

Dixon-Woods, M., 2011. 'Using framework-based synthesis for conducting reviews of qualitative studies'. BMC Medicine, 9(3), 39–40.

Dixon-Woods, M., Agarwal, S., Jones, D., Young, B. and Sutton, A. J, 2005. 'Synthesising qualitative and quantitative evidence: A review of possible methods'. Journal of Health Services Research and Policy, 10(1), 45–53.

Dixon-Woods, M., Amalberti, R., Goodman, S., Bergman, B. and Glasziou, P. 2011. 'Problems and promises of innovation: Why healthcare needs to rethink its love/hate relationship with the new'. BMJ Quality and Safety 20(Suppl1), i47–i51.

Dixon-Woods, M., Bonas, S., Booth, A., Jones, D. R., Miller, T., Sutton, A. J., Shaw, R. L., Smith, J. A. and Young, B., 2006a. 'How can systematic reviews incorporate qualitative research? A critical perspective'. Qualitative Research, 6(1), 27–44.

Dixon-Woods, M., Cavers, D., Agarwal, S., Annandale, E., Arthur, A., Harvey, J., Hsu, R. Katbamna, S. Olsen, R., Smith, L., Riley, R. and Sutton, A. J., 2006b. 'Conducting a critical interpretive synthesis of the literature on access to healthcare by vulnerable groups'. BMC Med Res Methodol, 6(35).

Donato, R. and Lazerson, M., 2000. 'New directions in American educational history: Problems and prospects. Educational Researcher, 29(8), 4–15.

Dunkin, M. J., 1996. 'Types of errors in synthesizing research in education'. Review of Educational Research, 66(2), 87–97.

Dynarski, M., 2008. 'Bringing Answers to Educators: Guiding Principles for Research Syntheses'. Educational Researcher, 37(1), 27.

Eastabrooks, C. A., Field, P. A. and Morse, J. M., 1994. 'Aggregating qualitative findings: An approach to theory development'. Qualitative Health Research, 4(4), 503–511.

Edwards, T., 2000. '"All the evidence shows ...": Reasonable expectations of educational research'. Oxford Review of Education, 26(3&4), 299–311.

Eisenhart, M., 1998. 'On the subject of interpretive reviews'. Review of Educational Research, 68(4), 391–399.

Eisenhart, M., 2001. 'Educational ethnography past, present, and future: Ideas to think with'. Educational Researcher, 30(8), 16–27.

Eisenhart, M., 2005. 'Hammers and saws for the improvement of educational research'. Educational Theory, 55(3), 245–261.

Eisner, E. W., 1992. 'A Reply to Gabriele Lakomski'. Curriculum Inquiry, 22(2), 205–209.

Eisner, E. W., 1997. 'The promise and perils of alternative forms of data representation'. Educational Researcher, 26(4), 4–10.

Elmore, R. F., 1991. 'Comment on "Towards rigor in reviews of multivocal literatures: Applying the exploratory case study method"'. Review of Educational Research, 61(3), 293–297.

Ely, M., Vinz, R., Anzul, M., and Downing, M., 1997. On writing qualitative research: Living by words. Washington, DC: Falmer Press.

Engberg, M. E., 2004. 'Improving Intergroup Relations in Higher Education: A Critical Examination of the Influence of Educational Interventions on Racial Bias'. Review of Educational Research, 74(4), 473.

EPPI-Centre, 2009. The Evidence for Policy and Practice Information and Co-ordinating Centre (EPPI-Centre) [online]. the Social Science Research Unit, Institute of Education, University of London website. Available from: http://eppi.ioe.ac.uk/cms/Default.aspx [Accessed 1 September 2011].

EPPI-Centre, 2011. EPPI-Reviewer 4 (Verstion 4.2.1.0) [online]. the Social Science Research Unit, Institute of Education, University of London website. Available from: http://eppi.ioe.ac.uk/cms/Default.aspx?alias=eppi.ioe.ac.uk/cms/er4 [Accessed 1 September 2011].

Evers, C. W., 1999. 'From foundations to coherence in educational research' in Keeves, J. P. and Lakomski, G. eds. Issues in educational research. 1st ed. New York: Pergamon, 264–279.

Faulkner, R. R., 1982. 'Improvising on a triad' in Van Maanen, J., Dabbs, J. M., Jr and Faulkner, R. R. eds. Varieties of qualitative research. Beverly Hills: Sage, 65–101.

Finfgeld, D. L., 2003. 'Metasynthesis: The state of the art – So far'. Qualitative Health Research, 13(7), 893–904.

Finfgeld-Connett, D. and Johnson, E. D., 2012. 'Literature search strategies for conducting knowledge-building and theory-generating qualitative systematic reviews'. Journal of Advanced Nursing, Article first published online: 17 May 2012, DOI: 10.1111/j.1365-2648.2012.06037.x.

Fitzgerald, J., 1995. 'English as a second language learners' cognitive reading processes: A review of research in the United States'. Review of Educational Research, 95(2), 145–190.

Fleiss, J. L. and Berlin, J. A., 2009. 'Effect sizes for dichotomous data' in Cooper, H. M., Hedges, L. V. and Valentine, J. C. eds. The handbook of research synthesis and meta-analysis. 2nd ed. New York: Sage, 237–253.

Foster, P. and Hammersley, M., 1998. 'A review of reviews: Structure and function in reviews of educational research'. British Educational Research Journal, 24(5), 609–628.

Franklin, B. M., 1999. 'Discourse, rationality and educational research: A historical perspective of RER'. Review of Educational Research, 69(4), 347–363.

Gallagher, D. J., 2004. 'Educational research, philosophical orthodoxy and unfulfilled promises: The quandary of traditional research in US special education' in Thomas, G. and Pring, R. eds. Evidence-based practice in education. Buckingham: Open University Press, 119–130.

Gaskell, J., 1988. 'Policy Research and Politics'. Alberta Journal of Educational Research, 34(4), 403–417.

Gaskell, P. J., Hepburn, G. and Robeck, E., 1998. 'Re/presenting a gender equity project: Contrasting visions and versions'. Journal of Research in Science Teaching, 35(8), 859–876.

Gijbels, D., et al., 2005. 'Effects of problem-based learning: A meta-analysis from the angle of assessment'. Review of Educational Research, 75(1), 27–61.

Gillborn, D. and Gipps, C., 1998. 'Watching the watchers: Research, methods, politics and equity. A response to Foster & Hammersley'. British Educational Research Journal, 24(5), 629–633.

Glaser, B. G. and Strauss, A., 1967. The discovery of grounded theory: Strategies for qualitative research. Chicago: Aldine.

Glass, G. V., 1976. 'Primary, secondary, and meta-analysis of research'. Educational Researcher, 5(10), 3–8.

Glass, G. V., 2000. Meta-analysis at 25 [online]. Available from: http://www.gvglass.info/papers/meta25.html [Accessed 4 June 2012].

Glass, G. V., 2006. 'Meta-analysis: The quantitative synthesis of research findings' in Green, J. L., Camilli, G. and Elmore, P. B. eds. Handbook of complementary methods in education research. 3rd ed. Washington: American Educational Research Association, 427–438.

Glass, G. V., McGaw, B. and Smith, M. L., 1981. Meta-analysis in social research. Beverly Hills: Sage.

Glass, G. V. and Smith, M. L., 1979. 'Meta-analysis of research on the relationship of class-size and achievement'. Evaluation and Policy Analysis, 1, 2–16.

Gordon, B. M., 1999. 'Who do you believe – Me or your eyes? Perceptions and issues in educational research: Reviews and the journals that validate them'. Review of Educational Research, 69(4), 407–410.

Gough, D., Oliver, S. and Thomas, J., 2012a. 'Introducing systematic reviews' in Gough, D., Oliver, S. and Thomas, J. eds. An introduction to systematic reviews. London: Sage, 1–16.

Gough, D., Oliver, S. and Thomas, J., eds., 2012b. An introduction to systematic reviews. London: Sage.

Gough, D. and Thomas, J., 2012. 'Commonality and diversity in reviews' in Gough, D., Oliver, S. and Thomas, J. eds. An introduction to systematic reviews. London: Sage, 35–65.

Grant, C. A. and Graue, E., 1999. '(Re)viewing a review: A case history of the Review of Educational Research'. Review of Educational Research, 69(4), 384–396.

Green, J. L., Camilli, G. and Elmore, P. B., eds., 2006. Handbook of Complementary Methods in Education Research. Washington: American Educational Research Association.

Green, J. L. and Skukauskaite, A., 2008. 'Becoming Critical Readers: Issues in Transparency, Representation, and Warranting of Claims'. Educational Researcher, 37(1), 30.

Greenhalgh, T., Robert, G., Macfarlane, F., Bate, P., Kyriakidou, O., and Peacock, R., 2005. 'Storylines of research in diffusion of innovation: a meta-narrative approach to systematic review'. Social Science & Medicine, 61(2), 417–430.

Greenhouse, J. B. and Iyengar, S., 2009. 'Sensitivity analysis and diagnostics' in Cooper, H. M., Hedges, L. V. and Valentine, J. C. eds. The handbook of research synthesis and meta-analysis. 2nd ed. New York: Sage, 417–433.

Greenwald, R., Hedges, L. V. and Laine, R. D., 1996. 'The effect of school resources on student achievement'. Review of Educational Research, 66(3), 361–396.

Greenwood, D. J. and Levin, M., 2000. 'Reconstructing the relationships between universities and society through action research' in Denzin, N. K. and Lincoln, Y. S. eds. Handbook of qualitative research. 2nd ed. Thousand Oaks, CA: Sage, 85–106.

Guba, E. G. and Lincoln, Y. S., 1999. 'Naturalistic and rationalistic enquiry' in Keeves, J. P. and Lakomski, G. eds. Issues in educational research. New York: Pergamon, 141–149.

Gubrium, J. F. and Holstein, J. A., 1997. The new language of qualitative method. New York: Oxford University Press.

Gubrium, J. F. and Holstein, J. A., 2000. 'Analyzing interpretive practice' in Denzin, N. K. and Lincoln, Y. S. eds. Handbook of qualitative research. 2nd ed. Thousand Oaks, CA: Sage, 487–508.

Haggis, T., 2009. 'What have we been thinking of? A critical overview of 40 years of student learning research in higher education'. Studies in Higher Education, 34(4), 377–390.

Haig, B. D., 1999. 'Feminist research methodology' in Keeves, J. P. and Lakomski, G. eds. Issues in educational research. 1st ed. New York: Pergamon, 222–231.

Hammersley, M., 2000. 'The relevance of qualitative research'. Oxford Review of Education, 26(3&4), 393–405.

Hammersley, M., 2001. 'On "systematic" reviews of research literatures: A "narrative" response to Evans & Benefield'. British Educational Research Journal, 27(5), 543–554.

Hammersley, M., 2003. Systematic or unsystematic, is that the question? Some reflections on the science, art, and politics of reviewing research. Paper presented at the Department of Epidemiology and Public Health, University of Leicester.

Hammersley, M., 2004. 'Some questions about evidence-based practice in education' in Thomas, G. and Pring, R. eds. Evidence-based practice in education. Buckingham: Open University Press, 133–149.

Hammerstrøm, K., Wade, A. and Jørgensen, A.-M. K., 2010. Searching for studies: A guide to information retrieval for Campbell Systematic Reviews. Campbell Systematic Reviews 2010: Supplement 1 [online]. The Campbell Collaboration website. Available from: http://www.campbellcollaboration.org/ [Accessed 20 September 2011].

Hannes, K. and Lockwood, C., 2011a. 'Pragmatism as the philosophical foundation for the Joanna Briggs meta-aggregative approach to qualitative evidence synthesis'. Journal of Advanced Nursing, 67(7), 1632–1642.

Hannes, K. and Lockwood, C., 2011b. Synthesizing qualitative research: Choosing the right approach. 2nd ed. Hoboken: John Wiley & Sons.

Hannes, K., Lockwood, C. and Pearson, A., 2010. 'A comparative analysis of three online appraisal instruments: Ability to assess validity in qualitative research'. Qualitative Health Research, 20(12), 1736–1743.

Hannes, K. and Macaitis, K., 2012. 'A move to more systematic and transparent approaches in qualitative evidence synthesis: update on a review of published papers'. Qualitative Research, 12(4), 402–442.

Harlen, W. and Crick, R. D., 2004. 'Opportunities and challenges of using systematic reviews of research for evidence-based policy in education'. Evaluation and Research in Education, 18(1–2), 54–71.

Hatch, J. A., 2006. 'Qualitative studies in the era of scientifically-based research: Musings of a former QSE editor'. International Journal of Qualitative Studies in Education 19(4), 403–407.

Hattie, J., 2009. Visible learning: A synthesis of over 800 meta-analyses relating to achievement. London: Routledge.

Hattie, J. and Timperley, H., 2007. 'The power of feedback'. Review of Educational Research, 77(1), 81–113.

Hedges, L. V., 2009. 'Statistical consideration' in Cooper, H. M., Hedges, L. V. and Valentine, J. C. eds. The handbook of research synthesis and meta-analysis. 2nd ed. New York: Sage.

Hedges, L. V. and Olkin, I., 1985. Statistical methods for meta-analysis. Orlando: Academic Press.

Hedges, L. V., Shymansky, J. A. and Woodworth, G., 1989. A practical guide to modern methods of meta-analysis. Washington, DC: National Science Teachers Association.

Hemsley-Brown, J. and Sharp, C., 2003. 'The use of research to improve professional practice: A systematic review of the literature'. Oxford Review of Education, 29(4), 449.

Henry, A., 2006. 'Historical studies: Groups/institutions' in Green, J. L., Camilli, G. and Elmore, P. B. eds. Handbook of complementary methods in education research. 3rd ed. Washington: American Educational Research Association, 333–355.

Herman, R., et al., 2006. 'Reply to Comments from the What Works Clearinghouse on "What doesn't work"'. Educational Researcher, 35(2), 22–23.

Heron, J. and Reason, P., 1997. 'A participatory inquiry paradigm'. Qualitative Inquiry, 3(3), 274–294.

Heyvaert, M., 2011. 'Mixed methods research synthesis: definition, framework, and potential'. Quality and quantity.

Hildebrand, G. M., 2001. 'Re/Writing science from the margins' in Barton, A. C. and Osborne, M. D. eds. Teaching science in diverse settings: Marginalized discourses & classroom practice. New York: Peter Long, 161–198.

Hodder, I., 2000. 'The interpretations of documents and material culture' in Denzin, N. K. and Lincoln, Y. S. eds. Handbook of qualitative research. 2nd ed. Thousand Oaks, CA: Sage, 703–715.

Hodkinson, P. and Smith, J. K., 2004. 'The relationship between research, policy and practice' in Thomas, G. and Pring, R. eds. Evidence-based practice in education. Buckingham: Open University Press, 150–163.

Hofer, B. K. and Pintrich, P. R., 1997. 'The development of epistemological theories: Beliefs about knowledge and knowing and their relation to learning'. Review of Educational Research, 67(1), 88–140.

Howe, K. R., 2005. 'The question of education science: Experimentism versus experimentalism'. Educational Theory, 55(3), 307–321.

Husen, T., 1999. 'Research paradigms in education' in Keeves, J. P. and Lakomski, G. eds. Issues in educational research. 1st ed. New York: Pergamon, 31–39.

Hustler, D., Edwards, A. and Stronach, I., 1998. Editorial. British Educational Research Journal, 24(5), 499–501.

Jackson, M., 1998. Minima ethnographica: Intersubjectivity and the anthropological project. Chicago: University of Chicago Press.

JBI, n.d. The Joanna Briggs Institute [online]. Faculty of Health Sciences at the University of Adelaide, South Australia. Available from: http://www.joannabriggs.edu.au/ [Accessed 3 July 2012].

Jensen, L. A. and Allen, M. N., 1994. 'A synthesis of qualitative research on wellness-illness'. Qualitative Health Research, 4(4), 349–369.

Jensen, L. A. and Allen, M. N., 1996. 'Meta-synthesis of qualitative findings'. Qualitative Health Research, 6(4), 553–560.

Kaestle, C. F., 1997. 'Recent methodological developments in the history of American education' in Jaeger, R. M. ed. Complementary methods for research in education. 2nd ed. Washington, DC: American Educational Research Association, 119–129.

Kaestle, C. F., 1999. 'Historical methods in educational research' in Keeves, J. P. and Lakomski, G. eds. Issues in educational research. 1st ed. New York: Pergamon, 121–131.

Kastner, M., et al., 2012. 'What is the most appropriate knowledge synthesis method to conduct a review? Protocol for a scoping review'. BMC Medical Research Methodology, 12(1), 114.

Kasworm, C. E., 1990. 'Adult undergraduates in higher education: A review of past research perspectives'. Review of Educational Research, 60(3), 345–372.

Kelly, A. E. and Lesh, R. A., 2000. 'Trends and shifts in research methods' in Kelly, A. E. and Lesh, R. A. eds. Handbook of research design in mathematics and science education. London: Erlbaum Associates, 35–44.

Kemmis, S., 1999. 'Action research' in Keeves, J. P. and Lakomski, G. eds. Issues in educational research. New York: Pergamon, 150–160.

Kemmis, S. and McTaggart, R., 2000. 'Participatory action research in Denzin, N. K. and Lincoln, Y. S. eds. Handbook of qualitative research. 2nd ed. Thousand Oaks, CA: Sage, 567–605.

Kennedy, M. M., 2007. 'Defining a literature'. Educational Researcher, 36(3), 139–147.

Kennedy, M. M., 2008. 'Contributions of qualitative research to research on teacher qualifications'. Educational Evaluation and Policy Analysis, 30, 344–367.

Kennedy, M. M., 2010. 'Attribution error and the quest for teacher quality'. Educational Researcher, 39(8), 591–598.

Keogh, J. and Garrick, B., 2011. 'Creating Catch 22: zooming in and zooming out on the discursive constructions of teachers in a news article'. International Journal of Qualitative Studies in Education, 24(4), 419–434.

Kirk, R. E., 1996. 'Practical significance: A concept whose time has come'. Educational and Psychological Measurement, 56(5), 746–759.

Kress, T. M., 2011a. 'Inside the "thick wrapper" of critical pedagogy and research'. International Journal of Qualitative Studies in Education, 24(3), 261–266.

Kress, T. M., 2011b. 'Stepping out of the academic brew: Using critical research to break down hierarchies of knowledge production'. International Journal of Qualitative Studies in Education, 24(3), 267–283.

Kuhn, T. S., 1962. The structure of scientific revolutions. Chicago, IL: University of Chicago Press.

Kuhn, T. S., 1970. The structure of scientific revolutions. 2nd ed. Chicago, IL: University of Chicago Press.

L'Hommedieu, R., Menges, R. J. and Brinko, K. T., 1988. 'Validity issues in meta-analysis: Suggestions for research and policy'. Higher Education Research & Development, 7(2), 119–128.

La Paro, K. and Pianta, R., 2000. 'Predicting children's competence in the early school years: A meta-analytic review'. Review of Educational Research, 70(4), 443–484.

Lakomski, G., 1999. 'Critical theory and education' in Keeves, J. P. and Lakomski, G. eds. Issues in educational research. 1st ed. New York: Pergamon, 174–183.

Lather, P., 1986. 'Issues of validity in openly ideological research: Between a rock and a soft place'. Interchange, 17(4), 63–84.

Lather, P., 1993. 'Fertile obsession: Validity after poststructuralism'. The Sociological Quaterly, 34(4), 673–693.

Lather, P., 1996. 'Troubling clarity: The politics of accessible language'. Harvard Educational Review, 66(3), 524–545.

Lather, P., 1999. 'To be of use: The work of reviewing'. Review of Educational Research, 69(1), 2–7.

Lather, P., 2004a. 'Scientific research in education: A critical perspective'. British Educational Research Journal, 30(6), 759–772.

Lather, P., 2004b. 'This is your father's paradigm: Government intrusion and the case of qualitative research in education'. Qualitative Inquiry, 10(1), 15–34.

Lather, P., 2006. 'Paradigm proliferation as a good thing to think with: Teaching research in education as a wild profusion'. International Journal of Qualitative Studies in Education 19(1), 35–37.

Lawson, M. J., 1997. 'Concept mapping' in Keeves, J. P. ed. Educational research, methodology and measurement: An international handbook. 2nd ed. New York: Pergamon, 290–296.

Layton, D., 1994. 'STS in the School Curriculum: A movement overtaken by history?' in Solomon, J. and Aikenhead, G. eds. STS Education: International Perspectives on Reform. N.Y: Teachers College Press, Columbia University, 32–44.

Leander, K. M., Phillips, N. C. and Taylor, K. H., 2010. 'The changing social spaces of learning: Mapping new mobilities'. Review of Research in Education, 34, 329–394.

LeCompte, M. D., 1995. 'Some notes on power, agenda, and voice: A researcher's personal evolution toward critical collaboration research' in McLaren, P. L. and Giarelli, J. M. eds. Critical theory and educational research. New York: State University of New York Press.

LeCompte, M. D. and Goetz, J. P., 1982. 'Problems of reliability and validity in ethnographic research'. Review of Educational Research, 52(1), 31–60.

LeCompte, M. D. and Preissle, J., 1993. Ethnography and qualitative design in educational research. 2nd ed. San Diego: Academic Press.

Light, R. J. and Pillemer, D. B., 1984. Summing up: The science of reviewing research. Cambridge: Harvard University Press.

Light, R. J., Singer, J. D. and Willett, J. B., 1994. 'The visual presentation and interpretation of meta-analyses' in Cooper, H. M. and Hedges, L. V. eds. The handbook of research synthesis. New York: Sage, 439–454.

Lincoln, Y. S. and Guba, E. G., 1985. Naturalistic inquiry. Beverly Hills, CA: Sage.

Lincoln, Y. S. and Guba, E. G., 1986. 'But is it rigorous? Trustworthiness and authenticity in naturalistic evaluation' in Williams, D. ed. Naturalistic evaluation. San Francisco, CA: Jossey-Bass, 73–84.

Lincoln, Y. S., Linham, S. A. and Guba, E. G., 2011. 'Paradigmatic controversies, contradictions, and emerging confluences, revisited' in Denzin, N. K. and Lincoln, Y. S. eds. The Sage handbook of qualitative research. 4th ed. Thousand Oaks, CA: Sage, 97–128.

Lipsey, M. W., 2009. 'Identifying interesting variables and analysis opportunities' in Cooper, H. M., Hedges, L. V. and Valentine, J. C. eds. The handbook of research synthesis and meta-analysis. 2nd ed. New York: Sage, 147–158.

Lipsey, M. W. and Wilson, D. B., 2001. Practical meta-analysis. Thousand Oaks, CA; London: Sage.

Livingston, G., 1999. 'Beyond watching over established ways: A review as recasting the literature, recasting the lived'. Review of Educational Research, 69(1), 9–19.

Lloyd Jones, M., 2004. 'Application of systematic review methods to qualitative research: Practical issues'. Journal of Advanced Nursing, 48(3), 271–278.

Lou, Y., P. C., Spence, J. C., Poulsen, C., Chambers, B., and d'Apollonia, S., 1996. 'Within-class grouping: A meta-analysis'. Review of Educational Research, 66(4), 423–458.

Louis, T. A. and Zelterman, D., 1994. 'Bayesian approaches to research synthesis' in Cooper, H. M. and Hedges, L. V. eds. The handbook of research synthesis. New York: Sage, 411–422.

Lucas, S. R. and Beresford, L., 2010. 'Naming and classifying: Theory, evidence and equity in education'. Review of Research in Education, 34, 25–84.

Luke, A., Green, J. and Kelly, G. J., 2010. 'What counts as evidence and equity?' Review of Research in Education, 34, vii–xvi.

MacLure, M., 2005. '"Clarity bordering on stupidity": Where's the quality in systematic review?' Journal of Education Policy, 20(4), 393–416.

Major, C. H. and Savin-Baden, M., 2010. An introduction to qualitative research synthesis: Managing the information explosion in social science research. London: Routledge

Marshall, J. and Peters, M., 1999. 'Postmodernism' in Keeves, J. P. and Lakomski, G. eds. Issues in educational research. New York: Pergamon, 242–248.

Mason, J., 2002. Researching your own practice: The discipline of noticing. London: Routledge.

Matt, G. E. and Cook, T. D., 1994. 'Threats to the validity of research synthesis' in Cooper, H. M. and Hedges, L. V. eds. The handbook of research synthesis. New York: Sage, 503–520.

Matt, G. E. and Cook, T. D., 2009. 'Threats to the validity of generalized inferences' in Cooper, H. M., Hedges, L. V. and Valentine, J. C. eds. The handbook of research synthesis and meta-analysis. 2nd ed. New York: Sage, 537–560.

Maxcy, S. J., 2003. 'Pragmatic threads in mixed methods research in the social sciences: The search for multiple modes of inquiry and the end of the philosophy of formalism' in Tashakkori, A. and Teddlie, C. eds. Handbook of mixed methods in social & behavioral research. Thousand Oaks, CA: Sage, 51–90.

Maxwell, J. A. and Loomis, D. M., 2003. 'Mixed methods design: An alternative approach' Tashakkori, A. and Teddlie, C. eds. Handbook of mixed methods in social & behavioral research. Thousand Oaks, CA: Sage, 241–272.

Mayer, R. E., 2000. 'What is the place of science in educational research'. Educational Researcher, 32(3), 29–36.

Mayer, R. E., 2001. 'Resisting the assault on science: The case for evidence-based reasoning in educational research'. Educational Researcher, 30(7), 29–30.

Mays, N., Pope, C. and Popay, J., 2005a. Details of approaches to synthesis. A methodological appendix to the paper: Systematically reviewing qualitative and quantitative evidence to inform management and policy making in the health field [online]. the Canadian Health Services Research Foundation website. Available from: http://www.chsrf.ca/funding_opportunities/commissioned_research/projects/ msynth_e.php [Accessed 4 July 2006].

Mays, N., Pope, C. and Popay, J., 2005b. 'Systematically reviewing qualitative and quantitative evidence to inform management and policy making in the health field'. Journal of Health Services Research and Policy, 10(1), 6–20.

Meacham, S. J., 1998. 'Threads of a new language: A response to Eisenhart's "On the subject of interpretive reviews"'. Review of Educational Research, 68(4), 401–407.

Mertens, D. M., 2005. Research and evaluation in education and psychology: Integrating diversity with quantitative, qualitative, and mixed methods. 2nd ed. Thousand Oaks, CA: Sage.

Mertens, D. M., Bledsoe, K. L., Sullivan, M., and Wilson, A., 2010. 'Utilization of mixed methods for transformative purposes' in Tashakkori, A. and Teddlie, C. eds. Sage handbook of mixed methods in social & behavioral research. 2nd ed. Thousand Oaks, CA: Sage, 193–214.

Miles, M. B. and Huberman, A. M., 1984. 'Drawing valid meaning from qualitative data: Toward a shared craft'. Educational Researcher, 13(5), 20–30.

Miles, M. B. and Huberman, A. M., 1994. Qualitative data analysis: An expanded sourcebook. 2nd ed. Thousand Oaks: Sage.

Miller, N. and Pollock, V. E., 1994. 'Meta-analytic synthesis for theory development' in Cooper, H. M. and Hedges, L. V. eds. The handbook of research synthesis. New York: Sage, 457–484.

Moss, P. A., 2005a. 'Toward "epistemic reflexivity" in educational research: A response to Scientific Research in Education'. Teachers College Record, 107(1), 19–29.

Moss, P. A., 2005b. 'Understanding the other/understanding ourselves: Toward a constructive dialogue about "principles" in educational research'. Educational Theory, 55(3), 263–283.

Murray, F. B. and Raths, J., 1996. 'Factors in the peer review of reviews'. Review of Educational Research, 66(4), 417–421.

Murray, F. B., Raths, J. and Blanteno, L., 1996. 'The decoupling of RER articles, critiques, and rejoinders in the educational literature'. Review of Educational Research, 66(4), 657–658.

Nisbet, J., 1999. 'Policy-oriented research' in Keeves, J. P. and Lakomski, G. eds. Issues in educational research. 1st ed. New York: Pergamon, 64–78.

Noblit, G. W. and Hare, R. D., 1988. Meta-ethnography: Synthesizing qualitative studies. Newbury Park: Sage.

Norris, J., 2003. Arts-based research is for everyone: Exploring the methodological potential of arts-based research. Banff, Canada. (Powerpoint file and Audiotape available from Kennedy Recordings).

Oakley, A., 2003. 'Research evidence, knowledge management and educational practice: Early lessons from a systematic approach'. London Review of Education, 1(1), 21–33.

Oancea, A., 2005. 'Criticisms of educational research: key topics and levels of analysis'. British Educational Research Journal, 31(2), 157–183.

Ödman, P. and Kerdeman, D., 1999. 'Hermeneutics' in Keeves, J. P. and Lakomski, G. eds. Issues in educational research. 1st ed. New York: Pergamon, 184–197.

Ogawa, R. T. and Malen, B., 1991a. 'A response to commentaries on "Towards rigor in reviews of multivocal literatures ..."'. Review of Educational Research, 61(3), 307–313.

Ogawa, R. T. and Malen, B., 1991b. 'Towards rigor in reviews of multivocal literatures: Applying the exploratory case study method'. Review of Educational Research, 61(3), 265–286.

Oliver, S., Dickson, K. and Newman, M., 2012. 'Getting started with a review' in Gough, D., Oliver, S. and Thomas, J. eds. An introduction to systematic reviews. London: Sage, 66–82.

Oliver, S. R., et al., 2008. 'A multidimensional conceptual framework for analysing public involvement in health services research'. Health Expectations, 11(1), 72–84.

Onwuegbuzie, A. J. and Teddlie, C., 2003. 'A framework for analyzing data in mixed methods research' in Tashakkori, A. and Teddlie, C. eds. Handbook of mixed methods in social & behavioral research. Thousand Oaks, CA: Sage, 351–384.

Orwin, R. G., 1994. 'Evaluating coding decisions' in Cooper, H. M. and Hedges, L. V. eds. The handbook of research synthesis. New York: Sage, 139–162.

Orwin, R. G. and Vevea, J. L., 2009. 'Evaluating coding decisions' in Cooper, H. M., Hedges, L. V. and Valentine, J. C. eds. The handbook of research synthesis and meta-analysis. 2nd ed. New York: Sage, 177–203.

Papaioannou, D., Sutton, A., Carroll, C., Booth, A., and Wong, R. , 2010. 'Literature searching for social science systematic reviews: Consideration of a range of search techniques'. Health Information & Libraries Journal, 27(2), 114–122.

Pascarella, E. T. and Terenzini, P. T., 2005. How college affects students a third decade of research. 1st ed. San Francisco: Jossey-Bass.

Paterson, B. L., Thorne, S. E., Canam, C., and Jillings, C., 2001. Meta-study of qualitative health research: A practical guide to meta-analysis and meta-synthesis. Thousand Oaks, CA: Sage.

Patton, M. Q., 1991. 'Towards utility in reviews of multivocal literatures'. Review of Educational Research, 61(3), 287–292.

Patton, M. Q., 1999. 'Myths as normative frames for qualitative interpretation of life stories'. Qualitative Inquiry, 5(3), 338–352.

Patton, M. Q., 2002. Qualitative research and evaluation methods. 3rd ed. Thousand Oaks, CA: Sage.

Paugh, P. and Robinson, E., 2011. 'Keeping a "vigilant critique": Unpacking critical praxis as teacher educators'. International Journal of Qualitative Studies in Education, 24(3), 363–378.

Paul, J. L. and Marfo, K., 2001. 'Preparation of educational researchers in philosophical foundations of inquiry'. Review of Educational Research, 71(4), 525–547.

Pawson, R., 2006. Evidence-based policy: A realist perspective. London: Sage.

Pawson, R., Greenhalgh, T., Harvey, G., and Walshe, K. , 2005. 'Realist Review: A new method of systematic review designed for complex policy interventions'. Journal of Health Services Research and Policy, 10(1), 21–34.

Peile, C., 1994. The creative paradigm: Insight, synthesis and knowledge development. Sydney: Avebury.

Peshkin, A., 2001. 'Angles of vision: Enhancing perception in qualitative research'. Qualitative Inquiry, 7(2), 238–253.

Petticrew, M. and Roberts, H., 2006. Systematic reviews in the social sciences: A practical guide. Malden, MA: Blackwell.

Phillips, D. C., 2006. 'A guide for the perplexed: Scientific educational research, methodolatory, and the gold versus platinum standards'. Educational Research Review, 1(1), 15–26.

Phillips, R., McNaught, C. and Kennedy, G., 2012. Evaluating e-learning: Guiding research and practice. NY: Routledge.

Pigott, T. D., 2009. 'Handling missing data' in Cooper, H. M., Hedges, L. V. and Valentine, J. C. eds. The handbook of research synthesis and meta-analysis. 2nd ed. New York: Sage, 399–416.

Popay, J., Rogers, A. and Williams, G., 1998. 'Rationale and standards for the systematics review of qualitative literature in health services research'. Qualitative Health Research, 8(3), 341–351.

Pope, C., Mays, N. and Popay, J., 2007. Synthesizing qualitative and quantitative health evidence: A guide to methods. Maidenhead, England: Open University Press.

Popkewitz, T. S., 1999. Reviewing reviews: RER, research and the politics of educational knowledge'. Review of Educational Research, 69(4), 397–404.

Popkewitz, T. S., 2004. 'Is the National Research Council Committee's report on Scientific Research in Education scientific? On trusting the manifesto'. Qualitative Inquiry, 10(1), 62–78.

Popper, K. R., 1965. Conjectures and refutations: The growth of scientific knowledge. New York: Harper & Row.

Posavac, E. J., 1992. 'Communicating applied social psychology to users: A challenge and an art' in Bryant, F. B., J. Edwards, R. S. Tindale, E. J. Posavac, L. Heath, E. Henderson and Y. Suarez-Balcazar eds. Methodological issues in applied social psychology. New York: Plenum Press, 269–293.

Rees, R. and Oliver, S., 2012. 'Stakeholder perspectives and participation in reviews' in Gough, D., Oliver, S. and Thomas, J. eds. An introduction to systematic reviews. London: Sage, 17–34.

Richardson, L., 2000a. 'Evaluating ethnography'. Qualitative Inquiry, 6(2), 235–255.

Richardson, L., 2000b. 'Writing: A method of Inquiry' in Denzin, N. K. and Lincoln, Y. S. eds. Handbook of qualitative research. 2nd ed. Thousand Oaks, CA: Sage, 923–948.

Richardson, L., 2001. 'Getting personal: Writing-stories'. Qualitative studies in education, 33–38.

Ridgway, J., Zawojewski, J. S. and Hoover, M. N., 2000. 'Problematising evidence-based policy and practice'. Evaluation and Research in Education, 14(3&4), 181–192.

Riessman, C. K., 1993. Narrative analysis. Newbury Park, CA: Sage.

Ritchie, S. M. and Rigano, D. L., 2007. 'Solidarity through collaborative research'. International Journal of Qualitative Studies in Education, 20(2), 129–150.

Rosenthal, M. C., 1994. 'The fugitive literature' in Cooper, H. M. and Hedges, L. V. eds. The handbook of research synthesis. New York: Sage, 85–94.

Rosenthal, R., 1980. 'Combining probabilities and the file drawer problem'. Evaluation in Education, 4, 18–21.

Rothstein, H. R., College, B., Turner, H. M., and Lavenberg, J. G., 2004. The Campbell Collaboration information retrieval policy brief [online]. The Campbell Collaboration website. Available from: http://www.campbellcollaboration.org/MG/IRMGPolicyBriefRevised.pdf [Accessed 5 June 2006].

Rothstein, H. R. and Hopewell, S., 2009. 'Grey literature' in Cooper, H. M., Hedges, L. V. and Valentine, J. C. eds. The handbook of research synthesis and meta-analysis. 2nd ed. New York: Sage, 103–125.

Ryan, K. E. and Hood, L. K., 2004. 'Guarding the castle and opening the gates'. Qualitative Inquiry, 10(1), 79–95.

Sandelowski, M. and Barroso, J., 2002. 'Reading qualitative studies'. International Journal of Qualitative Methods.

Sandelowski, M. and Barroso, J., 2007. Handbook for synthesizing qualitative research. New York Springer.

Sandelowski, M., Voils, C. I., Leeman, J., and Crandell, J. L. , 2012. 'Mapping the Mixed Methods–Mixed Research Synthesis Terrain'. Journal of mixed methods research, 6(4), 317–331.

Schmid, C. H. and Lipsey, M. W., 2011. Author guidelines: Research Synthesis Methods [online]. Available from: http://onlinelibrary.wiley.com/journal/10.1002/%28ISSN%291759-2887/homepage/ForAuthors.html#general [Accessed 23 September 2011].

Schoenfeld, A. H., 2006. 'What doesn't work: The challenge and failure of the What Works Clearinghouse to conduct meaningful reviews of studies of mathematics curricula'. Educational Researcher, 35(2), 13–21.

Schön, D. A., 1992. 'The Theory of Inquiry: Dewey's Legacy to Education'. Curriculum Inquiry, 22(2), 119–139.

Schwandt, T. A., 1998. 'The interpretive review of educational matters: Is there any other kind?' Review of Educational Research, 68(4), 409–412.

Schwandt, T. A., 2005. 'A diagnostic reading of scientifically based research for education'. Educational Theory, 55(3), 286–305.

Seale, C., 1999. The quality of qualitative research. London: Sage.

Segall, A., 2001. 'Critical ethnography and the invocation of voice: From the field/in the field – single exposure, double standard?' Qualitative studies in education, 14(4), 579–592.

Shadish, W. R., n.d. Links to meta-analysis software [online]. The School of Social Sciences, University of California, Merced website. Available from: http://faculty. ucmerced.edu/wshadish/Meta-Analysis%20Software.htm [Accessed 4 July 2012].

Shimpuku, Y. and Norr, K. F., 2012. 'Working with interpreters in cross-cultural qualitative research in the context of a developing country: systematic literature review'. Journal of Advanced Nursing. Article first published online: 15 MAR 2012, DOI: 10.1111/j.1365-2648.2012.05951.x.

Sholle, D., 1992. 'Authority on the left: Critical pedagogy, postmodernism and vital strategies'. Cultural Studies, 6(2), 271–289.

Shulha, L. M. and Wilson, R. J., 2003. 'Collaborative mixed methods research' in Tashakkori, A. and Teddlie, C. eds. Handbook of mixed methods in social & behavioral research. Thousand Oaks, CA: Sage, 639–670.

Silverman, D., 2000. 'Analyzing talk and text' in Denzin, N. K. and Lincoln, Y. S. eds. Handbook of qualitative research. 2nd ed. Thousand Oaks, CA: Sage, 821–834.

Sipe, T.-A. and Curlette, W. L., 1997. ''A meta-synthesis of factors related to educational achievement: A methodological approach to summarizing and synthesizing meta-analyses'. International Journal of Educational Research, 25(7), 583–698.

Sirin, S. R., 2005. 'Socioeconomic status and academic achievement: A meta-analytic review of research'. Review of Educational Research, 75(3), 417–453.

Slavin, R. E., 1986. 'Best-evidence synthesis: An alternative to meta-analytic and traditional reviews'. Educational Researcher, 15(9), 5–11.

Slavin, R. E., 2002. 'Evidence-based education policies: Transforming educational practice and research'. Educational Researcher, 31(7), 15–21.

Slavin, R. E., 2008a. 'Evidence-Based Reform in Education: Which Evidence Counts?' Educational Researcher, 37(1), 47–50.

Slavin, R. E., 2008b. 'Perspectives on evidence-based research in education—What works? Issues in synthesizing educational program evaluations'. Educational Researcher, 37(1), 5–14.

Smith, M. L. and Glass, G. V., 1977. 'Meta-analysis of psychotherapy outcome studies'. The American psychologist, 32(9), 752–760.

Smyth, J. and Hattam, R., 2000. 'Intellectual as hustler: Researching against the grain of the market'. British Educational Research Journal, 26(2), 157–175.

SRSM, nd. Society for Research Synthesis Methodology [online]. Available from: http://www.srsm.org/AboutSRSM.htm [Accessed 22 September 2011].

Stake, R. E., 1998. Case studies in Denzin, N. K. and Lincoln, Y. S. eds. Strategies of qualitative inquiry. Thousand Oaks, CA: Sage, 86–109.

Stock, W. A., 1994. 'Systematic coding for research synthesis' in Cooper, H. M. and Hedges, L. V. eds. The handbook of research synthesis. New York: Sage, 125–138.

Stock, W. A., Benito, J. G. and Lasa, N. B., 1996. 'Research synthesis: Coding and conjectures'. Evaluation and the Health Professions, 19(1), 104–117.

Strathern, M., 2000. 'The tyranny of transparency'. British Educational Research Journal, 26(3), 309–321.

Strauss, A. and Corbin, J., 1998. Basics of qualitative research: Techniques and procedures for developing grounded theory. 2nd ed. Thousand Oaks, CA: Sage.

Strike, K. A. and Posner, G., 1983. 'Epistemological problems in organizing social science knowledge for application' in Ward, S. A. and Reed, L. J. eds. Knowledge structure and use: Implications for synthesis and interpretation. Philadelphia: Temple University Press, 47–83.

Stronach, I. and MacLure, M., 1997. Educational research undone: The postmodern embrace. Buckingham: Open University Press.

Suri, H., 1999. A methodologically inclusive model for research synthesis. Joint conference of AARE and NZARE, Melbourne.

Suri, H., 2007. Expanding possibilities within research syntheses: A methodologically inclusive research synthesis framework. PhD Thesis. The University of Melbourne.

Suri, H., 2011. 'Purposeful sampling in qualitative research synthesis'. Qualitative Research Journal, 11(2), 63–75.

Suri, H., 2012. 'Epistemological pluralism in qualitative research synthesis'. International Journal of Qualitative Studies in Education (DOI:10.1080/0951839 8.2012.691565).

Suri, H. and Hattie, J., in press. 'Meta-analysis and research synthesis in education'. Oxford Bibliographies Online.

Suri, H. and Patel, F., 2012. 'Ethical considerations in online research methods' in Silva, C. ed. Online research methods in urban and planning studies: Design and outcomes. Hershey PA: IGI Global, 394–408.

Sutton, A. J., 2009. 'Publication Bias' in Cooper, H. M., Hedges, L. V. and Valentine, J. C. eds. The handbook of research synthesis and meta-analysis. 2nd ed. New York: Sage, 435–452.

Tashakkori, A. and Teddlie, C., 2003. 'The past and future of mixed methods research: From data triangulation to mixed model designs' in Tashakkori, A. and Teddlie, C. eds. Handbook of mixed methods in social & behavioral research. Thousand Oaks, CA: Sage, 671–702.

Tashakkori, A. and Teddlie, C., eds., 2010. Sage handbook of mixed methods in social & behavioral research. Thousand Oaks, CA: Sage.

Taylor, C., 1982. 'Interpretation and the sciences of man' in Bredo, E. and Feinberg, W. eds. Knowledge and values in social and eduational research. Philadelphia: Temple University Press.

Te Manatu Taonga Ministry for Culture and Heritage, 2005. Review of Cultural Well-Being Related Activity [online]. The Ministry for Culture and Heritage with Local Authorities website. Available from: http://www.mch.govt.nz/cwb/pdfs/review-of-cultural-wellbeing-activity.pdf [Accessed 19 February 2006].

Teddlie, C. and Tashakkori, A., 2003. 'Major issues and controversies in the use of mixed methods in the social and behavioral sciences' in Tashakkori, A. and Teddlie, C. eds. Handbook of mixed methods in social & behavioral research. Thousand Oaks, CA: Sage, 3–50.

The Cochrane Collaboration, 2011. The Cochrane Collaboration [online]. The Cochrane Collaboration: Working together to provide the best evidence for health care. Available from: http://www.cochrane.org/ [Accessed 20 September 2011].

Thomas, G., 2004. 'Introduction: Evidence and practice' in Thomas, G. and Pring, R. eds. Evidence-based practice in education. Buckingham: Open University Press, 1–18.

Thomas, J. and Harden, A., 2008. 'Methods for the thematic synthesis of qualitative research in systematic reviews'. BMC Medical Research Methodology, 8, 45–54.

Thompson, B., 2006. 'Research synthesis: Effect sizes' in Green, J. L., Camilli, G. and Elmore, P. B. eds. Handbook of complementary methods in education research. 3rd ed. Washington: American Educational Research Association, 583–603.

Thorne, S., 2001. 'Conceptual and theoretical challenges in meta-synthesis'. Advances in Qualitative Methods Conference. Edmonton Alberta.

Tierney, W. G., 2000. 'Undaunted courage: Life history and postmodern courage' in Denzin, N. K. and Lincoln, Y. S. eds. Handbook of qualitative research. 2nd ed. Thousand Oaks, CA: Sage, 537–553.

Torrance, H., 2004. 'Using action research to generate knowledge about educational practice' in Thomas, G. and Pring, R. eds. Evidence-based practice in education. Buckingham: Open University Press, 187–200.

Tuchman, G., 1998. 'Historical social science: Methodologies, methods, and meanings' in Denzin, N. K. and Lincoln, Y. S. eds. Strategies of qualitative inquiry. Thousand Oaks, CA: Sage.

Valentine, J. C., 2009. 'Judging the quality of primary research' in Cooper, H. M., Hedges, L. V. and Valentine, J. C. eds. The handbook of research synthesis and meta-analysis. 2nd ed. New York: Sage, 129–146.

Van Maanen, J., 1988. Tales of the field: on writing ethnography. Chicago: University of Chicago Press.

Veenman, S., 1995. 'Cognitive and noncognitive effects of multigrade and multi-age classes: A best-evidence synthesis'. Review of Educational Research, 65(4), 319–381.

Walker, J. C. and Evers, C. W., 1999. 'Research in education: Epistemological issues' in Keeves, J. P. and Lakomski, G. eds. Issues in educational research. 1st ed. New York: Pergamon, 40–56.

Ward, S. A., 1983. 'Knowledge structure and knowledge synthesis' in Ward, S. A. and Reed, L. J. eds. Knowledge structure and use: Implications for synthesis and interpretation. Philadelphia: Temple University Press, 21–42.

Warschauer, M. and Matuchniak, T., 2010. 'New technology and digital worlds: Analyzing evidence of equity in access, use, and outcomes'. Review of Research in Education, 179–225, vii–xvi.

White, H. D., 2009. 'Scientific communication and literature retrieval' in Cooper, H. M., Hedges, L. V. and Valentine, J. C. eds. The handbook of research synthesis and meta-analysis. 2nd ed. New York: Sage, 51–77.

Wickens, C. M., 2010. 'The investigation of power in written texts through the use of multiple textual analytic frames'. International Journal of Qualitative Studies in Education, 24(2), 151–164.

Wideen, M., Mayer-Smith, J. and Moon, B., 1998. 'A critical analysis of the research on learning to teach: Making the case for an ecological perspective on inquiry'. Review of Educational Research, 68(2), 130–178.

Wilczynski, N. L., Marks, S. and Haynes, R. B., 2007. 'Search strategies for identifying qualitative studies in CINAHL'. Qualitative Health Research, 17, 705–710.

Willinsky, J., 2005. 'Scientific research in a democratic culture: Or what's a social science for?' Teachers College Record, 107(1), 38–51.

Wilson, D. B., 2009. 'Systematic coding' in Cooper, H. M., Hedges, L. V. and Valentine, J. C. eds. The handbook of research synthesis and meta-analysis. 2nd ed. New York: Sage, 159–176.

Windschitl, M., 2002. 'Framing constructivism in practice as the negotiation of dilemmas: An analysis of the conceptual, pedagogical, cultural, and political challenges facing teachers'. Review of Educational Research, 72(2), 131–175.

Wink, J., 1997. Critical pedagogy: Notes from the real world. New York: Longman.

Wiseman, A. W., 2010. 'The uses of evidence for educational policymaking: Global contexts and international trends'. Review of Research in Education, 34, 1–24.

Wortman, P. M., 1994. 'Judging research quality' in Cooper, H. M. and Hedges, L. V. eds. The handbook of research synthesis. New York: Sage, 97–110.

Wright, S. and Coultas, S., 2007. The Cochrane Qualitative Methods Group. Faculty of Health & Medicine, Lancaster University website. Available from: http://www.lancs.ac.uk/shm/dhr/research/public/cochrane.htm [Accessed 20 September 2011].

Yeager, D. S. and Walton, G. M., 2011. 'Social-Psychological Interventions in Education: They're Not Magic'. Review of Educational Research, 81(2), 267.

Yin, R. K., 1991. 'Advancing rigorous methodologies: A review of "Towards rigor in reviews of multivocal literatures ..."'. Review of Educational Research, 61(3), 299–305.

Yu, K., 2011. 'Exploring the nature of the researcher-practitioner relationship in qualitative educational research publications'. International Journal of Qualitative Studies in Education (First published on: 06 January 2011 at iFirst).

Zhao, S., 1991. 'Meta-theory, meta-method, meta-data-analysis: What, why, and how?' Sociological Perspectives, 34(3), 377–390.

Zimmer, L., 2006. 'Qualitative meta-synthesis: A question of dialoguing with texts'. Journal of Advanced Nursing, 53(3), 311–318.

# Index

Page references in *italics* show a figure and those in **bold** indicate a table.